THE MAKING OF
A GREAT WINE

THE MAKING OF A GREAT WINE

GAJA AND SORI SAN LORENZO

Edward Steinberg

THE ECCO PRESS

The Ecco Press
100 West Broad Street
Hopewell, NJ 08525
Published simultaneously in Canada by
Penguin Books Canada Ltd., Ontario
Printed in the United States of America

Library of Congress Cataloging-in-Publication Data
Steinberg, Edward.
The making of a great wine: Gaja and Sori San Lorenzo
originally published as The vines of San Lorenzo: the making of
a great wine in the new tradition
/ by Edward Steinberg.
p.   cm.
ISBN 0-88001-284-6 (hardcover)
ISBN 0-88001-505-5 (paperback)
1. Wine and wine making—Italy—Barbaresco.   2. Gaja, Angelo.
I. Title.
TP559.I8S75   1992
641.2'223'09451—dc20   92-26642

Designed by Debby Jay
The text of this book is set in 11½ point Bembo.
9 8 7 6 5 4 3 2 1
FIRST PAPERBACK EDITION

To my wife's parents,
Jussi and Liisa Tenkku,
and
to the memory of my own,
A. D. and Sadye Steinberg

ACKNOWLEDGEMENTS

Angelo Gaja understood the idea right away: to describe the making of wine in general—not only the technical details, but their historical background and human context as well—by telling the story of a particular one. My greatest debt is to him for giving me the run of his winery and vineyards, thereby enabling this book to materialize. I am also deeply grateful to him, his wife, Lucia, and the entire Gaja family for their hospitality and the graciousness with which they accepted my frequent intrusions into their lives.

I also wish to thank all the other people in Barbaresco who helped me in various ways: among others, Federica Boggero, Giuseppe Botto, Luigi Cavallo, Ernesto Giacosa, Valerio Grasso, Angelo Lembo, Pietro Rocca and his family, and Rino and Roberta Rocca. Aldo Vacca was a congenial companion who took care of many practical matters. Federico Curtaz and Guido Rivella accepted my relentless poking into their work with unfailing good humor and were extremely generous in sharing their knowledge and connections. I am also greatly indebted to them, their wives, Daniela and Maria Grazia, and the rest of their families for going out of their way to make me feel at home.

Many people elsewhere helped: M. Daffy and the other *fendeurs* I met in France; the Ganau and Molinas brothers and the other cork producers I met in Sardinia; Rocco Di Stefano, Franco Mannini, Franco Marchini, Robert Mondavi, Alberto Orrico, the

Ragnedda brothers, Paolo Ruaro and Luciano Sandrone, as well as the staffs of the Istituto Sperimentale per l'Enologia in Asti, the National Archives in Turin, and the Scuola di Viticoltura e Enologia and the public library in Alba. Special thanks are due Lorenzo Corino, Eugenio Gamba, Camille Gauthier, Vincenzo Gerbi, and Albino Morando for their hospitality and all the time they so generously devoted to me.

Thanks are also due Barbara Edelman and her staff at Barbara Edelman Communications, Inc., in New York for help connected with the publishing of this book; and to Bill Crager, Chris Kingsley, and their colleagues at The Ecco Press for producing it in often trying circumstances.

Finally, I wish to express my gratitude to four people who were crucial to the realization of this enterprise: Clara Viscogliosi, for introducing me to Angelo Gaja and for all the tastings at the old Enoteca Roffi Isabelli in Rome; Pat Conroy, for the sustaining friendship of a writer who is also a fellow southerner; Daniel Halpern, for rescuing the book at a critical moment and bestowing on it the attention of a publisher who is also a poet; and my wife, Marja, for more reasons than there are grape varieties.

THE MAKING OF
A GREAT WINE

*I*N SILENCE AND DARKNESS, in the depths of the soil, the slumbering vine begins to stir. Rootlets grow, water and minerals are absorbed, sap inches upwards.

Many feet above, in the bud eyes at the nodes of a cane, ensconced in padding and protected by two hard, dark scales, embryonic shoots await the welcoming warmth of spring. The eyes grow plump, the scales drop off, and the tender tip emerges with its tiny, folded leaves. The shoot stiffens as it grows. More leaves appear. Coiling tendrils. Inflorescences that look for all the world like miniature clusters of grapes.

An inflorescence is composed of dozens of diminutive flowers, each attached by a stem to a larger stalk and covered by a five-petaled cap. The cap slips off, pouches at the tips of the stamens split open, and grains of pollen drift down onto the stigma below. Enchanting the nose as well as the eye, the hermaphrodite fertilizes itself. A grape is born, the pollinated ovary of a single flower. Unfertilized flowers fall to the ground. The hard, green pinheads that remain, the newborn bunches, slowly start to grow.

Suddenly, one here, one there, apparently at random, the grapes change color as if scarlet or yellow fever were spreading through the vineyard. The race to ripeness has begun. They darken, soften, sweeten.

Harvesters come and go. By now the shoots are wooden canes. The leaves explode in a riot of color, the final fireworks before they fall and the vine sinks slowly back into slumber.

"In the end," writes Émile Peynaud, the most influential enologist of our time, "it's everywhere like in Bordeaux." Despite the infinite variations possible, the story of the growing of grapes on one plot of land and their subsequent transformation is the story of Everywine.

October 26, 1991

*B*RAVO!" booms a voice.

"Bravissimo!" chimes another.

More than a thousand people are on their feet. It's a standing ovation.

On the stage, as if taken by surprise, the performer seems uncertain of what to do. At the theater next door, the Richard Rodgers, or the one across the street, the curtain would have come to his rescue by now. The video camera continues to roll.

On the long tables in front of each row of seats lie sheets of paper with notes on the show. The applause is a crescendo already two minutes long. The reviews will surely be raves.

This is Broadway, but the star seems uneasy about taking a bow. And the rest of the cast is out in the audience, in thousands of glasses and hundreds of small spittoons.

This is the New York Wine Experience, where agriculture drops its first two syllables. No light entertainment here. No Lambrusco, Beaujolais nouveau, or white Zinfandel. The seminars are serious stuff: swirl and sniff, sip, study, spit. But no less than the people who will soon be filing into the stadium out in Minneapolis for the sixth game of the World Series, the students here are fans. Emotions run deep.

Playing here two days ago was Burgundy's most prestigious producer, the Domaine de la Romanée-Conti. Yesterday it was Penfolds from Australia and its Grange Hermitage, perhaps the New World's greatest wine. Tomorrow it will be Château Latour, one of the grandest glories of Bordeaux.

The applause goes on. In the Bacchanalia of Broadway, the man on stage has stolen the show.

The video replay would no doubt leave the uninitiated wondering what all the ado was about. There he is, Angelo Gaja, in his dark suit, putting on his reading glasses behind the lectern. Unlike when he first visited the United States seventeen years ago, he is now a well-known figure. Wine writers no longer have to tell their readers that his name is pronounced "guy-ah," with the accent on the first syllable. But he still takes nothing for granted. Matter-of-fact, he starts from scratch.

After a few remarks about Italian wine today, he moves on to speak about his own winery, founded in Barbaresco by his great-grandfather in 1859. The village is located in the northwestern corner of Italy in the region of Piedmont, about thirty miles southeast of the country's fourth-largest city and former capital, Turin, where Fiat automobiles are made.

The winery is not large. Production is about 250,000 bottles a year, half of which is Barbaresco, made from the Nebbiolo grape: a regular bottling and three single-vineyard ones. Then several other red wines made from local grapes such as Barbera and Dolcetto and small amounts of red and white from international varieties. In 1993 they'll release the other major Nebbiolo wine, Barolo, which they hadn't produced since they decided thirty years ago to stop buying grapes from other growers. It comes from a vineyard they purchased just three years ago in the district of that denomination on the other side of the nearby town of Alba.

Angelo is speaking with the aid of only a few notes. The English he has learned as an adult stumbles now and then as the pace quickens. He introduces his winemaker, Guido Rivella, and his vineyard manager, Federico Curtaz, both of whom are sitting in the front row.

Now for some slides. Here are the steep, vine-covered hills of the area around Alba, on the right bank of the Tánaro River. Called the Langhe, the region is famous for truffles as well as wine. That's Barbaresco perched on top of the hill with its tower. The Tanaro is flowing past below.

On to the tasting. Gaia & Rey 1990. This Chardonnay is named after his older daughter and his paternal grandmother. "What's the price?" someone asks. "Sixty-five dollars," he replies. The audience murmurs. Gaia & Rey 1983. "Our first vintage of this wine." Vignarey 1988. "Barbera is a grape usually associated with cheap, inferior wine, but it's finally showing what it can do if given a chance." Darmagi 1986. Angelo smiles for the first time as he tells a story about his father's reaction when he had Nebbiolo vines ripped up right below their house in order to plant Cabernet Sauvignon there. The audience laughs. Sorì Tildìn 1985. "If you want to like Barbaresco, you have to love tannin." More laughter. He does not mention that when this vintage came out, *The Wine Spectator,* which organizes the Wine Experience, wrote that it was "a wine of incredible depth, suppleness, and elegance," perhaps "the finest Italian red ever made." With the other two single-vineyard Barbarescos, Sorì San Lorenzo and Costa Russi, it's his most expensive wine. Coming up are older Barbarescos—the 1971, 1961, and 1955. In 1955, Angelo was a fifteen-year-old schoolboy.

Seated in the front row is Michael Broadbent, head of Christie's wine auctions and one of the most eminent figures in the world of wine. Although the notes he is so intently writing now will not make it into the revised edition of his monumental *The Great Vintage Book of Winetasting,* which is just being published, he does praise several of Angelo's wines in the eight pages dedicated to Italy. That may seem pitifully few compared to the two hundred eighty on France, but it is still eight more than when the collection of notes was first published in 1980.

The book reflects the history of wine. The wines Christie's deals in are overwhelmingly French. Two hundred years ago, in 1792, one of Broadbent's predecessors was already auctioning the 1785 vintage of Château Latour. Sixty years ago, when Angelo's father, Giovanni, started to help out at the family winery, the connoisseurs' consensus on Italian wine was reflected in Julian Street's popular book, *Wines,* published in 1933. There are ten pages on Italy and seventy-three on France; Barbaresco is not discussed at all. "The fine points of wine-growing are wearisome details to Italians," Street writes. Their wines are characterized by "quantity rather than elegance. Compared to French wines, they are coarse."

For an Italian producer to be treated as the peer of the greatest of France would have been as unthinkable as teams from places like Atlanta and Minnesota playing a World Series. Indeed, the situation was very much like that of baseball in the United States at the time. Membership in the two eight-team major leagues had not changed since 1903, and there were no teams west of St. Louis or south of Washington, D.C. In the world of wine, the major leagues were called Burgundy and Bordeaux.

When Angelo started to work in 1961, the situation had not changed. Even ten years later, Hugh Johnson's pioneering *The World Atlas of Wine* granted France a seventy-two-page chapter to itself, while Italy was relegated to a catchall one on "Southern and Eastern Europe and the Mediterranean" and dispatched in fourteen pages, nine fewer than Germany got.

Nor were greater claims being made for the wines by the leading authorities on Italian food. In the 1963 edition of her classic *Italian Food,* Elizabeth David still advised readers to approach Italian wine "in a spirit of optimism and amiable inquiry, rather than with harsh comparisons to the wines of France," while Waverley Root's *The Food of Italy,* published in 1971, damned Italian wines with the defensive claim that they were better with Italian food. "Who would think of drinking a fine Médoc with a dish of spaghetti and tomato sauce?" he asked rhetorically, thereby inadvertently ridiculing the food as well.

The tasting is over; the cheering is on. In the World Series of wine, Angelo has hit a grand slam.

From Barbaresco to Broadway: things have changed indeed since he started out. Could the young man of twenty-one have dreamed of this swift succession of scenes during a brief Manhattan stay?

Lunch in a popular downtown café. Along with dessert the waiter brings an unordered bottle of Château d'Yquem. "From the gentleman over there," he explains, nodding toward a table at the other end of the room. The gentleman owns a wine shop in Detroit.

Dinner in a French restaurant on the Upper East Side that has just been rated the best in the country by the Gault-Millau guide. The owner comes to the table. There are some people in the other room who are drinking a bottle of Angelo's wine. They've heard he's here. Would he be so kind as to autograph the label?

Dinner after the performance in a fashionable midtown steakhouse. "Here he is!" announces a waiter as Angelo walks in. "The king of Italy." The owner is beaming as he shows him to his table. "When are you going to run for President?" he asks. After the referendum of 1946, will Italy have to choose again between monarchy and republic?

Back at Angelo's hotel, where the Wine Experience is taking place, an Italo-American comes up to him as he waits for the elevator. "I gotta have your wine for my restaurant," he blurts out with moist eyes. "What you did out there today made me feel proud to be Italian."

Upstairs in the lobby, an American is telling a Japanese acquaintance that he's leaving for Italy the next day. He has some business in Turin.

"Turin?" asks the Japanese. "Where's that?"

"You know," explains the American. "It's near where they make Barolo and Barbaresco."

The Japanese nods, but it's obvious that the map has still not quite come into focus. Then a broad grin suddenly flashes across his face.

"Ah, Barbaresco!" he exclaims as his head bobs up and down. "Gaja!"

Great wine works wonders and is itself one.

What do you have to do to make a great wine? Is there a secret?

In 1977 André Mentzelopulous bought one of the most famous wine estates in Bordeaux, Château Margaux, which had not produced a great wine since 1961. He engaged Émile Peynaud as a consultant and told him that he wanted to make the best wine in the world.

"That's not so hard," Peynaud replied. "All you have to do is give me the best *grapes.*"

October 7, 1988

*T*HE LAST CONTAINER of grapes has been loaded and the tractor starts off down the narrow road that runs along the bottom of the vine-clad slope.

To someone familiar only with table varieties, the grapes might seem almost as "unpromising" as those at Château Margaux did to the English writer Angus Reach a century and a half ago. They were a "homily against appearances," he wrote. "If you saw a bunch in Covent Garden you would turn from them with the notion that the fruiterer was trying to do you with overripe black currants." Not only are they smaller than table grapes, they are sweeter, too. Your hand becomes sticky right away if you crush one with your fingers. They are juicier and less crunchy when you bite into them, with a higher ratio of skin to pulp.

There are numerous varieties of all food plants, and the differences can be dramatic. Uncle Ben's may be OK to boil, but like the rice you use when cooking Chinese, it will ruin your risotto. Carnaroli and Vialone Nano are two varieties that can make it a delight.

Most people have tasted only a tiny fraction of the extant varieties of the fruits and vegetables they eat, not to speak of those that no longer exist. Sometimes a variety simply degenerates and disappears, as happened in England during the nineteenth century to the bittersweet Redstreak apple, from which the celebrated Herefordshire cider used to be made. More often it is economic factors that sound the death knoll. Commercial interests determine that most varieties are cultivated for reasons other than excellence and individuality of flavor: high yields, resistance to pests and disease, uniformity of appearance, ease of harvesting and transportation. The name of the insipid Moneymaker variety of tomato says it all.

A British potato enthusiast, Donald Maclean, once had more than four hundred varieties growing in his collection, but just six account for over 80 percent of commercial production in the United States. Who writes about the differences between the common varieties of potatoes and rarer, more interesting ones like the Pink Fir Apple, and how many consumers are willing to pay the difference in price?

Grapes are one of the few crops that can fetch a price that rewards the growing of demanding, low-yielding varieties: the ones that can make wine an "experience."

You can make decent wine out of other fruits: apples, for instance, or currants. Robert Parker, America's most influential wine writer, reviews the apple wines made in Vermont by Joseph Cerniglia and gives them high scores. They, too, vary with the variety, but it is doubtful that wine lovers will ever get worked up debating the relative merits of Granny Smith, Macintosh, and Northern Spy. Delightful as they are when young, these wines should be drunk within a year of the harvest and will not live to develop the complexity that is part of greatness.

The grapes moving down the road belong to the *vinifera* species of the genus *Vitis: Vitis vinifera,* "the wine-making vine," from which over 99 percent of all the wine in the world is made. In the United States you can still purchase brands such as Manischewitz and Mogen David that are made with the Concord variety of the native *Vitis labrusca.* When Mae West gave her legendary order in the movie *I'm No Angel* ("Beulah, peel me a grape!"), one hopes for Beulah's sake that the species in the bowl was the slipskin *labrusca. Vinifera* skins adhere tightly to the pulp.

It was the United States that heightened the world's awareness of wine grape varieties. As long ago as the post-Prohibition thirties, the influential writer and importer Frank Schoonmaker labelled his selections of California wines with varietal names rather than place names made famous by French and other European wines, as was standard practice in those days. Eventually "varietal" became a noun and a synonym of fine wine as opposed to the cheap jug wines that had tarnished the image of those places in the consumer's eye. Thus "Cabernet Sauvignon" became a code word meaning "This is *really* like Bordeaux."

The road has now begun to curve and climb as it finally takes on the hill. The grapes in tow behind the tractor are one of Italy's countless varieties of *vinifera*. There are so many that the ancient Roman poet Virgil wrote that numbering them would be like counting the waves of the sea or the grains of sand blown by the wind in the desert.

Two men are sitting on the tractor and talking. You may have studied Dante in the original, know Verdi's operas by heart, and have no trouble conversing with the natives in Rome, but you wouldn't understand a word they're saying. And that's not because of the noise the engine is making as it strains up the slope. They are speaking Piedmontese, the dialect of Piedmont.

Until the unification of Italy in 1861, Italian was only the third language of the region. Since 1720 Piedmont had been part of the Kingdom of Sardinia, which included not only Italy's second-largest island, but Savoie and Haute-Savoie, and the city of Nice in present-day France as well. Dialect was the language of private life and everyday business, while the educated used French for public affairs. The main architect of Italian unity and first prime minister of the Kingdom of Italy, Cavour, was described in school as distinguished in French, but mediocre in Italian. He was an accomplished orator in the former language, but stiff in the latter. "You realize he's translating," a contemporary wrote. In the exciting days of the birth of the new state, one Piedmontese town after another voted to conduct its affairs in Italian, which, as one resolution declared in French, *"est la langue de notre patrie"* ("is the language of our country").

The tractor passes below one of the local landmarks, known

simply as the Bricco, the Hill. Rising out of the vines is the modern, dark red house where Angelo Gaja lives with his wife, daughters, and parents.

The road has now become via Torino, Turin Street. On the left, at number one, lives Federico Curtaz's predecessor as Angelo's vineyard manager, seventy-five-year-old Luigi Cavallo, who is sitting in his courtyard. Cavallo has never been to Turin. "I've always been here," he says. Up to the end of the nineteenth century, peasants from this world apart, the Langhe, could be heard referring to Piedmont as if one had to cross the Tanaro River to get there. "We're going to Piedmont," they would say. "In Piedmont they do this and that."

The tractor is now driving through what locals refer to as the "square," where the two roads leading into town converge after skirting the opposite sides of the Bricco. It is heading toward that stretch of via Torino that is lined on both sides by buildings and is the only part of town where the visitor feels with any confidence that this is it, that this is Barbaresco, with its six hundred or so inhabitants.

Up ahead, at the end of the street, is the tower. From the top of its one hundred twenty-five feet, on a clear day, with the Alps staring you in the face, you can see over into the Barolo area and even make out the hill of Superga just outside Turin. You can follow the course of the Tanaro as it bends around Alba, snakes past below, and flows on to the town of Asti, not quite twenty miles away, and beyond.

On the left, as tractor and grapes go by, is the little town hall. Its archives offer glimpses of a past in which both nature and man were often less than benign. Two hundred years ago hail ravaged the vineyards three years in a row. On top of that came the wars fired by the French Revolution and Napoleon. Austrian artillery units got stuck in the mud a few miles down the road and villagers had to go with their oxen to haul them out. Barbaresco was ordered by the French to supply them with "bread, wine, munitions, straw, four oxen and forty-four pairs of shoes." The French general Flavigny had all the bells in town melted down to make cannons. Not many years later, even a happy event turned to sorrow. On October 1, 1821, a bonfire welcoming King Vittorio Emanuele I to the Langhe destroyed the roof of Barbaresco's tower.

At number thirty-six, on the right, the tractor turns off the street and honks in front of a huge red metal door. Folding and rumbling as it goes, the door rolls slowly back. The tractor moves forward.

The courtyard of the Gaja winery is ringing with Piedmontese. "We're not talking about the Concorde or one of those high-speed trains they've got in Japan," a voice exclaims. "I just want a photocopier that works!" To the left of the door, wearing a multi-colored sweater and blue jeans, Angelo is talking to a man near the low wooden building that houses the winery office. The fierce intensity of his expression is tempered by an incipient smile.

Halfway down the courtyard on the right, standing in his gray smock by the pitlike bin next to the cellar steps where grapes are unloaded, is Guido Rivella. His gentle face is even thinner than usual, the toll that every harvest takes.

At the far end of the courtyard two men are conversing next to the railing that overlooks the paved area outside the lowest level of the cellar far below and the sloping vineyards beyond. One of them is thirtyish Aldo Vacca, who takes care of visitors and foreign correspondence at the winery. The other is Angelo's father, Giovanni, known to everyone as "the *geometra*," after the profession he practiced in addition to running the winery before Angelo took over. A *geometra* is not a geometrician, but someone with the basic skills of a land surveyor and an architect.

Still jaunty at just over eighty, Giovanni Gaja remembers the courtyard as it was sixty years ago, when it belonged to four different owners.

Right there, where he's standing with Aldo, were trees and grass. The courtyard faded into the hillside, which was excavated almost forty years later when they enlarged the cellar. There, in the middle of the courtyard, was the cistern where rainwater collected. They didn't have running water in Barbaresco until 1964, when he had been mayor for six years. Over there, across from Guido, instead of the storeroom was the stall where his father, the first Angelo, kept the mule that brought the grapes he bought back to the winery. Most of the office was the house where the Gajas lived at that time. The room where Aldo works was the kitchen, while Angelo's office was part of another family's house. Where the entrance is now, with its sliding door, was a small building on the street front.

The tractor stops and backs up toward Guido. Aldo walks over with Giovanni Gaja and tastes a grape. "They look real good," he says. "The best since '85."

When that vintage made its debut, two of Germany's leading wine experts, Armin Diel and Joel Payne, wrote that it had "a multifaceted structure, enormous extract, concentrated fruit, unbelievable richness and a magnificent finish." Robert Parker described it as "exotic, compelling and incredibly complex." Its bouquet, he wrote, "is reminiscent of what a fictional blend of Romanée-Conti and Mouton-Rothschild might taste like."

"What is it?" asks the *geometra*.

"Nebbiolo," Aldo replies. "From San Lorenzo."

October 27, 1988

*O*BSERVED FROM THE HILL across the valley, Fasèt, Sorì San Lorenzo is like a stage where the lights go on early and are turned off late. You master your first word of the local dialect: *sorì,* a slope facing south, a slope that catches the most sun. In this relatively northern climate—the latitude is that of Bordeaux, well north of New York—and at an altitude of over eight hundred feet, the slow-ripening Nebbiolo grape needs all the sun it can get.

The vine is more sensitive to site than any other fruit-bearing plant. In the world of wine, the lexicon of land is rich in subtle distinctions.

The importance of site was expressed prosaically in the seventeenth century by the English philosopher John Locke, who marvelled that the mere "width of a ditch" separated the great Bordeaux vineyard of Haut-Brion from the lesser one next door, and poetically in our own by the French writer Colette. "The vine makes the savor of the earth intelligible to man," she wrote. "It senses, then expresses in its clusters, the secrets of the soil."

Which is more important—the variety or the site? As with marriage, it's the match that counts, the mutual exaltation. Over a

[14]

hundred years ago, Robert Louis Stevenson described the court-ship process in California's Napa Valley, where there was no long-standing tradition to dictate one's mate. "One corner of land after another is tried with one kind of grape after another," he wrote in 1883. "This is a failure, that is better, a third best." Centuries earlier, Cistercian monks had done the same thing in Burgundy.

Sorì San Lorenzo looks out upon an open valley. It is ventilated and thus less subject to excessive heat and humidity and the consequent danger of rot than it would be otherwise. Off to its right is the Tanaro, which a dam transforms into a quasi-lake just as it flows by the vineyard, increasing its temperature-moderating influence. The crown of the hill protects the vines from cold northern winds. You don't have to be an expert to note these features and understand their importance.

But there are puzzling details, too. The vines of San Lorenzo are planted in horizontal rows that follow the curve of the slope, while those of a contiguous plot run straight up and down it. When you look attentively at the two plots, it definitely seems that the neighboring vines are planted closer together. Then there is the foliage. The vines of San Lorenzo are still full of light green leaves, so a small leafless plot wedged into them on the Tanaro side stands out in its stark bareness, while across the slope is a vineyard where the green of the leaves is blatantly bright.

October 28, 1988

ℱEDERICO CURTAZ squats down and picks up a clump of freshly turned earth.

"The poverty of this soil is priceless!" he exclaims.

From somewhere up there, Saint Lawrence must have a look now and then at this vineyard that bears his name. Versed as he is in paradox, he would understand. When, as treasurer of the Church, he was ordered by the prefect of Rome to hand over the Church's valuables, he assembled the poor and sick and presented them to the official. "Here," he said, "is the Church's treasure."

Wine may end in the poetry of tasting, but it begins in the prose of the soil. From the way he's beaming, you'd think Federico were examining nuggets of gold, or at least one of those famous truffles. He talks about soil as passionately as wine lovers discuss the finer points of Pauillac and Pomerol.

Federico was born not quite thirty years ago in the Valle d'Aosta, near the French and Swiss borders, but he grew up partly in nearby Asti, his mother's hometown. While still a schoolboy he participated precociously in the radical politics and strenuous ideological confrontations of the seventies. "If you want war,"

Angelo told him when he started to work at the winery in 1983, "you'll have it."

No shot was ever fired. Reflecting on his self-portrait of the viticulturist as a young man, Federico shakes his head. "I'm beginning to think that when you're sixteen you might be better off spending your time in a discothèque," he sighs.

His parents eke out a living from what is not much more than subsistence farming. The soil is in his blood, too, but his perspective is different from theirs. After graduating from a technical school, he worked on a farm in Wales, growing hops and squash. He spent time in London. "Travel is the real school," he says. People and museums encountered far from home have left their mark on him.

Vineyard workers are the forgotten men and women of wine. Leading producers are stars. Top winemakers make not only wine, but a name for themselves as well. Keepers of the vine work far from the limelight.

"You can't do this job with a trade union mentality," says Federico, who had to skip his vacation this year. Work in the vineyards fell far behind schedule because of bad weather in the spring and he had to scramble throughout the summer to catch up. "You also have to have a long-term perspective. It takes years before you see the results of what you're doing."

Federico breaks the clump with his hands. It splits open perfectly. "Like an orange," he says with a broad grin. His results are beginning to show.

To the ignorant feet of a layman, the soil of a vineyard is merely the stuff one walks on there. Little does he suspect in his pedestrian plodding what lies beneath the surface.

"Structure is the most important thing, but the least considered." Federico's voice is fervent. Vines growing in a great vineyard are the aristocrats of the vegetable kingdom, but they have the same physiological needs as their plebeian brethren. Structure determines how soil handles the vital elements of water and air.

The structure of a given soil is related to its texture—the relative proportions of sand, silt, and clay it contains. Sand particles are the largest and clay the finest; silt is in between. Structure refers to the arrangement of particles into aggregates and how they hold together. Neither light, single-grained sandy soil nor heavy, massive clayey soil would split as Federico's clump did. Neither one has structure. Clay swells with water, the pores close, it doesn't drain. Water stagnates around the roots of the vine and deprives them of vital oxygen. Sand doesn't retain water. If drought is prolonged, as it can be in Barbaresco, the vine will cease to function and eventually die in sandy soil. Tension, to use one of Federico's favorite words, is what you need.

"Drain, but retain!" Federico chants. "That's the refrain." He doesn't suspect that the English language has made him a rhymester.

"The soil of San Lorenzo is 10 percent sand, 20 percent coarse silt, 40 percent fine silt, and 30 percent clay," he says. "It's the silt that gives it its great balance."

Federico has a rodlike device with which he can measure the depth of the soil and obtain a cross section. He plunges it into the ground and pushes it down as far as it will go. The scale reads 28 inches. The soil at the bottom of the rod is rather compact; there are specks of limestone. He walks over to the next passageway and then a few rows down the slope, where the vines have a slightly more exuberant foliage and their trunks are slightly thicker. He strains as he pushes the rod down again: 32 inches.

"There are more temptations for the vine here," he says with amusement. "The more goodies there are in the fridge, the fatter we get, too. This deeper soil increases the vigor of the vine."

It's clear from the way he says *"vigore"* that it's a four-letter word and has no place in a proper viticultural vocabulary. "Weak" is a term that glows with praise. Weakness is a strength.

Like parents who dedicate so much time and energy to their jobs that they have little left over for their children, vigorous vines grow so furiously and so long into the season that they detract sustenance from the grapes. Ripening is delayed. Skins remain fragile and less resistant to disease. Thick, tangled foliage creates problems for cultivation. Clusters are larger and grapes are less concentrated in flavor.

The vigor of a vine can be measured by the length of the shoots it puts out in one season and by the thickness of its trunk. You can weigh it.

Federico is at once clinical and paternal as he examines the foliage. "The vines of San Lorenzo give you balanced vegetation," he says with quiet admiration in his voice. Some of them were planted before he was born and, with vines as with people, nothing tempers vigor like age. But his eyes begin to bulge and his tone turns animated when he talks about some vines in the vineyard that Angelo recently bought over in the Barolo area, in Serralunga. He's going to rip them up.

"There's one spot there where the soil is just too deep for Nebbiolo. It's almost Californian." Federico says "Californian" with a mixture of awe and disdain. "When I was there a few years ago, I saw trunks as thick as trees!" he exclaims, indicating the girth with his hands. He shakes his head. "Vines like that are real Mike Tysons: all brawn and no finesse."

Vigor is in great part a function of water and nitrogen. Limit them and you limit vigor.

Federico pulls out a sheet of paper with the results of a soil analysis he's just received from a laboratory. Printed on the form are the percentages of nitrogen that make a soil "poor," "sufficient" or "rich." "Poor" is less than 0.12 percent; the soil of Sorì Lorenzo contains 0.073 percent. According to the laboratory, the vineyard is destitute, a pauper. They recommend the get-rich-quick approach of heavy fertilization.

"The recommendations are standard for other crops," he snorts. "They're OK for corn."

Balance is once again the key. "Staying trim shouldn't mean malnutrition," Federico says, wrinkling his brow. "The way some wine writers carry on about making the vine suffer, you'd think it was the Marquis himself who wrote the standard work on viticulture." An impish grin steals across his face. "I've read de Sade, you know."

He points across the slope in the direction away from the Tanaro. "Take that vineyard over there. The leaves are bright green because the vines have been heavily fertilized with nitrogen." He swivels around and gestures with his head toward the river. "Then there is that enclave that doesn't belong to us. The

[19]

leaves fell off early there because the overcropped vines simply ran out of gas."

Between the rows of vines, Federico has planted broad beans and vetches, leguminous plants that "doe manure and fat the soil where they be sowed," as an elegant seventeenth-century translation of the Roman naturalist Pliny the Elder words it. But they make nitrogen available to the vines, as Federico says, "in a properly parsimonious fashion." And the "green manure" delights not only the dietician. After it is mowed in the late spring while in full bloom and turned over into the soil, it will decompose into humus, one of Federico's valiant allies in the struggle to maintain structure. By binding the soil's particles into relatively stable aggregates, humus keeps it permeable to water and air.

"Organic matter is a remedy for almost all the ills of the soil," Federico says, and proudly announces that he's just found a good source of manure—a nearby farm. If that's not the equivalent of striking it rich with a lottery ticket for him, then it's the next best thing. With fewer and fewer animals around, it's not so easy these days. There's manure, and there's *manure*. A lot of the stuff contains antibiotics, which are detrimental to the bacteria that are so vital to the health of the soil. (Federico is pleased that on the farm he's just discovered they don't put antibiotics in the calves' fodder.) You also have to see how much straw is mixed in, he notes. And beware pig manure: a real nitrogen bomb!

Eyes that follow Federico around the vineyard soon wish their vision were less superfical.

The semiotician of the soil points to a sign from the subterranean world: a bulge just above the ground on each trunk. It becomes harder to follow what Federico is saying. He hasn't shifted into dialect, but rather into some kind of jargon or code: "420A," "Kober 5BB," "S04." The upshot of it all is that these proud European aristocrats are unable to stand on their own feet and are totally dependent for survival on humble immigrants from America. The bulge is a graft.

After stowing away on botanical specimens shipped by steamer from the United States, the phylloxera louse disembarked clandestinely in France around 1860 and proceeded to devastate the vineyards of Europe as it chewed its way through them, feeding off the roots of the vines. The microscopic marauder seemed invincible, and *Vitis vinifera* appeared doomed to extinction. A solution was finally found, which was radical in both the common and botanical senses of the word: grafting *vinifera* vines onto the roots of phylloxera–immune American species.

The question was hotly debated; experts were divided. Would there not be contagion, perhaps some viny V.D.? What if those foreigners brought in other pests with them?

In 1881 the Italian government created an experimental nursery of American rootstocks and appointed as its head Domizio Cavazza, director of the newly founded Royal School of Enology and Viticulture in Alba, who was later to be the prime mover behind Barbaresco's cooperative winery. As a precautionary measure, the nursery was quarantined on the island of Montecristo. Even then the protests failed to subside, and shortly thereafter the government decreed the destruction of the nursery.

Not all these fears were unfounded. A vine disease that was new to the Continent, the so-called "downy" form of mildew, eventually slipped into Europe with the migrating masses. But the grafting movement could not be stopped.

The deepest fear was that the partnership with proletarians would debase the noble *vinifera* wine. But the Americans turned out to be okay. They supported their partners discreetly, staying out of sight and not interfering directly with the grapes themselves. Venerable *vinifera*'s blood remained blue.

The alliance against phylloxera was one of the greatest examples of transatlantic cooperation in history. That nineteenth-century NATO, the North Atlantic Transplant Operation, is still going strong. Billions of American rootstocks are entrenched in European soil, and European nurseries turn out millions of replacements every year.

But not all the tales within the larger success story had a happy ending. Many of the foreigners had trouble adapting to their new environment, and couples frequently proved to be incompatible.

Cavazza had already noted that although it was "easy to see that American roots are thin, tough, hard to cut, and resistant when you pull them; in short, much stronger than ours," it was not so obvious that each species had its own degree of compatibility with the different *vinifera* varieties and adapted more or less well to the different environments of Europe. "They have to live, as well as resist phylloxera!" Cavazza exclaimed.

American vines evolved in more fertile, less arid soils than those of most European vineyards, and the less vigorous ones find the going rough in the limestone-rich Langhe. Of the three American species of *Vitis* most used as rootstocks—*riparia, rupestris,* and *berlandieri*—the first is the least vigorous and most sensitive to limestone; the last is the most tolerant of limestone, but is very vigorous and roots poorly. *Rupestris* has deep-striking roots and is the most resistant to drought. These differences and other important ones were not understood at first, and indiscriminate use led to failures.

The ultimate solution was to crossbreed: usually two American species, more rarely an American with *vinifera*. Federico's jargon refers to the resultant hybrid rootstocks. S04? Selection number four from the research institute in Oppenheim, Germany. Kober 5BB? One of Mr. Kober's crosses. The two most common rootstocks in Barbaresco are the 420A and the Kober 5BB, both *riparia* x *berlandieri,* as the botanists write it.

There are actually many advantages to grafting. You can tailor the rootstock to the needs of *vinifera* variety and soil. And you can restrain vigor. *Vinifera* vines are more vigorous on their own fleshier, more extensive roots, which is one of the reasons for the negative attitude to manuring that one encounters in nineteenth-century pre-phylloxera works on viticulture. Growers in Monterey County, California rediscovered that vigor after they had planted thousands of acres with ungrafted vines.

(What's more, they have discovered that their area is not immune to phylloxera. And even growers in prestigious Napa and Sonoma are beginning to reel from the realization that they will have to replant about 65 percent of their vines very soon. In 1985 the University of California at Davis identified a mutant of the phylloxera louse—biotype B—which is ravaging with incredible speed vines grafted onto AxR#1 rootstock, a cross between *rupestris* and the *vinifera* variety Aramon. Because of its *vinifera* component, the rootstock is more vulnerable than all-American ones even to the original biotype A, but growers favored it because its greater productivity more than made up for its briefer lifespan.)

The other *vinifera* varieties may have been shocked as well as relieved when they were first grafted, but for Nebbiolo it was no novelty. When vineyards are planted or replanted, cuttings are used. While the vine is dormant, one-year-old canes are cut into sections with two or more bud-eyes. In pre-phylloxera days, the cuttings were planted without further ado. Nebbiolo's exceptional vigor created problems, however. Lorenzo Fantini, a *geometra* from the Langhe whose writings constitute our most important source of information on viticulture and enology in the area during the second half of the nineteenth-century, noted that "Nebbiolo cuttings bear fruit only after five or six years and most of the time they put out many shoots and no grapes. So Nebbiolo is no longer planted and instead growers plant Dolcetto and Moscatello [two less vigorous varieties of *vinifera*]. After the fourth year they graft Nebbiolo onto the rootstock and the same year they get their grapes."

Federico smiles knowingly.

"That's Nebbiolo's vigor for you," he says as he examines another clump of earth, "It's a truly noble vine only when it lives in poverty like San Lorenzo's."

*F*OR THE FAITHFUL of winedom, a great vineyard is holy land. But a pilgrimage to Sorì San Lorenzo before 1964 would have saddened the soul. Sacred soil was being profaned.

The vineyard was then an anonymous part of a hillside farm providing income for the benefice of the cathedral of Alba and run by a sharecropper. Giovanni Gaja purchased the entire property, which is still referred to as *masuè*, dialect for "sharecropper."

The tractor alley up and down that privileged part of the slope now called San Lorenzo, after the patron saint of Alba, was much more than just a path for getting in and out of the vineyard. On a detailed map of the fifties it is indicated as Strada Montà, the "street" or "road" leading up to the village from the ferry crossing on the Tanaro, the "port of Barbaresco." The ferry was still running at that time, day and night, and was the quickest way to get to the other side of the river. It was used not only by pedestrians, but by farmers with animals and wagons as well. The road was lined with oaks, elms, and poplars. Guido Rivella remembers it well from frequent visits to his grandfather, who lived just across the river.

The entire hillside is now planted with vines, but until 1964 there was a large meadow, which served as a pasture for the farmer's livestock, his main concern. "Animals were the sharecropper's piggybank," says Angelo. "They could be sold any time he needed cash." There were also fruit and hazelnut trees in the meadow.

Between the rows of vines other crops were planted. "It was subsistence farming in those days," explains Pietro Rocca, a grower who worked with Angelo in the sixties. "Grapes were really a secondary crop. Wheat was the main one, because it meant bread and pasta for the family." Angelo harvested more than grapes in 1964. He had twenty people helping him mow over ten tons of wheat in his new vineyard.

Sharecropping was widespread in Barbaresco. When three years later his father bought the farm called Roncagliette, including what are now the famous vineyards of Sorì Tildìn and Costa Russi, the situation was even more depressing. Costa Russi was not even planted to vines at the time.

"The whole property was in ruins," says Angelo. "It was owned by an engineer at Fiat, who was always grumbling about how much the place was costing him. And his sharecropper complained that he was forced to do somersaults to make ends meet. Nobody wanted to spend a lira."

In the Barbaresco of those days, there was nothing glamorous about growing grapes, and nothing strange about plebeian plants, not to speak of calves, rubbing elbows with aristocratic vines. Why was the precious poverty of San Lorenzo's soil being squandered so?

The vineyard was on the wrong side of those Alps you can see so well from Barbaresco on a clear day. Beyond them, in France, a plant knew its place. What a nineteenth-century French agronomist called the "liberty, equality, and fraternity of vegetables" was unthinkable in a great vineyard there, where even the tiniest blade of grass was not suffered to compete with vines for water and nourishment. Who can imagine Romanée-Conti corn or bread made with wheat from Château Latour?

With an occasional exception, such as Vintage Port, fine wine meant French. Roman legions had spread viticulture to France in ancient times, but when the age of modern wine dawned in the second half of the seventeenth century, Italy was left far behind.

Until then, wine had been an agricultural product like any other and little importance was attributed to its precise place of origin. The price of a wine of any given year usually took a nose dive as soon as the following vintage was available, for it was in all likelihood well on its way to vinegar by then.

The transformation of an alcoholic beverage into something one "experiences" was due to the concomitance of several factors: a strong, cylindrical bottle; a cork to close it; the great wine estates of Bordeaux, created by ambitious urbanites; and a wealthy market thirsty for wine. The market was England; London set the prices and bought the wine. As recently as the 1950s one heard in Bordeaux the saying "If the weather's good in London during the month of August, it'll be a good year for wine."

The predominance of French wines on the English market went all the way back to 1152, when Bordeaux became part of the English royal domain through the marriage of Henry II and Eleanor of Aquitaine. In the 1660s, at the beginning of the era of modern wine, Arnaud de Pontac, an influential public figure in Bordeaux and ambassador to London, began to promote his Haut-Brion, the first Bordeaux wine to be sold under the name of the estate where it was produced: the estate to which John Locke was to make his pilgrimage in 1677. He made his wine known to people who could create a demand, who not only appreciated it and could afford it themselves, but who would spread the word and influence others. "Ho Bryan," as Samuel Pepys referred to it in his famous diary, led the way for other French estates that were to become famous.

France established the international vinous canon. Bordeaux and Burgundy became household words as colors. The wine a young Italo-American singer like Frank Sinatra got no kick from was Champagne, not the ancestral Asti Spumante. Even modest French wines glowed with the reflected glamour of aristocratic-sounding and long-familiar names, while even the best Italian ones were guilty by association with the likes of Lambrusco.

During her frequent wars with France, England would levy discriminatory duties on imports from the enemy and seek alternative sources of wine, which is how Port got its foot in the important door. It was in this way that early in the eighteenth century, Barolo, Barbaresco's neighbor, got its chance. Documents in the National Archives in Turin reveal that English merchants were interested in a deal, but getting the wine to them was a problem. There was no road leading to the port of Nice suitable for the transportation of heavy barrels, while the Republic of Genoa, with its more accessible ports, would have taxed the wine out of the market.

Italy's geographical isolation and lack of political unity sealed the fate of wines like Barbaresco. The Langhe remained a region of backward farmers making wine for strictly local consumption.

A wine without a demanding international market is like a dancer or musician who performs only for a hometown audience, without competition and critical reviews. French success in the long run was due not only to geography and marketing, but also to the quality of the wines.

The state of the future Sorì San Lorenzo on the eve of its purchase by Giovanni Gaja would not have surprised Lorenzo Fantini, who knew the vineyards and cellars of the Langhe first-hand and yet observed them from a much broader perspective than that of the peasant grower. He began his main work, *Enology and Viticulture in the Province of Cuneo,* in the early 1880s and was still adding to it as late as 1895, when the once elegant handwriting of his never-to-be-printed manuscript had become almost illegible.

In the middle of the nineteenth century, writes Fantini, "the state of wine making was miserable, with procedures going back to the good patriarch Noah." The main cause of the situation was "the almost total lack of trade," which in turn was due to "the scarcity and sometimes total lack of roads." It was a vicious circle. "In those times, to speak of exporting was like speaking Sanskrit and frequent were the years in which producers were forced to drink their own wines for want of buyers. That explains the phenomenal generosity with which our grandfathers poured wine for their friends!"

He acknowledges that progress has been made since then, but finds that the wines of the province "are still unable to compete worthily with those of our transalpine neighbors."

A contemporary of Fantini's from nearby Casale Monferrato, Ottavio Ottavi, founder of Italy's first viticultural and enological journal and author of major works on both subjects, is even more critical. "It is an undeniable fact," he writes, "that at present we make little fine wine, much poor wine, and a lot of vinegar." And to top it all off, even the best wines are plagued by inconsistency. "One bottle is worthy of a Pope's palate, even Paul III's, while another is barely fit for cooking bell peppers."

Fantini emphasizes sharecropping as a major reason why more progress has not been made since that period. "A sharecropper who is a good viticulturist is as rare as the phoenix," he writes. "And no owner who has a sharecropper running his property is tempted to invest in improvements."

Mixed crops even in prime sites for growing grapes was another consequence of the precarious economic situation. The great fear of humanity had always been not having enough to eat, and Fantini is eloquent on the farmer's reluctance to put all his eggs in the grape basket and his consequent determination "to harvest a bit of everything." He tells the story of a farmer not far from Barbaresco who tried leaving a few rows in his vineyard free of other crops.

"The result was sensational. The difference between the grapes in those rows and the ones in the rest of the vineyard, where he had continued to plant other crops, was too great not to be noticed and duly acknowledged. And so, the following year, he did not plant any wheat at all in the vineyard. Would that he had never done it! His family, his friends, and everybody else wanted to stone him. He had to start planting wheat again."

Ottavi also decried "the marriage of Bacchus and Ceres." It created competition for water and nutrients, shaded the vines, caused humidity and made vineyard work difficult. Both he and Fantini urged farmers to separate their vines from the other crops, but to no avail. According to statistics of the Ministry of Agriculture, Industry, and Commerce, in 1896 mixed crops were grown in 99.5 percent of all vineyards in the Alba area.

France was way ahead in all respects. Writing to his father from Toulouse in 1910, a young peasant from Barbaresco, Pietro Musso, described the marvels of technology that local farmers used to prepare the ground for planting a new vineyard. "They have two large pulleys that haul a big plow back and forth. You're not always just digging away with a hoe like we do at home. The ground is broken up by this big machine and in a few days is ready to be planted." His father admonished him not to tell anybody about it when he came back to Barbaresco: "Nobody would believe you and we'd soon be the laughingstock of the town."

The times themselves were not propitious to progress. World War I hit hard. Outside the town hall of Barbaresco, a marble plaque dedicated to the village's "brave sons who fell for their country" has fifty-four names engraved on it. The autarkic fantasies of fascism, epitomized by Mussolini's "Battle for Grain," led farmers to plant even more cereal crops in their vineyard sites. And during World War II, not only were the farmers of Barbaresco sent off to fight on distant battlefields, as they had been only twenty-five years before, but the village itself was caught up in the conflict.

There had been brief moments, such as the founding of the cooperative winery under the directorship of Domizio Cavazza in 1894, when it seemed that Barbaresco and its wine were on their way to better days. But on the whole, more than fifty years later, not much had changed. And the essence of Fantini's analysis of the situation still rang true. "The prevalent economic factor is labor," he had written, "and rarely do you find it combined with the other two, capital and applied intelligence."

January 24, 1989

*A*S HE TALKS on the phone, Angelo glances out the window of his temporary office in the former tasting room. A BMW with Swiss license plates is parked just across the courtyard. Sitting with him is the car's owner, an elegantly dressed man with salt-and-pepper hair.

A construction worker is shouting from the courtyard railing to someone down below. Every time the office door is opened, sounds of banging and drilling unmuffle as they come in out of the cold.

Work is under way to enlarge the cellar, which the Serralunga vineyard has made too small. The office is being demolished to make way for a new one. Two giant cranes have reared their heads above the winery and the town.

The voice on the phone is speaking English with a British accent. Aldo Vacca enters the room with a fax. "Those people from London are coming on Tuesday," Angelo whispers to him as his ear continues to listen and his eyes begin to read.

Another day has begun.

Born six miles away in Alba, where he lived until 1963, Angelo came frequently to Barbaresco for family gatherings on Sundays and holidays and for longer stays before school in the fall. He remembers Christmases with "snow so deep you couldn't go outdoors," and an uncle who was always teasing his father. "The minute you have a little extra cash in your pocket," he would say, "you spend it on barrels and other stuff for the cellar."

He hardly knew his grandfather Angelo, who died in 1944, but a special place in his memories is occupied by his father's mother, Clotilde Rey. Born in a village just three miles from the French border, she had studied to be a schoolteacher. She brought a gentler culture to the family and had a vision of the winery that dimly foreshadowed her grandson's. Her dowry went to buy a small vineyard, and when she later urged Angelo's father to buy more of them, she insisted on the very best. It was she who attended to the whole commercial side of the winery, tending to the accounting, dealing with customers, and taking care of the correspondence. Above all, Angelo remembers her drumming the notion of quality into his head. "She was a missionary," he says.

Tender amusement steals over his face as he recalls her rituals. "She would set grapes aside in the fall which weren't to be touched until Easter, when the whole family got together. Then she would proudly bring out a few bunches that by then were half-rotten." Clotilde Rey's thriftiness was proverbial. "She wasn't stingy," Angelo says, making a distinction less and less meaningful in the credit-card-happy society he knows all too well. "She saved." He pauses to reflect. "She came from mountain people, who had never had anything. Maybe she simply didn't know how to enjoy what she eventually had here."

By the time she died in 1961, the Gaja winery had become the leading one in Barbaresco. It was among the very few to bottle at least some of its own wine. The big merchant houses, which were located in Alba and in the Barolo area, would "adjust" their Barbaresco by blending it with lesser years or with Barbera, a lesser wine. "In my grandfather's and father's bottles, you would find only Barbaresco of the year on the label," he says. "They had a policy of quality."

They were able to stick to it because Angelo's father had his own profession and an income that did not depend on the winery. Poor years could be sold off in bulk. A higher price could be asked for a good one without having to worry about selling it all right away.

The Gaja winery may have been the leading one in Barbaresco, but that wasn't saying much at that time if you had a more than local perspective. Sales were still mainly in Piedmont and direct to customers in anonymous demijohns. But Angelo's perspective was broader. For one thing, he hadn't grown up just anywhere. He had grown up in Alba.

At the beginning of the fifties, Alba was the least industrialized town in the province of Cuneo. By the end of the decade, which saw the spectacular rise to international stature of two industries created by local entrepreneurs, that position had been reversed.

Ferrero is now the second-largest sweets producer in Europe, with 3,500 workers in Alba itself and 5,000 more throughout the world. It grew from a little pastry shop started in 1946 by Pietro Ferrero, who hit on the idea of creating "the people's chocolate," hazelnut paste mixed with a little cocoa that cost one-fifth the price of chocolate itself in the immediate postwar years of poverty. The collective Italian sweet tooth, hungrier than ever after five years of wartime deprivation, responded voraciously to what is now known as Nutella. In 1951 Ferrero already had 300 workers; by 1961, 2,700. The story of Miroglio, the local company that is now one of Italy's five largest textile groups, is similar.

Alba in the fifties was a showplace of what came to be known as the Italian economic miracle. Population increased from 16,000 to 21,000, employment in industry more than tripled. A window on the world had been opened. Angelo grew up breathing a different air from that of Barbaresco.

The economic miracle was also connected to the enological one in a more direct way. The construction boom set off by Alba's rapid growth meant prosperity for Giovanni Gaja. Much more money was available for investing in vineyards than before, and Angelo's father eventually bought more than 125 acres of them.

In 1960, Angelo graduated from the school of viticulture and enology in Alba. He was starting out at the right time, for the sixties was the turning point for the consumption and production of fine wine in the world. The fifties had been depressed even in Bordeaux, where, in the words of one of the leading producers, "the whole Médoc was up for sale." In a sense, the sale of Château

Latour to a British concern in 1963 was a sign of the renaissance there: someone was actually willing to spend a lot of money buying and renovating a wine estate! The founding of the Robert Mondavi winery in Napa Valley in 1966 and the resumption by Christie's of its suspended wine auctions the same year were two more signals among many. Prices had started their steady climb upward. The wine revolution had begun.

An urge to travel took Angelo to London, where he wound up working in a fast-food place: fish-and-chips and the underground to work—"a useful lesson for life," he says. During the next ten years, he made many trips abroad, especially to France.

"Going abroad, I realized that Italy's image was nil," he says. He pauses to let the word sink in. "It was humiliating to read the wine lists in restaurants. There would be pages of wines from Bordeaux alone, but only a cheap Soave or generic Chianti from Italy."

Angelo had his work cut out for him.

"I wanted to understand the key to the success of French wines," he says. Visits to famous estates in Burgundy and Bordeaux gave him insights, but the courses for growers at Montpellier, in the south of France, were even more valuable. "The most famous regions had successful and highly codified traditions," he explains. "The South had a great deal in common with Italy. They, too, were trying to get out of the bulk and blending wine rut."

Back in Barbaresco, Angelo was working in the family vineyards. There was more and more to do as his father bought what are now considered the jewels of the Gaja crown: in 1961, the entire Bricco, where the Gajas also went to live in their new house three years later; in 1964, Masuè; in 1967, Roncagliette.

"The vineyard is a tough school," he says. "You learn to distrust appearances; you get used to having your hopes dashed. If the season is bad from the start, you have time to resign yourself. But in years like 1966, everything is fine until the fall, and then rain ruins beautiful grapes."

Older people in Barbaresco remember daredevil Angelo tearing through the village and vineyards on his tractor as if it were a racing car. He was in a hurry, and not only to get up and down the slopes. Major changes in policy were already in the works.

The Gajas decided that, beginning in 1962, they would no

longer buy grapes from other growers. "Earlier, in good years," Angelo says, "we were able to buy grapes that were as good as our own. But viticulture was changing fast, and for the worse."

Growers were using synthetic fertilizers with a heavier and heavier hand. With the prospect of a comprehensive wine law (the *Denominazione d'Origine Controllata* statute adopted in 1963) giving legal status and consequently greater prestige to wines such as Barbaresco, just as the *Appellation Contrôlée* legislation had done in France thirty years earlier, Nebbiolo was being planted in totally inappropriate sites, and on vigorous Kober 5BB rootstocks to boot. New sprays were coming on the market that increased the vine's vigor, rather than restraining it as the traditional copper sulfate did.

"That was a tough decision!" Angelo exclaims. "It meant that we were cut out of the more famous Barolo area, where we owned no vineyards. But we could say to people, 'Hey, look! We do it all ourselves, from grape to bottle.'"

The quality line was held at a critical time, and reinforced by another major decision two years later.

"I noticed that whenever Dad would talk about a certain vintage as being exceptional," Angelo recalls, "it always turned out that the harvest had been exceptionally small, as in 1961, when hail the previous year reduced the crop by more than half. So I thought to myself, 'What if we halved production every year?'"

January 23, 1989

*T*HE NORTH-FACING SLOPE of Fasèt is still white with the light snowfall of yesterday. Vine dressers in Burgundy would have thanked their patron, Saint Vincent, whose day it was. But whoever sent the frosty fluff, this winter's first, the local growers are grateful. As snow melts, the water seeps slowly through the topsoil and into the strata below—emergency moisture deep roots can tap during the desperate days of drought.

The observer's feet may be standing in snow, but his eyes see no trace of it on the slope of San Lorenzo. Patches stand out here and there on contiguous plots. When the cooperative winery of Barbaresco was founded, it classified as prime those vineyards where snow melted first. It knew its Nebbiolo. "The principle that the same variety does better or worse according to where it is planted is admitted and undeniable for all grapes," observes Fantini, "but for Nebbiolo it is really an axiom."

Federico and his crew are at San Lorenzo for the winter pruning. "This is nothing," he responds to a shiverer's lament. "When we did the pruning here four years ago, it was seventeen below." On the Fahrenheit scale, that's about zero.

Working next to Federico is Angelo Lembo. Although he is the fairer of the two, Lembo is from Sicily.

Italian historians still debate whether the process of national unification, which culminated in the proclamation of the Kingdom of Italy in 1861, was a war of liberation led by Piedmont against foreign rulers, as the official version had it at the time, or the covert conquest of the rest of the country by Italy's Prussia. One thing is certain: Vittorio Emanuele II, the second ruler of the Kingdom of Sardinia to bear that name, saw no reason to change the ordinal when he became the first sovereign of the Kingdom of Italy. In his mind, evidently, the new kingdom was merely an extension of the old.

The Piedmontese and other northern leaders knew little or nothing of the South. It was not only geographically that Turin was closer to London than to Lembo's birthplace. Cavour himself admitted that he was much more familiar with England and that he had thought Sicilians spoke Arabic. When southern Italy had been annexed to the new state, one of his close associates, the future prime minister Luigi Carlo Farini, went down to observe the situation. "You call this Italy?" he soon wrote in disbelief. "This is Africa!"

Angelo Lembo left Sicily in the mid-sixties at the age of sixteen, part of a massive wave of emigration to the North. At first he worked at the Fiat automobile plant in Turin. When he started to work at the winery in 1968 the local workers gave him a hard time with their teasing. Luigi Cavallo was especially rough on him. "I can still hear him," says Lembo with a chuckle, "screaming his head off in dialect about southerners not speaking proper Italian!"

Lembo has been pruning these vines for twenty years now. "He knows them so well he calls them by name and talks to them," chortles Federico. "In Piedmontese, of course."

Just as we all still bear signs of our simian past, even the noblest vines are marked by their origins as forest creepers and climbers. Under natural conditions a vine must compete with other plants. Not having a thick trunk to hold it above the ground, it has evolved other means of ensuring itself a place in the sun. It grows rapidly and over a long period of time. Tenacious tendrils enable it to cling to trees and make its way to the top of them.

Nathaniel Hawthorne was fascinated by the vines he saw in Tuscany in 1858. "Nothing can be more picturesque," he wrote in his notebook, "than the spectacle of an old grape-vine . . . clinging round its tree, imprisoning within its strong embrace the friend that supported its tender infancy, converting the tree wholly to its own selfish ends, stretching out its innumerable arms on every bough, and hardly allowing a leaf to sprout except its own."

But the writer also recorded his suspicion that "the vine is a pleasanter object of sight" growing in this way than it is "in countries where it produces a more precious wine, and therefore is trained more artificially."

Hawthorne's suspicion was well-founded. Great wine grapes are the product of strict viti*culture:* of nature highly nurtured. With vines as with us, culture directs the course of nature toward ends of its own.

In the vineyard, where it does not have to compete with trees and can be propped up by a trellis or other support, the vine's vigorous growth has no value. It no longer has to be among the fittest to survive. But the vine has not yet adapted to this civilized mode of existence. It still has the instincts of its forest forebears.

Federico nods his head. The wine lover's view of Nature is too enocentric.

"Nature couldn't care less about wine," he says. "She's interested in seeds."

Like all fruits, grapes are essentially a device of seed dispersal, ensuring the survival of the species. In a sense, the sugar is merely a surplus left over after the seeds have received all the nourishment they need. The more seeds a grape has, the less sugar and more acid it will contain. And since they produce hormones that diffuse into the pulp and stimulate its growth, more seeds mean larger berries and ultimately less concentrated wine.

From nature's point of view, the more grapes the merrier. But a vine produces only a certain amount of the substances that will give the wine color, scent, and flavor. If that amount is spread among many bunches rather than few, the wine will be diluted. Doing what comes naturally, vines are like parents who conceive more children than they have the means to bring up properly.

"If you care about the kids," says Federico, "you have to impose strict discipline." He pauses before making his painful point. "And that includes mutilation."

Perhaps the most striking example of the diversion of natural instincts for epicurean ends used to be seen in the cultivation of tobacco. The tobacco plant's metabolism is geared to nourishing the flower cluster at its top and channels the most nutrients in that direction. In the days when rich-tasting tobacco was in demand among connoisseurs, the inflorescence would be cut as soon as it began to develop, in order to divert the upward-moving savory substances to the highest leaves, which would then be used as wrappers for the finest cigars. Reproduction was sacrificed to enrich the inedible leaves, the prized part of the plant as far as cigars are concerned.

Discipline in the vineyard is imposed through training and pruning. A vine is trained to give a certain form to its permanent and semipermanent parts. It is to this form that pruning returns the vines each year, as a trim periodically does for a haircut. The possible forms are many: close-cropped or expansive; high off the ground or low; freestanding or supported by a vertical or horizontal trellis. The choice depends on the climate, the vigor of the variety, and the kind of wine you want to make.

The vines of San Lorenzo have been trained so that each has a trunk about two feet tall, from which the tangled canes now emerge. Each year's growth and crop of grapes is supported by a trellis over six feet high, which consists of four wires, end posts, and intermediate stakes.

Pruning regulates the vine's annual growth. In strict viticulture, it sacrifices quantity for quality.

It was the Greeks who brought viticultural discipline to Italy. The traveller and geographer Pausanias relates that there was a place where his fellow countrymen venerated the statue of a donkey. The animal had eaten part of a vine, which produced tastier grapes after the mutilation. (Hanging high from an undisciplined, tree-trained vine somewhere else in Greece, the grapes in Aesop's famous fable may not have been sour, as the fox claimed, but they certainly would not have made very good wine.) In Italy, the Etruscans treated grapevines like the cousins of Tarzan's lianas they are, training them on trees and letting them grow freely. Hawthorne's vine was an example of the Etruscan approach, which was still common in central Italy until the 1960s.

The number of buds left on the vine at pruning is the main determinant of the size of the crop. There is no magic number, though. If you leave too many buds, you'll have a large crop of inferior grapes. "But you don't want to prune too short, either," warns Federico. "With too few buds, the vine's energy is channeled into shoot and leaf production. A few years ago, Angelo wanted to reduce his Cabernet Sauvignon crop even further. So we pruned back to just six buds. The vines produced shoots like mad!" What you aim for is an equilibrium between reproduction—that is, grapes—and vegetative growth. Balance is all.

"It all depends" is one of Federico's refrains. The number of buds you leave depends on the variety of the vine, its age, how it has performed in the past, and the soil.

Nebbiolo vines, for instance, rarely produce grapes from the first two buds on a cane, those nearest the trunk. A memory spreads amusement over Federico's face. When he was in California he saw some Nebbiolo vines trained to the widespread cordon spur system, where many short canes, called spurs, are left on the vine, each with only two buds.

"You should have seen them!" he exclaims. "The vines went haywire. They didn't produce a single grape, but what an orgy of leaves!"

The Gaja crew did not do the pruning in the Serralunga vineyard last year because the purchase took place in July. The former owner left an average of 18 buds per vine, but Federico will reduce the number only gradually. "If we started right away pruning there like we do here," he says, "the vine would get fat." It has to get used to producing less. It has to find its balance.

"The best balance is that of old vines," he says. "They have a lot of self-discipline." They're "sagacious" and "restrained"; young ones are "headstrong" and "obstreperous." One of these days, when he has the leisure, Federico will no doubt compose a poem in praise of old vines. But you can be sure they won't be trained Etruscan-style like "the vines that round the thatch-eves run" in Keats's ode "To Autumn."

By nature, Nebbiolo is anything but restrained.

[39]

"It's the wildest horse in the rodeo," Federico says. "A real bucking bronco. Reining it is usually a big problem."

But the vines of San Lorenzo are old and the soil is poor.

"You don't have to go to great lengths to figure out how to prune here. You could leave these vines twenty buds and they'd still give you very few bunches." He gestures toward some un-pruned vines. "You don't see those monstrously long canes here that you do in many Nebbiolo vineyards."

The pruning cuttings of an average vine at San Lorenzo weigh around ten pounds, while those of young Nebbiolo vines in richer soil might weigh thirty or more—the weights of weakness and vigor.

Like a barber about to cut into a shock of shaggy hair, Angelo Lembo sizes up a vine. It is now a tangle of about a dozen wooden canes, all but two of which started out last spring as tender tips of shoots peeking timidly out of bud eyes.

He clips away the "past," the by-now two-year-old canes that bore last year's shoots and crop. Then he selects one of the two remaining one-year-old canes as the "present," the one that will bear this year's shoots and crop, and trims it so that only eight eyes are left. This cane will be tied along the bottom wire of the trellis and the new shoots will emerge from the dormant buds which formed on the cane during the past growing season. Finally, he cuts back the other cane to a spur with only two buds. This is the "future," from which two shoots will grow. One will be chosen during next winter's pruning as the "present" to bear the grapes for Sorì San Lorenzo 1990 and the other as the new "future."

This is known as cane-and-spur pruning, and the particular version that Federico and his crew are using is called Guyot, after the nineteenth-century French agronomist Jules Guyot, who propagandized it. But the system had already been around for a long time. What could be clearer than the instructions written in 1670 by Sir Thomas Hanmer, who owned a vineyard in, of all places, Wales?:

Leave . . . one chiefe or master branch . . . let this master branch be left half a yard or a yard long, according to the strength of the vine, and let it be the principal among the branches . . . the lowest of the other branches must be pruned very low or short, leaving only one eye or budd, or two at the most . . . and this short branch . . . is to serve to send forth a master branch for the next year, cutting off the master branch which was left last year. This vine being thus pruned, cut away all the other branches except the two aforesaid.

Federico is working nearby. "We'd like to prune even shorter," he says, "so we could plant more densely. When we replant here, we'd like to bring the density up to over two thousand vines per acre. Like the Merlot over there." He nods in the direction of a plot further along the slope of Masuè. "But to do that we need really weak vines." Greater density increases competition among the roots for nutrients and thus reduces vigor. Sorì San Lorenzo now has just over 1,600 vines per acre.

Federico leaves only seven buds as he trims the "master branch" of a vine. "It's struggling," he explains. "This will help the vine get its energy back."

It turns out that the vines are not all that healthy. "In fact," he says, "a lot of them are sick. They have a virosis." The news sounds terrible, but Federico is nonchalant.

The virosis is called leaf roll because the edges of the leaves curl. As long as the case isn't severe it doesn't affect the quality of the wine, just the vigor and longevity.

"Or rather," says Federico, "by decreasing the vigor it helps produce *better* grapes." He pauses pensively. "Those virus-free vines they've been developing through clonal selection and heat treatment are hard to restrain. Just look at those yields a lot of people are getting nowadays."

Health can be harmful. The paradox is profound.

Federico himself seems tired. Vine after vine, he and his men have been pruning since November.

"Ideally," he says, "it would be better to start later." After the leaves fall, the vine shifts its metabolism and transfers food reserves to the trunk, where they will be stored and thus available to boost the new growth off to a good start in the spring. The transfer takes time. "But there's simply too much work to do. We can't prune all the vines in just a few weeks. So we do the most important vineyards late and rotate the others."

With the new vineyard at Serralunga, the winery now has more than 300,000 vines. "If you put all those cuttings together, you'd have quite a pile of wood!" Federico exclaims.

Some varieties are easier to prune than others. "With Merlot you can prune a vine a minute," says Federico. Its wood is relatively soft and it doesn't present any particular problems. Sauvignon and its Cabernet cousin require the most physical strength. Their tendrils are tenacious and the wood is very tough. Indeed, an old synonym for Cabernet Sauvignon in Bordeaux is Vidure: *vigne dure,* hard vine.

In many vineyards, Nebbiolo is hard to prune, though its wood is tender. "The problem is *how* to prune it," Federico says. "Prune Chardonnay short and it simply produces that much less. If you prune Nebbiolo short, it might produce just a couple of clusters and not even ripen those."

As the snip and snap of the pruners' shears moves steadily down the slope, the line of demarcation is clear. Nature's tangle retreats before the advance of symmetry. Literally on the cutting edge of civilization, the shear-toting sheriffs impose law and order on the wild frontier. Brutal they may be, but even the gentlest lover of wine would hardly think it wrong. In the vineyard, at least, the end justifies the means.

Vigorous pruning is based on two assumptions; if they turn out to be wrong, the grower will grumble. One is that there is a market that will reward his sacrifice of quantity by paying him more for his wine. The other is that nature will do no pruning of her own. A low percentage of fertilization at flowering means an even smaller harvest and hail can reduce it further.

Great wine requires not only the repression of the instincts of the vine, but those of the grower as well. Quantity gratifies immediately; the pleasures of quality are deferred. They are experienced only in the wine and, of course, the price it fetches. No wonder, then, that civilization in a vineyard can create discontent.

Like the vines they tend, vineyard workers can be deeply rooted in history. "Even today," says Federico, "some of them have trouble adjusting when they start to work here. Notions like quality and fine wine are abstractions to them, and they find it hard to understand why abundance should be sacrificed." He smiles wryly. "After all, they don't dash off to comparative tastings after work!"

Until after the Second World War, yields in Barbaresco were tiny by even the highest standards of today. This was not because growers had a commitment to quality as that notion is currently understood, but rather because they lacked the means to produce more. Once they had the means, peasants did not want to miss the historic opportunity to make their dreams of abundance come true.

Aldo Vacca has two uncles who are growers. One of them has a vineyard with six rows of Nebbiolo. "Last year I thinned out the crop in the three bottom rows, the ones that usually produce less ripe grapes," Aldo says, "and got over half a degree more alcohol than in the other rows. You could taste the difference." He scratches his head as he reflects. "My uncles understand the quality issue abstractly, but they have an attachment to quantity that's hereditary. It's in their blood!"

Pietro Rocca's voice is smooth and finely modulated as he talks about Angelo's decision in the mid-sixties to lower yields drastically. "Angelo's doings were looked upon by most people as anything but angelic," he says with a twinkle in his eye. "In fact, they were considered downright diabolical. In those days, even eighteen buds a vine were thought to be miserably few, and it was common to have two and even three canes with twelve buds each." He chuckles. "You still see vines like that. They're real museum pieces."

Cutting back to twelve buds per vine as Angelo had decided to do meant sacrificing an enormous amount of grapes. Even *one* bud per vine less would have meant a reduction of about 1,600 clusters per acre. The comments of workers at the local tavern expressed doubts about Angelo's sanity. Giovanni Gaja was mayor of Barbaresco at the time and attentive to what people were saying.

"One day he rushed into the house all upset," recalls Angelo. "Everyone in the village is saying we have so few grapes that we're going to go bankrupt!' he exclaimed. 'How on earth are we going to pay the workers?' "

When Angelo Lembo started to work at the winery, the Battle

of the Buds was still raging. "Angelo would give us pruning instructions," he says, "but as soon as he had turned his back, Gino and the rest of them would do as they pleased."

Angelo smiles as he sighs. "Ah, Gino! Luigi Cavallo was a pillar of the winery. His dedication was total. He would talk about 'my vines' and 'my grapes.' He would have died rather than miss a day's work because of illness. When it was harvest time, he'd be on the spot before dawn and get furious with the other workers for arriving later." Angelo shakes his head. "But it was quite a battle. He always had an excuse for not pruning shorter. I can still hear the litany. The Kober rootstock is too vigorous; you won't get any grapes. What if flowering is poor? What if it hails?"

The battle didn't end with the buds. There were the root-stocks to be planted in the new vineyards. Angelo wanted the 420A to restrain Nebbiolo's vigor; Cavallo liked vigorous plants and the Kober 5BB gave him what he wanted. There was also the wicker that was traditionally used to tie up canes and shoots to the trellis in the spring.

"Gino would start gathering and stripping reeds in the fall. Months in advance. When spools of wire became available, which enabled you to do the job in a fraction of the time, he wouldn't hear of it. If you gave him a spool, he'd take it and throw it away. You practically had to put it by his bedside and let the idea sink in slowly while he slept! After three years, he started to use wire. Reluctantly."

In those days Angelo was an impetuous young man setting out to conquer the world. Luigi Cavallo was a middle-aged ex-sharecropper who had never been to Turin, but was used to commanding in the vineyard. The conflict was real, but the battle never got bloody.

The young man had come to live in Barbaresco and had learned the dialect he had never spoken at home. Ambitious, but good-natured, he had an intuitive understanding of the people working for him. He took Cavallo out to dinner now and then, talked things over, and tried to get him involved in his plans. If Barbaresco wouldn't bustle, the young man in a hurry would wait.

In the few words that Angelo stood up to say while dessert and coffee were being served during the annual dinner for winery employees just before Christmas, there was, as always, "a warm welcome for Gino Cavallo, who for so many years was a pillar of the winery." Cavallo had a leg amputated a few years ago and doesn't get around much anymore. But he sits almost every day in his courtyard with the beret from which he is never separated on his head. He looks you in the eye and proudly tells the story of how things changed at the winery when Angelo came on the scene.

"I went up to see Angelo at his home when he was starting to take over. He explained to me what he wanted. 'I'm not interested in having a whole lot of grapes,' he said. The difference between Angelo and his father was like that between night and day."

Cavallo stresses his words with a gesture of his hand, holding his palm down when he says "night" and turning it up when he comes to "day."

"The *geometra* just wanted us to bring in grapes, period. We harvested everything. With Angelo, the music changed completely. We picked only ripe grapes. We went through the vineyard several times if necessary.

"One Sunday in July Angelo dropped in on me and said that there were too many grapes on the vines down at San Lorenzo. So the next day we started to cut off bunches. People thought he was crazy. The peasants snickered. One of them said, 'I get four times as many grapes in my vineyard!' They didn't understand anything then and they don't understand anything now.

"People came to work here from other places who didn't know anything about this job. I even had to teach a southerner how to do things. Now he really knows his stuff. He's a good man."

Snip! go the shears: the last vine's future has been clipped. San Lorenzo's once dishevelled shocks are now neat and trim. But the crewcut won't last long.

May 10, 1989

J UST LOOK AT THEM!" Federico exclaims. "They're already roaring down the runway." He has been working around the trunk of a vine and stands up to take a break.

The temperature has climbed close to eighty as the afternoon sun floods Saint Lawrence's *sorì*, but surely it isn't hot enough to have affected Federico's lucidity. His madness must be metaphor.

The different stages of a vine's seasonal growth, its phenological phases, become those of an airline flight. The airplane vine leaves the gate when it begins to stir after winter dormancy and taxis to the runway. At budbreak it's off and gathering speed. Flowering is the takeoff, a critical moment of tension between vegetative thrust and reproductive needs. Once the grapes have formed, they and the vine can cruise: a relatively calm and uneventful period. Then, at the *invaiatura,* the grape's change of color, the long descent begins. If the weather's good, if it's sunny and dry, the grapes descend to deliciousness, the vine to depletion.

Vineyards and airports are two places where talk about the weather is more than idle chatter. Federico was worried in the

[46]

weeks after pruning. It snowed only that once, and in February and March it hardly rained at all.

"The vine did weep, though," he chirps. "In the second week of March."

Has Federico suddenly come under the spell of the Marquis? He shakes his head with a grin. As it rises in the spring, sap flows through the vine's pruning wounds. "You might think the vine is in mourning or even bleeding to death," he says. "But those are really tears of joy, a sign that it won't go thirsty. After prolonged drought, the vine is so sad it doesn't weep at all."

March was almost summery. During the last week the buds burst as the temperature rose as high as it is now. The vines of San Lorenzo left the gate and started down the runway ahead of schedule.

"Enough of metaphor!" Federico says abruptly, putting an end to the flight of his imagination. This botanical bard has his feet on the ground.

"See the Sauvignon over there?" he asks, pointing to a plot farther along the slope of Masuè. "Those vines bud after the Nebbiolo here, but last year we harvested them on August 24. The Nebbiolo wasn't picked until October 7, over six weeks later."

Cabernet starts out after Nebbiolo, but catches up later in the season. In a nearby vineyard like Pajorè, which is 300 feet higher up than San Lorenzo, Nebbiolo itself passes through every phase ten days later than here.

After an exceptionally rainy April, Federico is less concerned. If he knew the song, he would undoubtedly break out into "April Showers." But whatever the month, Federico is always singing the praises of rainfall in the spring. Summer rain is usually torrential; a brief, violent downpour that runs right down the slope and creates erosion. Rain in the spring comes mainly in the form of gentle showers that are absorbed by the soil without runoff.

Federico is at San Lorenzo today for the first of various tasks known as green pruning that will be done throughout the summer. He and his men are removing suckers from the rootstocks and any adventitious shoots that may have emerged on the vines.

"We didn't spend all that time pruning in January just to let these suckers have a field day now," he growls with a grin.

[47]

Green pruning is one of his major concerns between winter pruning and the harvest.

"It's like cleanliness in the cellar or housework at home," Federico says. "Just humdrum, everyday drudgery. Nothing as showy as harvesting or winter pruning." He pauses as he pulls a sucker. "But it's crucial, like defense."

Defense! Federico says it offhand, but the word explodes like a bomb. *Difesa* expresses the seriousness of the task of protecting the vines and grapes from harm. Federico also uses the word *lotta,* as in the "fight" against cancer. No doubt these words are more stirring to the vineyard's worker-soldiers than the usual English-language term. Would "disease and pest control" rouse them to resistance?

Defense is central to what Federico sees as the ultimate goal of his work. "My job," he says, "is to enable the wine maker to decide freely when to harvest." If the grapes are healthy, he can pick when their ripeness is optimal. But if they're starting to rot, his choice is only Hobson's.

Federico's goal is only apparently modest. A harvest with healthy grapes is a viticultural V-Day.

Keeping a grape healthy means above all keeping its skin intact. "Once the skin breaks," Federico says with a wince, "that's the ball game." With the grape it's as with us. If we cut a finger and break our skin, we risk an infection. "But unfortunately," he observes, "we can't just rinse off the grape and stick a Band-Aid on it." As the great Swiss wine scientist Hermann Müller-Thurgau noted long ago, a grape with a ruptured skin has about forty times as many microorganisms on it as does a healthy one.

Defense must be diligent. But that means more than merely being alert. It means taking the initiative and making conditions more difficult for the potential invader. "It's just like in sports," says Federico. "The best defense is a good offense."

Federico has to defend not only the vines, but also the soil. "You always come back to that sooner or later," he insists. "The preservation of the soil is the great challenge to viticulture."

He has worked his way to the end of the row and is now on the edge of Sorì San Lorenzo, facing vines that run straight up and down the slope. This way of planting, called *rittochino,* has been used by the winery since 1978. The *rittochino* method goes back to pre-modern times in the Langhe, but was gradually abandoned in favor of *girapoggio,* where the rows of vines follow the contours of the slope, as at San Lorenzo. Thomas Jefferson explained the advantages of the latter method in a letter to a friend almost two centuries ago.

"We now plant horizontally, following the contours of the hills," he wrote. "Every furrow thus acts as a reservoir to receive and retain the waters . . . The horses draw much easier on the dead level and it is in fact a conversion of hilly ground into a plain."

There was an additional advantage for the peasants of the Langhe: they could exploit the ground between the rows for planting other crops.

But *rittochino* also has its reasons. The oxen of old, like Jefferson's horses, may have found the footing easier in a *girapoggio* vineyard, but tractors work better moving up and down the slope. And in a vineyard with a southern exposure, both sides of the rows receive direct sunlight because they run north and south.

A disadvantage of *rittochino* is that it means more erosion. That explains in part why there is grass growing in the vineyards.

"Not so long ago," says Federico, "there was a bodybuilding concept of the vineyard." He strikes a pose and flexes his muscles. "The Schwarzenegger style. It was thought that vines should be vigorous and that they shouldn't have any competition. Grass was the big bugaboo. There was frequent tilling to keep weeds down."

Tilling leads to the oxidation and destruction of organic matter, especially if it's deep or carried out in the heat of summer. Tilling is detrimental to structure.

Federico ponders as he plucks. "Weedkillers can take the place of tilling," he says, "but they impoverish the soil, too."

He often talks about his friend, Lorenzo Corino, an expert on soil conservation who works at the research institute in Asti. "Lorenzo tells me that 15 years ago the French kept their vineyards totally clean with weedkillers." Federico chuckles as he remembers Corino's words. " 'We tried for years to keep up with the French,' he says in that deadpan way of his, 'but luckily we had problems. Now we're ahead because we fell behind.' "

[49]

Heavy rainfall on a clean-cultivated slope causes erosion; grass hinders runoff and increases its absorption.

"Grass can be a precious ally," say Federico. "But it all depends. If you have it in the wrong place at the wrong time, it can be a dangerous enemy."

One yearns for an old-fashioned fight in which friends are friends and foes are foes. Weedkillers? It all depends.

"It's like medicine," he says. "You do without it if you can, but you take it if necessary to avoid something worse. Sometimes, in a pinch, weedkillers can save you from going into the vineyard with heavy machinery. People think you can do anything at any time with machines, but you can't. If the soil is wet, they'll compact it."

"Compact" comes out of Federico's mouth invested with all due solemnity. Compaction is a crime against the soil. It's murderous for structure.

"If you have to get in to do something urgent like spraying," he says, "then there's got to be grass. A tractor on bare, wet soil will destroy it."

He wrinkles his brow. "Last year it rained a lot in the spring and there was still grass in the vineyards on June 20. Angelo had been away on a trip and when he came back he got all upset. 'What's this grass doing here this late in the season?' he asked. I know everyone dreams of immaculate vineyards like those you see in the Médoc. They impress visitors. But Barbaresco isn't Bordeaux. We had to get into the vineyards to spray and I wasn't about to do so on bare, drenched soil." He gives the ground a knowing look. "The grass saved the structure of the soil."

When the workers are through suckering here, they'll move on to another vineyard. They're always on the move. In Barbaresco alone they tend twenty-one different vineyards, fourteen of which are planted with Nebbiolo. There are other vineyards in Alba and in the nearby village of Treiso, not to mention more distant Serralunga, with its seventy acres of vines.

"Ah, Serralunga!" exclaims Federico. "Just one big vineyard. It's easy over there." He stops in his conversational tracks and backs up. "Well," he says, "relatively easy. In fact, a lot of people think we're crazy here. They do much more of the work with machines in Bordeaux. The famous vineyards of Burgundy seem almost flat compared to ours. And in California a lot of vineyards are on land that *is* flat." He gestures down the steep incline of San Lorenzo. "You can grow Cabernet on the valley floor, but just try growing Nebbiolo there!"

Federico looks pensively at a vine.

"I guess our real madness is in cultivating this vine at all. I'm often amazed that peasants have continued growing it over the years when there's so much less green pruning and other work with easy varieties like Barbera and Cabernet."

Actually, many peasant growers gave up long ago. Nebbiolo was once widely planted throughout Piedmont and elsewhere in northwestern Italy, sometimes alias Spanna, Chiavennasca, Picotener, and several other names. But it has been in constant retreat at least since the beginning of the eighteenth century. After such natural disasters as the terrible frost of 1709, the fungus disease oidium in the middle of the nineteenth century, and phylloxera several decades later, when peasants replanted they often replaced Nebbiolo with hardier and more prolific, if less noble, varieties.

A good example is the area of Asti, where as long ago as 1330 Nebbiolo was described as being much praised. At the beginning of the twentieth century, it was still planted in about 20 percent of the vineyards in a town such as Costigliole. Now there is none at all.

Fantini noted a century ago that cultivation of Nebbiolo had been retreating to those few privileged sites which produced grapes of such exceptional quality that the effort to grow them was economically worthwhile. In the Langhe, Nebbiolo was replaced more and more by an outsider, Barbera. According to Fantini, Barbera made its first appearance there around 1875. In 1883 he observed that it "is grown in a few places in the Langhe, but the quantity produced is negligible." By 1895 it had "an important place in our viticulture, and more and more of it is planted every day." Barbera is now the area's most widely cultivated variety.

In his pamphlet *Barbaresco and Its Wine,* published in 1907, Domizio Cavazza lists all the charges that a peasant plaintiff would bring against Nebbiolo in a viticultural court. The following year, Barbaresco growers protested against their Nebbiolo vineyards being put into the highest tax bracket. "Given that the variety does not ensure a constant income," they noted, "in no vineyard is Nebbiolo grown by itself, but together with Barbera, Freisa, and Dolcetto."

Although it is still cultivated elsewhere in Piedmont and, here and there, even beyond, the vine's ultimate bastions are Barbaresco and Barolo. Nebbiolo is besieged. But it is not about to meet its Waterloo. Rather, another Belgian village comes to mind: Bastogne. There, during the Second World War's Battle of the Bulge, the commander of greatly outnumbered American forces gave a defiant answer when called upon by the Germans to surrender. Here the reply will be the same. "Nuts!" they will say, whatever that is in the dialect. "Nebbiolo, now and forever!"

"I've often thought about it," says Federico. "There's something religious in the attitude toward Nebbiolo around here. I know growers who'll spend all Sunday morning in the vineyard tending it instead of going to Mass. Maybe it's their way of worshipping God."

He looks around San Lorenzo.

"They're in awe of this vine."

*A*LDO VACCA perks up his ears. His smile is somewhere between sly and shy.

"That's right," he says. "With Nebbiolo, you're always in the vineyard."

Aldo is standing at the door of the temporary little tasting room near the cellar steps. The visiting tasters have come and gone. Scribbling notes amid glasses and bottles, Angelo looks up with an expression that seems to say, "And in the tasting room, too."

Nebbiolo needs explaining.

It is a venerable variety. The first documented reference to it goes back to 1268. In 1606, a connoisseur at the court in Turin called it "the queen of red grapes." And passing through Turin in 1787, Thomas Jefferson noted in his journal that he had tasted a wine made with "Nebiule," his transcription of the dialect.

As for the people of Barbaresco, they have been growing grapes and making wine for centuries. In the cathedral of Alba, which is dedicated to Saint Lawrence, a wooden stall in the choir dating from the late fifteenth century has an inlaid decoration depicting the village and its ancient castle under a bowl of grapes.

Angelo is impish. "Sure, the wines from around here are ancient," he says. "But until recently, so was the wine making."

Though Jefferson wrote that the wine he had drunk in Turin was "pleasing," it would have wine lovers today clamoring for a refund. "As sweet as the silky Madeira, as astringent on the palate as Bordeaux, and as brisk as Champagne," reads his tasting note.

The tradition of sweet and often bubbly Nebbiolo was to last for another century or two. When growers of Barbaresco formed an association in 1908 to discuss ways of protecting their wine from fraud, they acknowledged that "in past times . . . most of it was little better than those sickly sweet, semisparkling or frothy Nebbiolos that delighted the unsophisticated palates and the stronger stomachs of our forefathers." Even though there had been a few pioneers, "a real direct production of a notable quantity, constant in quality and highly reputed in commerce, did not exist before 1894—that is, when the Cooperative Winery of Barbaresco was founded." Four years later, the bulletin of the Piedmontese Wine Producers' Association carried an article by its correspondent in the United States describing how, for tax purposes, Nebbiolo wine was imported in bulk and transformed in New York into thousands of cases of "the ideal sparkling and semisweet red wine." And in 1933 Julian Street wrote that, although "it was not in a class with the great wines of other wine growing regions," the finest Italian wine he had ever drunk was a thirty-one-year-old slightly sweet, but no longer sparkling, "Nebbiolo Spumante."

The Barbarescos on the tasting room table go all the way back to 1961: Angelo's biography in bottles. It was in 1961 that he started working at the winery and that they last bought grapes from other growers.

Pietro Rocca and Guido Rivella's father had sold grapes to the winery that year, and there were even some from Masuè in the wine. Hail the year before had damaged the vines, so the yield was tiny. The wine had got off to a great start in the vineyard.

"Grandeur and misery of Nebbiolo," says Angelo with a sigh as he sniffs a glass of the '61. The wine has had many admirers. Even Michael Broadbent was lavish with praise. "One of the most glorious Italian wines I have ever drunk," a note of his from 1984 reads.

"Soft, with a flavor that opened up into a crescendo." Broadbent tasted the wine when it was twenty-three years old. What would he have said about it back in the sixties?

"Who knows which '61 he would have drunk?" retorts Angelo. "Some of it took years to complete the fermentation. And, as always back then, we bottled it in small lots of one thousand bottles at a time. Some lots stayed in the wood years longer than others. The differences were great."

The wine is an example of Barbaresco at its best in those days, but Angelo's evaluation is less than enthusiastic.

"Sure," he admits, "the wine is rich. It's certainly great in its own way. But I'd like a cleaner, fresher bouquet—one that's less musty and muted. I want purer fruit."

Barbaresco at less than its best had little appeal to any but a local market.

As Angelo sees it, the '61 was great despite the wine making. But it also had another problem: it was made with Nebbiolo.

When Angelo talks about Nebbiolo, he sounds like the father of a gifted son who has yet to live up fully to his promise. Pride and exasperation mingle in his tone. His expectations are still great, but he no longer has any illusions to lose.

The most quoted tasting note in all of wine literature is the one on Haut-Brion from the diary of Samuel Pepys, dated April 11, 1663: "Drank a sort of French wine called Ho Bryan, that hath a good and most particular taste I ever met with."

To make a name for itself, a wine must be distinctive, "particular."

Like foods, however, wines can be too distinctive to be universally appealing. Such was the predicament of great Nebbiolo wines, as exemplified by Broadbent's comments on a much later Gaja wine, the 1982 Sorì Tildìn. He describes it as "rich," "intense," and "immensely impressive," but also notes that it is "strange" and "idiosyncratic for those inured [sic!] to Bordeaux."

"When I started travelling abroad," says Angelo, "I realized right away that Nebbiolo had little in common with other varieties. On the one hand, I was pleased. It meant that we had something all our own. But on the other, it meant isolation. Nebbiolo was to

[55]

the great French varieties as our traditional sport here in the Langhe—what we call elastic ball—is to sports like soccer and basketball that are played around the world."

International taste had been formed by French wines and grapes. You might even "beat" the French at a competition, as two wines from Napa Valley did in a historic showdown in Paris in 1976. But you had to play their game, which usually meant, as in Paris, Cabernet Sauvignon and Chardonnay. These varieties were the vinous equivalents of the English language. Making a wine with Nebbiolo was like speaking Finnish. (Cabernet was so well-known it was familiarly referred to as "Cab," but who called Nebbiolo "Neb?"

Even among wine experts notions of Nebbiolo could be nebulous indeed. As late as 1976 such an eminent authority as Maynard Amerine, who taught at the University of California at Davis for almost forty years and published more technical books and articles on wine than any other author in the English language, could write with co-author Edward B. Roessler in *Wines: Their Sensory Evaluation:*

> Nebbiola [sic] is the predominant grape in much of northwestern Italy. There it makes a variety of wines, none of which we find outstanding . . . Barolo appears most often bitter-astringent when young and also when old. Even at fifteen to twenty years, the aging does not produce an outstanding bouquet. We do not know whether it is grown elsewhere but apparently not (and justifiably so).

Given such knowledge of Nebbiolo, it is just as well that the book does not even mention Barbaresco!

"Nebbiolo is just as obstreperous in the cellar as it is in the vineyard," says Angelo.

"Toughness is the essence of Nebbiolo," British wine writer Jancis Robinson states bluntly. "No other grape is quite so cussedly high in tannin, acid, and dry extract."

Robert Parker writes about "furiously tannic, unyielding wines" that are "often forbidding and savage in their youthful rawness."

[56]

But unlike Amerine, these writers know that there are treasures beneath the toughness, that age might deliver one of those bouquets which, as Robinson puts it, "have non-wine-drinkers screeching with incredulous mirth when they read the classic descriptions." Between the two of them, they come up with an impressive list: violets, licorice, peppery spices, truffle-scented fruit, leather, tar, and tobacco.

Angelo wanted to make a Barbaresco that was more tempting than terrifying. "I would come back from France full of enthusiasm," he recalls, "but it would vanish after a few days of beating my head against the wall of Tradition."

The "depository of Tradition" at the Gaja winery was Luigi Rama, who was in charge of the cellar.

"Rama was a fixture," says Angelo. "He slept in a room overlooking the courtyard and ate with the family. He looked after the wine as if it were his own. He might get up at two in the morning to see how a barrel was doing." Angelo pauses. "But he had no contact with the outside. He lived in a world all his own."

Angelo was getting more actively involved in the cellar, as well as in the vineyard. "It was not an easy coexistence," he admits. But that was only part of the problem.

"In France there was a constant exchange between research institutes and producers. A couple of the people teaching at Montpellier when I was there were producers themselves. Back home, you didn't know who to go to if you had a problem. Growers were so used to certain defects that they didn't even notice them." He chuckles. "It was also embarrassing. After all, we were the leading winery, weren't we?"

Angelo tried to involve his fellow growers. In 1964 he rented a bus and organized a trip to Burgundy. Forty of them went along.

He throws up his hands.

"It must have been some kind of defense mechanism. They rejected everything they saw. Our ways were the only ones."

Meanwhile, foreigners would tear apart wines that the locals thought were great. Angelo painfully remembers some scornful British remarks about their yellow tinge. " 'Salami skin,' they called it," he says. " 'Chicken skin.' "

"That was the old style," he sighs. "But it was typical."

His expression indicates that a sore spot has been touched: *tipicità,* typicalness, being true to type.

"The style that was so violently rejected by foreigners was defended in the name of *tipicità,* which was often just a euphemism for mediocrity."

He recalls his own family's approach to wine.

"My father would drink no more than one glass with his meals, but that was sacrosanct. He was convinced that his wine was better than anyone else's. When he thought a bottle was exceptionally good he would exclaim, 'This is a real Marsala!' That was the greatest compliment."

Marsala is an oxidized wine which resembles Sherry and Madeira more than classic table wines such as Bordeaux and Burgundy.

"I had a great aunt who always kept an opened bottle of Barbaresco locked up in a little cabinet. She would have a sip now and then. If you wanted to 'drink,' you drank something less fine, such as Barbera or Dolcetto diluted with water. That was the characteristic attitude around here. Fine wine was considered almost a medicine, something for the sick and elderly."

As in other traditional wine-producing countries, wine in Italy was simply a beverage, comparable to coffee in the United States in those days. Coffee was more or less fresh, more or less good, but rarely would it become the topic of more than desultory conversation. It was unlikely that consumers would be familiar with the difference between the *arabica* and *robusta* varieties, much less attribute any importance to the precise geographical origin of the beans. Who compared different shades of roast? Coffee was, and to a great extent still is, a habit; something "hot," something to "pick you up." Adding water to wine may sound strange, but it was no different from adding a sweetener or cream to coffee.

Wine in Italy at that time was considered food and put on the table as a matter of course along with the bread. Most people drank the same wine every day and often it was anonymous. Wine lists were rare in restaurants, and frequently patrons were simply asked "Red or white?" before they had even looked at the menu.

Angelo was developing another idea of wine, and not only on

trips abroad. One important influence was a restaurant owner in Genoa named Paroldi, who was a friend and customer of his father's.

"I used to eat in the kitchen," he recalls as his expression brightens. "He would open great Burgundies and Bordeaux for me. All those smells and flavors that were different! Those were exciting experiences." He pauses significantly. "But Paroldi was also a great fan of Barbaresco."

Angelo swirls the '61 and gives it an energetic sniff.

His conviction was growing that Barbaresco could be improved in the cellar as well as the vineyard. There was no doubt that Barbaresco was "particular." Could it be made so that even wine-lovers "inured" to French wines would want to drink it?

A similar problem had been identified in literature by one of the leading Italian writers of the postwar period, Cesare Pavese, who was born in the Langhe and lived in Turin. In an essay on the American writer Sherwood Anderson, "Middle West and Piedmont," he praised Anderson's ability to capture the uniqueness of the Middle West in a way that gave it universal significance. Pavese expressed his hope that Piedmont would one day have a literary work that "is not only greatly cherished by us, but truly achieves that universality and freshness that speaks to all men and women."

By providing the necessary financial rewards, the international wine market enables great wines to be made. But it can also be a threat to individuality. To make his wine a universal one without sacrificing its uniqueness—that was Angelo's challenge. Barbaresco had been transformed before; it could be transformed again. But he would need help.

Rama was ill and approaching retirement. It was time to act.

"I was looking for someone I could carry on a real dialogue with," Angelo says. "Someone to whom I could transmit what I was learning all the time from my experiences abroad, but who had ideas and a personality of his own. We had to learn from each other. It couldn't be just another employee."

*G*UIDO!"
     Angelo's voice resounds as he scampers down the steps, into the realm of Guido Rivella.

As you descend, you first go through the windowless old cellar, where there are huge cement tanks built right into the wall that were formerly used for fermentation, and rows of large barrels where wine is still stored. Built between 1969 and 1972, the new cellar has windows that look out onto the vineyards you see from the courtyard railing. On the highest of its levels are the fermentation tanks currently used—the older ones made of epoxy-covered steel, the newer ones of stainless—and the press. The wine is bottled on the next level down and then stored on the one below that. On the lowest level are the small casks in which much of the wine is aged.

"Some of my father's clients didn't like the new cellar," Angelo says. "It wasn't picturesque enough. Too much light. Too much steel. Too much technology."

He steps over a hose through which wine is flowing from one container to another.

"It's funny," he reflects. "In other fields, people understand that technology is a means. When they go to the dentist, they want the latest and the best if it will do the job quicker and with less pain." He nods at the hose. "Just think!" he exclaims. "This job used to be done by a man using a cone-shaped wooden container called a *brenta,* which contained over twelve gallons. He would fill it up with wine from one large barrel, carry it on his back up a ladder and empty it into another one. I guess there's something about the spectacle of physical labor that enchants sedentary city folk."

Handling the wine in that way was just one instance of the sheer drudgery involved in making wine until quite recently. It also splashed the wine around a lot, exposing it to the harmful effects of oxygen.

"The first pumps were really rough on the wine, too. Now we have more gentle ones. In the cellar under construction, we'll be able to move the wine around with less pumping, just by the force of gravity." His smile is satisfaction itself. "Now *that's* progress!"

Suddenly billows of steam rise from behind the fermentation tanks. You expect Guido to appear naked, with a towel around his waist. Angelo laughs. No, they aren't running a Turkish bath on the side.

The only place germs are feared more than in a well-run wine cellar is in a well-run hospital. After all, our understanding of disease in both wine and people stems from a common source: the discoveries of Louis Pasteur in the second half of the nineteenth century. Cleaning with steam at over 150 degrees Fahrenheit enables the winery to avoid using detergents, which could contaminate the wine. Angelo again evokes the "picturesque" past. "Can you imagine what a job it was to keep the cellar clean when all we had was water from the well?"

You can still hear Luigi Cavallo's voice and see his gestures just a hundred yards or so down via Torino. "Don't get me wrong," he insists. "The cellar had always been clean. But when Angelo came on the scene. . . ." Palm down, palm up.

Angelo Lembo also remembers the early years.

"Angelo kept urging us to clean the barrels scrupulously," he says, "but Rama would insist, 'Just give it a lick and a promise.' He thought Angelo was an overly fussy young man."

[61]

Dwarfed as he walks by the stainless steel tanks, Angelo shouts again.

"I'm up here!" cries a voice through the steam. High above, a figure scurries like a monkey on the catwalk behind the tanks and starts to climb down. Angelo goes over to confer with Guido. The names of faraway places punctuate the conversation—Germany, Stockholm, Japan—as they talk in the language of Luigi Cavallo.

On the far side of forty, with graying and thinning hair, Guido was born and bred in Barbaresco, in a tiny cluster of houses surrounded by a sea of vines: the *borgata* of Montestefano, just a stone's throw—if you throw it twice—from the village itself.

"We didn't have anything in those days," he says as he starts to recall his early years. But once he scratches the surface of the past, he's like a truffle dog that's scented one of those toothsome tubers. His face lights up. Buried down there are the greatest of riches: memories of a happy childhood.

Times have changed since then. You can see it in the truffles themselves, which nowadays cost $1,000 a pound around Alba. As a kid Guido would play with his uncle's dog. "Once in a while he would sniff a truffle and I'd dig it up. But I didn't really care for them. And it didn't pay to sell them. They weren't worth much and the only merchant back then was in Alba. What with the cost of the train ticket and the time someone had to take off from work, you'd wind up losing money rather than making a profit."

Guido grew up in the midst of vines. Wine has always been a part of his life.

"When I was an infant," he recalls, "my mother would take me into the vineyard with her when she harvested, just as all the other mothers did with their little ones. By the time I was eight I was already helping out."

His father sold some of their grapes to Angelo's father, and others to a big winery over in the Barolo area, Fontanafredda. They also made a little wine at home.

"We only had a hand pump then," he says. "I remember pumping away in the cellar for hours."

For the Rivellas, too, polyculture was taken for granted: "Grapes were just another crop."

Guido counts on his fingers. "Wheat, corn, chick-peas, beans—

you name it, we grew it. Right along with the grapes. Families wanted to make sure they survived."

There were animals, too. Guido's eyes sparkle like a child's.

"We used to play with the ox, a gentle, good-natured animal. I can still feel the calluses on its neck where the yoke was. Sometimes I would go off with it at four o'clock in the morning to work on my uncle's farm." He pauses. "My father kept his last ox until 1966."

He turns pensive.

"The pace was slow then. We didn't know what stress was. I guess I feel a bit nostalgic for those days from time to time." He slaps his knee, as if to put an end to his musings. "But not for the insecurity."

In the 1950s, prospects were poor for making a living out of wine. There had been a string of poor vintages. Hail and rot were big problems. His two older brothers went to work at the Ferrero factory when they were only in their mid-teens.

"Just think!" Guido exclaims. "They were bringing home two regular paychecks. That was something in those days."

With the economic boom in full swing, Guido himself attended the school of viticulture and enology in Alba. He had to walk over a mile in the morning to catch the train and even farther coming home from school after getting a ride partway. Right after graduation, he went to work for a big company in Milan.

"It was a real processing plant," he says. "There was no concern whatsoever for quality. We didn't even know where the grapes came from! We just stabilized the stuff and that was it. We even made vermouth."

Angelo would drop by to see him whenever business took him to Milan. He talked about his plans for the future. In February 1970 Guido started to work at the Gaja winery.

"Angelo's ideas were exciting," he says, "and I wanted to get back to Barbaresco."

There's something fraternal about their relationship that comes from long familiarity. Something a bit old-fashioned. Watching Angelo and Guido as they talk about up-to-date matters in the comfortable cadence of the dialect, it's hard to imagine one without the other. Love and marriage. Horse and carriage. Gaja and

Rivella. But fraternal does not mean free of friction. Luckily, their characters are complementary to a T.

"Guido is a great mediator," says Angelo. "I had what seemed to me a clear vision, but sometimes my head was really in the clouds. He had his feet on the ground for both of us. If I had found myself working with another revolutionary, that would have been the ball game then and there!"

"Angelo takes nothing for granted," says Guido. "He always comes back from trips with his head full of new ideas. He keeps me on my toes. Without him, I'd have probably settled into a routine like so many others. But he acts instinctively, and everything has to be verified in our particular context. Barbaresco isn't Bordeaux."

Angelo is a steady downpour of ideas; like the soil of San Lorenzo, Guido drains but retains. Angelo is close to customers and critics; Guido has to grapple with the grapes. With Angelo's foot on the accelerator and Guido's on the brake, they get where they want to go.

"There have been moments of tension," says Angelo. "Only one person represents the winery, so Guido has sometimes been left in the shade."

Being a world famous producer in a tiny village like Barbaresco, Angelo has to watch his step. Sensitive to potential conflicts of interest, he has never wanted to be involved in local politics. Guido once served as assistant mayor, but since then he has also maintained a low profile.

"Guido would probably have liked to be mayor," says Angelo, "and he would have made a terrific one, too." He pauses to reflect. "He may have wanted to do something on his own."

It's the dialogue that's been decisive. Undaunted by their differences, the team has stood the test of time.

The huddle breaks and the team goes up to the courtyard. Angelo dashes back to his office, while Guido walks into a narrow doorway at the top of the steps.

To the left is his lab, which Guido always refers to with quotation marks in his voice, a tiny room crowded with beakers and bottles. He glances back hopefully across the courtyard. When the renovation work is finished, he'll have a proper laboratory where he can do "serious experiments."

Up a flight of stairs is his office, with a small desk and a couple of shelves crammed with books, journals, and reprints. He makes a broad gesture toward them.

"Angelo is always saying that we should keep up more with research. And he's right. But most of this stuff isn't certainties. The Bible of wine making has yet to be to written."

He winks his eye.

"Sometimes when I read different studies, with contradictory claims, I get the feeling I don't know how to make wine anymore!"

Guido grew up with wine, but the word had a different connotation before he started working with Angelo. In May 1970, he went to Burgundy with a group of local wine people. The trip was a revelation.

"It was the first time I experienced a real wine culture," he says as his face lights up. "You breathed it in the air in Beaune. You saw it in the way the sommeliers poured wine in restaurants. Wine was more than just another beverage."

Guido and the winery have grown together, and he has had to work hard to keep up.

"When I started here, we made just five wines, all of them red," he says. "The vintage never began before September 20 and it lasted a month at most. Even that month wasn't as intense as things have become. Now we have the whites, the new red varieties, the new wines made with old varieties. Last year, we made wine with the Serralunga grapes for the first time. Then there are all those small casks, the *barriques*. They're a lot more work than a few big ones."

Guido takes a deep breath.

"Just think! Last year we harvested the Sauvignon on August 24, four weeks before we would have started a few years ago."

Guido is also in charge of worrying at the winery, and in that capacity works the night shift as well. The wines he makes get reviewed, compared, and numerically rated throughout the world. Given Gaja's prices and reputation, expectations are high.

[65]

"Gaja is like the Juventus," he says wryly, referring to Italy's most prestigious soccer team. "The Juve *has* to win!"

Guido may be condemned to win, but he hasn't lost his enthusiasm.

"There's still so much to learn!" he exclaims. "That's the great thing about wine—it always has a surprise for you!"

"People were amazed when Guido came to work here," says Angelo. "They were suspicious of enologists in general, because they associated them with the big industrial companies. Besides, it was unheard of for a smallish winery such as ours, with a young man in the family, to hire someone to make the wine."

Angelo chuckles.

"I'll never forget my mother's reaction when she heard about it. She was really puzzled. 'What about you?' she asked me. 'What are *you* going to do?' "

𝓗URTLING DOWN THE HIGHWAY in Germany, Angelo seems somber, even slightly fierce. He's a Taurus and sometimes looks it. With pursed lips and a glaring frown, when he raises his eyebrows you wonder if he's going to charge.

Back in the office, the phone is his boss, but he doesn't have one in the car. Travel is a time for thinking—"a time to be with myself." His concentration can be intense, as now.

Suddenly he snaps his fingers and says, "okay!" The decision descends like lightning and dissipates the clouds. He sits back, relaxed, with a smile as broad as the Autobahn.

Roads are important to Angelo. He spends a lot of time on them.

"Thank goodness," he says happily, "there are no politicians here telling you you can't do more than fifty-five miles an hour!" What a way to waste an hour! Low speed limits remain a mystery he's never fathomed; here there are no limits at all.

What would Fantini say if he could see these CN license plates from the province of Cuneo speeding along abroad, and all in the name of wine? He who was obsessed by the connection between poor wine and poor roads. "Why, in the century of progress," he wondered, "should so many roads be left as they were two centuries ago? What good is an abundant harvest if you can't get your grapes to the market?"

Fantini ends his outburst with what sounds like a fable.

"There once was a hillside that was hardly cultivated at all and produced almost nothing. Now a new road skirts it and in just a few years it has been completely transformed into luxuriant vineyards. Not a single lot of land has remained uncultivated. When you pass by that spot now, even the sky seems different!"

Highways are not Germany's only attraction for Angelo. The country is the world's largest importer of wine: about 250 million gallons a year, compared to the 165 of Great Britain and the 50 of the United States. It's Angelo's most important market and he's frequently here on tour.

Every tour is a tour de force. Whirling like the wind, he talks shop with his importers, surveys the scene with wine writers, pays his respects to restaurateurs, conducts tastings.

"Many people still think of this country as all beer and sausages," he says. "They haven't heard about the restaurant revolution." Germany has more Michelin-starred restaurants than any country in Europe except France.

He's been on the road for several days now and the schedule is beginning to take its toll. Marketing means miles and meals, and it's always a star-spangled spree.

NEXT STOP: a village in Baden, just north of Switzerland and across the border from France. The owner of the restaurant is one of the region's leading wine producers. He imports Angelo's wine and Angelo reciprocates. His son, who has been in Barbaresco, shows Angelo the vineyards and cellar, then leads him through a pre-dinner tasting of their wines.

During the two-star feast, the owner comes over from time to time to follow Angelo's prandial progress and see if he's doing his share. "You have to try this dish," he insists.

Angelo smiles and thanks him. It's all in a hard day's work.

[68]

DAWN'S EARLY LIGHT is still lingering over the landscape, but Angelo is already behind the wheel. He's heading for Wiesbaden, a city not far from Frankfurt.

He learned long ago that the world was not going to come to Barbaresco. He would have to go to it. "Unlike Bordeaux," he says, "we Italians didn't have a commercial network. We were forced to travel."

He frequently mentions the famous quotation from Samuel Pepys's diary. What he finds perhaps even more impressive than the quality of Haut Brion as described in the diarist's comment is the fact that he was able to get the wine at all.

"The only way was to take our wine to people and get them to taste it. I had to create enthusiasm, make my trademark known. It seemed the natural thing to do." It seems obvious now, but not many Italian producers were thinking that way when Angelo was already on the road.

"I learned that consumers weren't passive, that attitudes were changing, and that the highest quality was what paid, even in a wine like Barbera. It's getting out of your little niche that you discover things like that."

It wasn't easy in the beginning.

"The first question people would ask me was always, 'Does it taste like Burgundy or Bordeaux?' " Barbaresco had what nowadays would be called an image problem.

Barbaresco's affinities as a wine-producing area were with Burgundy rather than Bordeaux: numerous small growers, fragmented properties, a demanding grape variety. But Burgundy's image was glamorous. It was associated with famous figures like Napoleon; the anecdotes abound.

When Domenico Cavazza wrote his pamphlet on Barbaresco in 1907, he made a pathetic attempt to give the wine a bit of historical luster by citing a certain General von Melas, who, on November 6, 1799, had ordered wine from the village to celebrate an Austrian victory over the French in a nearby battle. "Von *who*?" his readers must have wondered. Sales of Barbaresco were not about to soar. The order was merely one of many military requisitions of the

[69]

period. Symbolically enough, in a much more important battle seven months later at Marengo, only thirty miles from Barbaresco, von Melas was defeated by none other than Napoleon himself. If the latter had celebrated his victory with Barbaresco, the wine might have become as famous as the chicken dish his cooks are said to have improvised for him on the battlefield.

But Barbaresco was not only on the wrong side of the Alps; it was on the wrong side of Alba, as well.

"Wherever I went," Angelo says, "I used to be introduced as 'the producer of a wine like Barolo.' "

Barolo wasn't Burgundy, but its image beat Barbaresco's. It was known in Italy as "the king of wines and the wine of kings" because of its association with kings Carlo Alberto and Vittorio Emanuele II. Nobles like Cavour and the Falletti family had promoted it among their well-placed acquaintants.

When the *Random House Dictionary of the English Language* was published in 1966, it had an entry for Barolo, but none for Barbaresco. An American aberration? The following year a popular book on Piedmontese cooking by one of Italy's leading food writers, Massimo Alberini, was published. The author dedicated three pages of anecdotes and rhetoric to Barolo. "It has gloriously entered the ranks of the great wines of Europe as a peer of the Médocs, Château Margaux, and even the numbered bottles of Château Lafitte [sic]," he wrote. Barbaresco was mentioned only in a list of "other wines," between the likes of Grignolino and Brachetto—not exactly a strong recommendation. Even wines are known by the company they keep!

Cavazza's solution to Barbaresco's Barolo problem was simple. If you can't beat them, he reasoned, join them, and in 1892 he proposed that what are now three officially recognized wines—Barolo, Barbaresco, and Nebbiolo d'Alba—all be grouped together under the region's most prestigious name. The failure of the proposal to win support convinced him to promote "Barbaresco" as the name of the wine. For although a few bottles had been produced that called themselves simply Barbaresco—the oldest-known dates from 1870—the wine had been known up to then mainly as Nebbiolo di Barbaresco.

The Gajas paid dearly for their decision not to buy grapes even from the Barolo area. "At the end of the sixties, a big German importer tasted our Barbaresco and was enthusiastic. He wanted to import it, but insisted on having Barolo, too, because it was better known. He wound up working with one of the big Barolo merchants."

Angelo smiles wryly.

"It took me twenty years to get over the Barolo problem."

WIESBADEN and one star. Angelo leaves the table for a while to talk with the owner. The wine steward produces a bottle of the 1984 Gaia & Rey. "This Chardonnay is one of the best whites in our cellar," he says while Angelo is away. "And we've got some great stuff down there."

At the table is a journalist who writes on both economics and wine for Frankfurt's daily newspaper, Germany's most prestigious. His wife is with him; she teaches French. The conversation is low-key and relaxed, shifting back and forth between English and French, with a few words of Italian thrown in.

"It's funny," the journalist observes. "The great Nebbiolo wines are very special. They can put you off at first. I didn't like them at all. But once they got a hold on me, I was stuck." His wife nods eagerly and smiles. "You become friends for life," she says.

ANGELO HEADS SOUTHEAST from Frankfurt, in the direction of Munich. There's a luxury hotel in the country about a hundred miles away.

"Friends for life," he says. "What a nice way to put it!" The Taurus sounds almost tender. "But there's no getting around it: it's always the foreigners. Only a foreigner would say a thing like that."

There are many topics that get Angelo going, and foreigners is one of them.

"It's the foreigners who have expanded the market for the fine wines of Italy. And not only abroad, but also in Italy itself." He snaps his fingers. "You bet!" he exclaims. *"Sicuro!"*

"Go to any of the top restaurants in the Langhe. What license plates do you see on the cars parked outside? Most of them are

German, Austrian, or Swiss. And who orders the top Barolos and Barbarescos? Foreigners!"

Angelo has worked up up a good head of steam.

"One evening last week I was in a restaurant near Barbaresco. A party of Germans came in, six of them, and sat down at the table next to ours. And you know what wines they ordered? A bottle of San Lorenzo and one of Giacosa's Santo Stefano!"

Saint Stephen is the patron saint of a vineyard in the town of Neive, and Bruno Giacosa's wine from there is the only Barbaresco that enjoys prestige comparable to that of Angelo's best. But when those saints go marching in and over to your table, don't be surprised if there's the devil to pay when it's time to pay your bill!

Angelo now sells about two-thirds of his wine abroad.

"The real breakthrough came only in the late seventies and early eighties," he says. Burton Anderson's pioneering book, *Vino,* came out in 1980. Italian wine started to get respectful attention from influential periodicals, especially in the United States and the German-speaking area of Europe. By the end of the seventies, more than one Gaja bottle out of four was being sold abroad.

There had been a moment a century earlier, around the end of the 1870s, when Italy had a chance to challenge French predominance on the international fine-wine market. The phylloxera invasion was proving to be as devastating in its own way as the Prussian one of 1870 had been. Up to 1870 France had exported eight times as much wine as it imported, but by the end of the decade the country was a net importer by three to one, a ratio that was to double in the next few years.

Phylloxera hit Italy later; its effects were less severe. The times seemed right, but the big step forward was not to be taken. Italy's total production doubled in the period from 1870 to 1890, but most of it was bulk wine from the south. Ottavi was as trenchant as ever. "Four-fifths of the wine we export is to be considered raw material for blending," he wrote, "and it is no merit of ours if such raw material is in demand."

The cheap wine heritage weighs heavily even now. Italy still sells 90 million gallons of wine a year to France, but over 95 percent of it is bulk wine for blending. The two countries annually export

[72]

roughly the same amount of wine, just over 300 million gallons, but the French sell theirs for three times more than the Italians.

"Ah, France!" exclaims Angelo. "That's the toughest market of all." Several three-star restaurants there have his Barbaresco, but that sounds better than the wine actually sells. At least he's got his foot in the door. "Or, rather," he says, "my toe."

"I'm not complaining, though. France taught the world to drink fine wine. And whoever drinks fine wine is a potential customer of ours."

IT'S THE FANCIEST PLACE so far, and the star count is now up to five. Angelo is dining with a young couple, ex-academics who both import and write about wine. They've brought a bit of the didactic side of their former calling to their new vocation.

"What's more fun, the world of wine or the groves of Academe?" Angelo asks. They loosen up and laugh, and a sip of racy Riesling provides a footnote to their answer. The wine scholars know their stuff.

"The older generation of wine writers is Francophile to the core," he says, "but the younger generation doesn't have any prejudices. Some of them actually know more about Italian wines and prefer them."

"Ten years ago," says she, "nobody knew anything about the better Piedmontese wines. Now they're really popular." She glances at Angelo. "Guess who deserves most of the credit for that?"

ON THE MOVE to Munich, Angelo is ripping along. Two meals await him there, and appointments in between.

Not many Piedmontese producers back in the sixties would have bet that one day Angelo would be getting credit for making their fine wines known in a country like Germany.

"Our winery was looked upon as a strange phenomenon," he says, "a castle of cards destined to collapse. Until 1970 or so, the dream of most producers was a big company. A couple million

[73]

bottles a year or so. People were predicting an increase in the consumption of wine in the lower price range. No one thought it possible for a small artisan to sell his wine abroad, and for a high price at that." He smiles. "Now that there is little demand for cheap, mediocre wine, small is beautiful."

Angelo's first major marketing move was to adopt his restaurant strategy. His father had sold much of his wine in large containers, demijohns, to customers who bottled it themselves and drank it in the privacy of their homes.

"Private customers helped us survive in difficult times," he says, "but it was as if our wine were being drunk in secret. A restaurant is a stage. If the patron likes the wine, he'll tell the owner. The word gets out."

During the second half of the sixties, more and more wine was bottled at the winery, and sales in demijohns were phased out.

The restaurant strategy had other consequences. The winery had begun to sell through agents in the mid-sixties. "They said we had to have other wines than Barbaresco, especially for restaurants. Less-expensive wines that could be drunk younger." Shipments were a minimum of five cases, and sixty bottles of Barbaresco was too expensive an order for many potential customers. In 1967 the winery bought a vineyard just outside Alba and started to make the wines the agents needed: Barbera, Dolcetto, and Nebbiolo d'Alba.

Another innovation was the creation of what Angelo calls the "Nebbiolo hierarchy." It was a way of defending the quality line as well as improving sales.

All wine made with Nebbiolo grapes from the legally delimited Barbaresco district and meeting certain minimum standards has a right to the name of the appellation. No distinctions are officially admitted. What was a quality-conscious producer to do with grapes which might be good enough for the law, but not for his own Barbaresco label? Surely there was a solution beyond the drastic alternatives of lowering the quality of his Barbaresco or selling the wine in bulk at a derisory price.

Angelo completed the construction of the hierarchy about ten years ago. At the base is Vinót, a wine to be drunk young, like a very superior Beaujolais nouveau and made with the same technique of vinification. The next level is Nebbiolo delle Langhe, which does not have a legally defined and protected status. Much higher, in both quality and price, is the "normal" Barbaresco, about 100,000 bottles a year. Finally, at the top of the pyramid are the single-vineyard Barbarescos, of which only about 30,000 bottles in all are made. His first single-vineyard bottling was the 1967 vintage of Sorì San Lorenzo.

Sometimes, of course, a producer can defend the prestige of his label only by sacrificing a large part, or even all, of a given vintage if it is not up to his standards. In 1987 Angelo bottled only half his normal amount of Barbaresco and in 1984 none at all.

He shakes his head as the outskirts of Munich begin to appear. "That decision about the 1984 was very painful."

LUNCH at a three-star restaurant. At Angelo's table is another journalist who writes about wine as well as economics. His wife is the daughter of a wine producer. "The second best in Franconia," he says with a grin. The talk is about one thing and another: a trip to Italy they're planning, how his book on Italian wine has done. Angelo is as attentive to figurative grapevines as he is to the ones Federico tends.

Worthy of each and every star, the lunch gathers momentum. The waiter smiles as he suggests a little of this and a little of that. The chef comes out and graciously makes his own proposals. Angelo is cheerful, accepting his fate with style. What else can he do when he's being killed with culinary kindness?

MUNICH is a moveable feast. A respite of work, and Angelo moves on to another star and a wine list not much shorter than *War and Peace*. It's in the hands of another of his importers, who shares his passion for speed as well as wine. A high-tech artisan, he transforms just a few hundred BMWs a year into high-performance cars: "the fastest four-door sedans in the world."

The first wine is German, a 1984. "It's not a big, blowzy vintage like '83," he says, "but this is better balanced; this will age." He's as lyric as a tenor, singing his love for Riesling.

What grapes could be more unlike than Riesling and Nebbiolo,

[75]

this German and that Italian? But the acidity of Riesling from way up north, from the Saar or the Ruwer, can be as tough as the tannin of Nebbiolo from Barbaresco. And just as Nebbiolo was losing ground to lesser vines not long ago, Riesling was being rolled back by the Müller-Thurgau grape, a plague worse than phylloxera. On the international market Riesling can't hold a candle to Chardonnay; its stock is as low as Nebbiolo's compared to Cabernet Sauvignon's. Riesling, too, takes time. But when it's right, you just may make a friend for life.

The aria is over; the food is served. The evening has just begun.

ON THE ROAD AGAIN, Angelo is off to Switzerland, a special place for him. The German-speakers there drink more Gaja wine per capita than any other people in the world.

The speedometer sizzles as the border draws near. "This car would go even faster if it had been transformed by my importer," he says. "But it would also be a lot more expensive."

Those cars are like the world's top wines. They are frightfully expensive, but there's a market for them—a market all their own. You pay for the quality, to be sure, but also for the prestige.

"Price was a big problem not so long ago," says Angelo. "Only in the last two or three years have people stopped asking the price first thing."

Italian wines, including Barbaresco, had little or no prestige. They were supposed to be cheap, and that was that.

"I'll never forget something that happened in the late seventies. My importer organized a presentation in Boston. He managed to get a good turnout and everything went smoothly until he mentioned the price." Angelo rolls his eyeballs. "The wine writer for the city's leading newspaper got up and walked straight out of the room, before the tasting had even begun!"

The highway is now winding its way through the mountains of Switzerland. He glances at his watch. Punctuality is one of his personal Ten Commandments.

"One of the issues was the difference in price between our wine and other Barbarescos."

Bordeaux and Burgundy had a hierarchy of quality, a pyramid

of prestige backed by either an official classification, as in the latter region, or a traditional one, as in the Médoc. It was accepted that Château Latour cost more than a simple Bordeaux or even other châteaux in Pauillac.

"In the seventies, there were industrial Barbarescos selling in the United States for a couple of dollars. 'Why should Gaja sell for ten?' people thought. I had to get them to actually taste the wine."

As Angelo entered the eighties, he was going full steam. The 1978 and 1979 vintages were excellent back-to-back years after three poor ones in a row (1972 had been such a disaster that no one produced any Barbaresco at all) and in 1977 he had founded Gaja Distribution, an import company.

"It all started by chance," he says. "A friend of mine asked me to suggest an importer for the wines of the Domaine de la Romanée-Conti. I mentioned a few names. He called me back later and said, 'Why don't you take on the job yourself?' "

Angelo has a glint in his eye.

"It enabled me to give a little luster to the name of an illustrious nobody." He laughs. "I became known in the United States as the Italian importer of Romanée-Conti!"

In 1987, Gaja Distribution expanded its activities. Angelo now has the "best" from all over the world and the list lengthens year by year. He is also the exclusive Italian importer of the famous Riedel wineglasses from Austria.

"Gaja Distribution has enabled me to visit wineries not as a tourist," Angelo reflects, "but as a client. I've learned a lot about production and marketing strategies. I've broadened my knowledge of other regions."

As he recalls the past, he suddenly slaps his forehead.

"That was my chance!" he exclaims. "It could have saved me at least ten years."

One day in 1965, on a hot summer afternoon, an American showed up at the winery wanting to purchase some wine. He had just tasted one of their Barbarescos in Milan and had been so impressed that he had gotten in his car and driven there.

"For my father, an American customer was something out of science fiction," Angelo chuckles. "He could have been from Mars!"

The visitor was Frank Schoonmaker, the most prestigious wine writer and importer in the United States at that time. In addition to his role in imposing varietal names for fine California wines, Schoonmaker had been a key figure behind estate bottling in Burgundy. Most extraordinary of all, he was the one influential wine figure in those days who was downright enthusiastic about Nebbiolo. In his *The Encyclopedia of Wine,* published in 1964, he had written that it was "the outstanding red grape of Italy, one of the world's best." Barolo was "definitely a great wine," Barbaresco "a wine of distinction and great class." And there he was, standing in the courtyard of the Gaja winery and talking with twenty-five-year-old Angelo in a mixture of English and French.

It turned out to be a comedy of errors. "A tragicomedy," says Angelo.

"Unfortunately, it was more a clash than a conversation. I was too young and inexperienced. He asked right off the bat, 'How many bottles do you have?' I thought he wanted to buy out the whole cellar. That big talk upset me." He pauses. "Now I realize that it was normal for an importer to get an idea of the quantity available."

Angelo still can't quite believe it.

"I had a lot of trouble just trying to understand him. He said that our label was more suitable for olive oil than wine and I thought he wanted to change it. Only later did I realize that he just wanted to add one of his stickers: 'A Frank Schoonmaker Selection.'"

"A Frank Schoonmaker Selection" on a bottle of Barbaresco! What a difference that would have made!

"I didn't have the vaguest idea at the time who he was. It was only a number of years later that I heard all about Frank Schoonmaker. I almost fainted!"

THREE MORE STARS for lunch. The count is up to twelve. The wine steward greets Angelo warmly. He's been in Barbaresco and glowingly recalls "the wonderful wines" he tasted there. Angelo looks over the wine list. His wines are on it—"a real satisfaction"—but they are listed under Tuscany! Angelo takes it

[78]

graciously. "Just an oversight," he says matter-of-factly. "It could happen to anybody."

A Swiss wine writer joins him at the table. "What's new in Switzerland?" Angelo asks, and then becomes all ears.

The procession of courses begins. Angelo is enthusiastic. "Perfect!" he exclaims. "It takes real genius to cook with such sophisticated simplicity."

But as the meal marches relentlessly on, Angelo looks more and more like a groggy boxer. He dodges a couple of courses, yet the outcome is never in doubt. The food doesn't need a heavy punch to floor him for the count: at length, even lightness weighs. As light as they are superb, these dishes are young Muhammad Alis, floating like butterflies and stinging like bees.

Angelo is on the ropes. It's Barbaresco or bust.

June 10, 1989

*O*BSERVED FROM FASÈT, the scene is disconcerting. Hissing and fuming, rumbling like a tank, a tractor sprays its way through the saintly *sorì*. The vineyard is the venue of what must be chemical warfare!

Defense is on the offensive, but even through binoculars the enemy is nowhere in sight. Could all this sound and fury be just a show of strength?

Federico insists that the danger is clear and present. But the enemy, it seems, is only an army of two, and such singular soldiers at that! With names straight out of an old Walt Disney movie, so cute you want to cuddle them: Powdery and Downy.

"Wolves in sheeps' clothing!" snaps Federico. Villains in disguise: Bugsy Siegels, not Bugs Bunnies. He knows those characters well. The only question is: Which is Vineyard Enemy Number One, and which is Number Two?

Along with phylloxera, powdery and downy mildew made up the trio of plagues that America inadvertently visited on European vineyards in the second half of the nineteenth century. The popular names of oidium and what the Italians call *peronospora* derive from the former's appearance on the vine as a grayish powder and the latter's as whitish downy patches. They are fungi, plants which, lacking chlorophyll, are unable to synthesize their own food and live as parasites.

These fungi are fatal, but they are only two of the 100,000 or so known species. There are good fungi, too, and look what they can do! The original antibiotic, *Penicillium notatum,* has saved countless lives; *Penicillium roqueforti* has enhanced countless others. Another fungus, *Botrytis cinerea,* is the Dr. Jekyll and Mr. Hyde of the vineyard. On most grapes it's called "gray rot" and is as ghastly as Mr. Hyde, but on those used to make certain luscious sweet wines the rot is rightly known as "noble." When you enjoy that marvelous match, a great Sauternes and Roquefort cheese, remember in all fairness that the feast is twofold fungal!

Although the maleficent mildews belong to the same division of the plant kingdom, *Mycota,* they are divided by class. As a member of the upper class *Ascomycetes,* oidium hobnobs with the likes of truffles, morels, and even yeasts, without which wine would not exist. Peronospora belongs to the same lower class, *Phycomycetes,* as the notorious late blight of the potato, which caused the Irish famine of 1845–1848.

But these parasites carry out their predatory activity in similar fashion. As their appalling pallor spreads over the vine, threadlike filaments penetrate the leaves through minute pores, the stomata, and rob the cells of their sap by means of knoblike organs called haustoria. The starved leaves lose their green, wither, and fall off the vine. Grapes fail to ripen. They may split and be attacked by gray rot.

Historically, oidium was the first to attack a European vineyard. When it struck the Langhe around the middle of the nineteenth century, probably via England on some botanical specimens shipped from the United States, it became known simply as "the vine disease" because it was the first one the European vine had ever experienced. It spread rapidly, for there were no defenses.

According to Fantini, most peasants thought the disease was "a punishment from God, against which it was stupid and senseless to fight." Even when pulverized sulfur had been discovered to be an effective preventive, many refused to use it—the Biblical brimstone—because of its association with Satan.

[81]

Ironically enough, it was the clergy who took the initiative of convincing farmers to combat oidium with sulfur. A Piedmontese bishop, Monsignor Losanna, published a pamphlet on the subject, while a parish priest in the village of Barolo, Alessandro Bona, fervently preached the Gospel of sulfur in his sermons.

By 1860 the crisis was over, but the consequences were desolating. "Entire areas where grapes had been the main source of income," wrote Fantini, "were reduced to the most wretched poverty. Numerous breweries arose to make up for the lack of wine. People even made wine from apples, pears, and other fruits." For Nebbiolo, as the authoritative *Italian Ampelography* was to write in 1882, oidium was the "coup de grâce" in many areas.

Great wine regions like Bordeaux had suffered, too. In 1852, when oidium was just beginning to spread there, the four châteaux that in the famous classification drawn up three years later were to be classified as first growths together made almost 60,000 gallons of wine. Two years later the total was little more than 5,000.

Peronospora struck thirty years later. At first, most peasants confused it with oidium. They blamed sulfur and even that recent arrival on the scene, the railroad. "The vine is sick," wrote Cavazza in 1884. "Myriads of microbes are flying in the atmosphere. At the present time, no vine is immune." According to Fantini, peronospora was "a plague that could turn this garden into a desert." In Bordeaux, Château Margaux was unaffected in 1884 and sold for 5,000 francs a *tonneau,* about 250 gallons, but fellow first growth Château Lafite was so badly hit that the wine was rejected by the Bordeaux trade and sold for only 1,500 francs a *tonneau.*

What was to become the traditional preventive of peronospora, copper sulfate, was discovered by chance by Pierre Millardet, professor of botany at the University of Bordeaux. At that time many growers sprayed it on the rows of vines near roads because it looked like the well-known poison verdigris and thus protected the grapes from thieves. Millardet happened to be passing by a vineyard in St. Julien one day and noticed that the sprayed vines had not been affected by the downy mildew that was evident in the rest of the vineyard.

Used with lime and water as "Bordeaux mixture," copper sulfate became an essential weapon in the grower's arsenal. During the

Second World War, when it was unavailable, peasants in Barbaresco ground or used acid to dissolve copper coins, pots, and pans to obtain the metal, which had become more precious than gold. "Some people even cut down telephone wires to get the copper out of them," recalls Luigi Cavallo. Peasants got so used to seeing their vines turn blue from spraying with copper sulfate that even more recently developed sprays still come in a blue version as well as a clear one.

The spray that Federico is using against peronospora today is clear.

"It lets the light through and interferes less with photosynthesis," he says. "But the old-timers prefer blue because you can *see* it. The message is clear. The blue says: 'The vineyard is well sprayed. You did a good job!' It's a symbol, like the banner you wave when you go to a soccer game."

Because it is toxic for the vine, especially at low temperatures, copper sulfate reduces its vigor. It thus became an important factor of quality in the vineyard. But its use also had less positive consequences. Growers used to spray it indiscriminately, even at flowering, when the shoots are still tender and it is likely to be cold at night.

"There were years," says Pietro Rocca, "when some peasants found themselves with no grapes at all. The vines had been burned." He pauses pensively. "But we also made a lot of mistakes with those new sprays that increased the vine's vigor. We didn't know anything then. Only what the salesmen from the chemical companies told us."

"Cavallo would spray regularly," Angelo recalls. "By the calendar. That's the way things were done." But he himself once went to the opposite extreme. One year he decided that peronospora was no longer a threat and did not spray. Guido vividly remembers the scene.

"There was a group of us sitting and talking in the square. All of a sudden a worker came running up to tell him. You should have seen the look on his face!"

When reminded of that incident, Angelo flushes slightly and slaps his forehead.

"What a blow that was!" he groans. "What a mess!"

Federico is a careful tactician on the botanical battlefield. He studies the enemy's patterns of behavior, relies heavily on intelligence, and makes no move at random. He always treats a few vines differently than the rest of a given vineyard. Comparison of the results enables him to avoid needless spraying. Like people, some vineyards are more prone to illness than others. He didn't spray this year for early oidium at Sorì San Lorenzo, for example, because the disease hadn't appeared there in the past few years.

When there are unusual problems, Federico gets advice from soft-spoken and scholarly Paolo Ruaro, a defense specialist who has a consulting firm in Alba. They also discuss the latest research: on the life cycle of the peronospora spore during the fall and winter, for example. The less it rains then, the less virulent the fungus is likely to be during the growing season.

"There are no certainties yet," Ruaro says, "but what we know enables us to act on the basis of probability."

Federico isn't spraying with copper sulfate now because he's afraid the temperature might still drop unexpectedly at night. He'll use it a little later in order to toughen the vine's leaves, making them more resistant to disease and pests.

Which of the duo is more destructive, oidium or peronospora?

"They're different," says Federico. "Peronospora is more like a regular army, oidium like guerrilla forces. Peronospora has more firepower and can inflict greater losses if it strikes. But it's also more predictable." Unlike peronospora, oidium has practically no limits. "The wind is its element," says Federico. "Even a little haze in the air can lead to an attack." No wonder that although California, with its drier climate, does not have to worry about peronospora, it does have to fight oidium, as Federico is doing now with sulfur.

"It's a less ancient disease than peronospora," he explains. It's like a new generation of criminals that doesn't play by the old rules, or even any rules at all.

"I think it's mutating, adapting to the sprays. It's been attacking later, when it's warmer. Last year, there was an attack in the middle of July, when the grapes were already large—something that wouldn't have happened a few years ago."

If Federico had not banned the flight metaphor, the vines would be cruising now. With binoculars you can make out the tiny clusters of grapes. Flowering began precociously, a few days before the end of May.

Federico grins. "Angelo couldn't believe his ears when I told him that flowering was almost over at San Lorenzo." By June 3 almost all the clusters had already formed, though there were still a few flowers here and there. "It can take as few as three days or as many as ten," says Federico. "It depends on the weather."

The grower's classic fear at flowering is poor fruit-set. A certain percentage of fertilization failure is normal and varies with the variety. The vine attains its maximum daily growth rate right around flowering, which creates strong competition for nourishment between the vegetative and reproductive cycles.

"You have two gaping mouths," says Federico, "the newborn embryonic grapes and the tips of the shoots. There simply isn't enough food to go around." Vigorous vines and rainy springs mean even fewer births. *Colatura*—what the French call *coulure*—denotes fertilization failure beyond what is normal for a given variety. It can be another of nature's ways of unintentionally helping to make a better wine, as in the great 1961 vintage in Bordeaux.

"Last year," says Federico, "we even sprayed one vineyard lightly with copper sulfate at flowering to encourage a little *colatura*. We wanted less compact bunches, with fewer grapes, in order to avoid problems with rot in the fall." Loose bunches allow air to circulate around the grapes.

Federico gazes at his vines across the valley as the tractor continues to spray.

"We'll have to tidy them up again in a couple of days," he says. "It's hard to keep up with them now."

He and his men tied the shoots to the trellises only two weeks ago, but they're already sprawling again. June is the month of maximum daily growth, which depends, among other things, on the temperature and the availability of moisture. The optimum temperature for photosynthesis is between eighty and eighty-six degrees; the process slows down sharply and will eventually cease altogether if it gets much hotter than one hundred. June is usually just hot enough—today is the first time this year that the temperature has gone over eighty-six—and there is sufficient moisture in the ground from those April showers.

"You read in textbooks that a vine will grow as much as an inch a day, or even a bit more, at this stage," says Federico. "Those authors evidently don't have Nebbiolo in mind. Take a young Nebbiolo vine, give it deepish soil, and it'll grow twice as fast. Our Cabernet Sauvignon shoots grow only about half as long in a season as Nebbiolo." He smiles knowingly.

"I remember working in a vineyard on Saturday in the middle of June 1984. It was hot; there was humidity at night. When I went back to finish up the following Monday, the shoots had grown a good foot! It was a violent explosion of vegetation!"

The preventive offensive at San Lorenzo, whose poor soil now seems more precious than ever, is winding down.

"Last year around this time," says Federico, "the fighting was a lot fiercer. Peronospora was preparing a massive attack. There were three days when the whole crop was in the balance." Federico's vines came out of it pretty much unscathed, but a lot of others suffered heavy losses.

The tactician is thoughtful.

"We shouldn't complain," he mutters grimly. "At least we can defend the vine against oidium and peronospora. Hail doesn't even give you a fighting chance."

He's referring to the violent hailstorm that hit Serralunga just a few days ago. The Gaja vineyard was spared, but a nearby one owned by a well-known producer of Barolo was devastated.

"Just think," says Federico. "His vineyard is not much more than a mile from ours. I went by there the other day. It looked as if it had been bombed. He won't harvest a single grape there this year."

Federico is upset.

"If 1989 turns out to be a great year for Barolo," he says bitterly, "ask Giovanni Conterno what he thinks of vintage charts."

June 11, 1989

OUR STARS!" raves Angelo as he digs into the large, deep bowl his wife has set before him. The huge green salad is the main course of his homecoming dinner. It is a leafy luxury he can never afford when he's away on tour.

Lucia Gaja knows her man. With her in his corner, even a groggy boxer can bounce right back and be raring to go at the bell.

Perky and pretty, Lucia was born and grew up in an outlying part of the village whose name you sometimes see, like Guido's Montestefano, on a Barbaresco label: Pajé, "straw stacks." She went to work in the winery office while still a teenager, in 1970, which thus became the year in which Angelo hired not only his winemaker, but also his future wife. They were married six years later.

"Lucia used to amble along like all the other girls from around here," says an old-timer in the village. "But once she started going out with Angelo, her pace quickened. Now she whizzes about just like him."

Angelo pours a Bordeaux he's decided to import. She takes a sip.

"What do you think of it?" he asks.

"Tell me how much we have of it," she says playfully.

[87]

"Maybe I went a bit overboard," he says. "There's a big ship-ment on the way."

"I like it a lot!" Lucia chirps. "I love this wine!" she coos.

"See why I married her?" asks Angelo with a grin.

Spirits are high. The banter blossoms. Body and soul are in tune.

In addition to working long hours in the winery office, which she now runs, Lucia takes care of their daughters, Gaia and Ros-sana, shops, and does her own cooking. She even finds time to worry that a well-fed guest is not getting enough to eat.

"Try some of this," she says as she puts a bowl on the table. "Coon-yáh" is how she pronounces the name. What could it be? "It's basically just grape juice boiled down until it's nice and thick," Lucia says. "Making it in the fall is a real ritual around here. It reminds me of my childhood."

She's not sure how you spell it, though. *Cugnà? Cougnà?*

"What are you talking about!" Angelo exclaims. "That long first vowel is always written as an *'o'* in the dialect." He cites other examples, including *sorì*. He's excited. He's in his element.

Explaining the marvels that could be accomplished with a simple lever, the Greek mathematician and physicist Archimedes told King Hieron II of Syracuse back in the second century B.C., "Give me a point of support and I shall move the world." Barbaresco is globetrotting Angelo's fulcrum, his Archimedean point. The lever-age is even in the language.

"In our family," says Lucia, "bread with *cognà* was considered a treat." She isn't even forty yet, but she's old enough to remember hard times.

"We never went exactly hungry, but the only time of year when you could really eat all you wanted was before Christmas, when the pig was slaughtered. It was a big event, with all the sausages and everything. Neighbors and friends would come over."

Angelo remembers the pig that his grandmother used to keep in the courtyard: "the terror in its eyes when the butcher came around." He shudders. "It may have been a gentler world back in those days," he says, "but in some ways it was certainly crueller, too."

It was a world that Angelo got a glimpse of as he was growing up, a world into which even Lucia was born and which existed until well into the fifties. The choral voice of the older citizens tells it like it was.

Even the custom of getting together in the barns on winter evenings lingered on. It was warmer there because of the animals. An important presence was that of the *cantastorie,* the singer of tales who would entertain the others with his stories. Some of them made a name for themselves and were much in demand.

There was still a flour mill in the group of houses along the road to Alba called Tre Stelle. Villagers would go there about once a month to have their wheat ground. In the village itself there was a store with a wood-fired oven where people would bring their dough in the evening to have it baked. The ferry across the Tanaro was run by four men working shifts of one week a month each, and the service was available around the clock. You could even wake the ferryman up in the middle of the night if you wanted to cross the river. On weekends and holidays, they played "elastic ball" in the square. The whole village would gather to cheer on the local team.

Sitting here this evening, with these images of the past presiding over the present and the gaiety of the Gajas radiating like the warmth of the wine itself, it's hard to imagine Barbaresco caught up in the brutality of the Second World War. But those images, too, gradually come into focus.

Alba was occupied by the Germans and bombed by the Allies. It was taken by partisan forces and held for twenty-three days. The Langhe became the scene of a civil war between the Resistance movement and diehard fascists, and the wartime death rate there was almost twice that of Italy as a whole.

Many young men from the village were sent off, ill-equipped, with the Cuneo Division to fight Mussolini's war alongside the Germans in the Soviet Union. The division was decimated.

On August 5, 1944, the Germans and their fascist allies conducted a roundup in Barbaresco, taking away thirty hostages who were to be shot if eleven prisoners held by the resistance movement were not released. Giovanni Gaja, who was in Barbaresco then and barely escaped arrest, vividly remembers the day. "Luigi Rama was

[89]

shaving at a window that overlooks the courtyard. When the fascists rushed in they saw him before he realized what was going on and took him off to Turin with the others."

Luigi Cavallo recalls acts of savagery. "One day I was working in a vineyard when my dog started to bark in a strange way. I followed him and found a young man, really just a teenager, buried with his pants pulled down and his buttocks sticking out of the ground." Cavallo later dug up two more bodies.

Aldo Vacca's father, who had joined one of the partisan groups, was walking down a path one day and managed to get rid of his weapon just in time before a fascist patrol caught him. He was arrested for desertion and sent to a concentration camp in Germany. In the last days of the war he became violently ill. "If the Americans hadn't arrived in the nick of time with antibiotics," he says, "I would have died."

Even idyllic Montestefano did not escape the violence. "Partisans would come and stay here," Guido's mother recalls. "Once they had to dash off and left their weapons behind." She rushed out with two of Guido's aunts and his grandmother to bury them in a nearby hazelnut grove. "If the fascists had discovered those weapons," she says, "they would have burned our homes to the ground."

There were amusing notes, though, as the Langhe met the Allies toward the end of the war. A former partisan recalls the parachutes used by Allied planes to drop supplies to his and other units. The morning after a drop "balconies all over the Langhe would be ablaze with the colors of homemade nylon lingerie." Another chuckles at a photo showing local eyes bulging as three black G.I.s stroll down a street in Alba. "They had more stuff in one of their packs than we had in all of ours put together," he says.

Although Angelo will be turning half a century old next year, his favorite tense is still the future. He can get excited about the past, but it takes a certain effort, like slowing down to fifty-five miles per hour.

He won't be long in Barbaresco now. Business trips beckon, but there's more, too. He'll soon be in Burgundy for several days with top French and California producers, an honorary Franco-American at a symposium on Chardonnay. Right now he's talking about an unusual event that will take place in a lakeside castle in Bavaria at the end of September.

A wealthy German wine lover has invited him to a re-creation of a famous event in gastronomic history: the so-called "dinner of the three emperors." Wilhelm I of Prussia, his son Friedrich III, and Alexander II of Russia dined together in Paris on June 3, 1867, at the most celebrated restaurant of the day, the Café Anglais. Angelo will be drinking the same wines that were served on that occasion, only one hundred twenty-two years and a few months older: "Grand Chambertin" Domaine de Grésigny 1846; Château Lafite 1848; Châteaux Latour, Margaux, and Yquem 1847; and others.

"I'll have to dress up in the style of the period," he tells Lucia. What could the latest fashion have been in the last years of the Second Empire?

He's used to quick changes of costume now, but if you catch him backstage, in a moment such as this, you can still get glimpses of the young man about the town of Barbaresco before he became a prominent figure on the international wine scene.

"In those days Angelo was a *normal* person," says Angelo Lembo, whose face expresses astonishment as the adjective comes out of his mouth. "He would drop by just like that and say, 'Let's go out to dinner.' Sometimes Gino Cavallo would come along, too."

"I can still see him sitting out in the square and chatting as if it were yesterday," says Guido. "Dropping by the tavern to play cards and joke around with the boys."

Pietro Rocca remembers him coming over to his house for a cup of coffee every Sunday after lunch. "Angelo would sit with us puffing on one of those cigars he used to smoke. His father would never have allowed that in his home." Rocca's smile sparkles. "Angelo was really the life of the village in those days. He organized festivities and even took care of the details."

Such scenes became less frequent as Angelo started to travel more. Now there are periods in which one trip is barely over when another has already begun. But one trip that has remained vivid in his memory is his first one to California, in 1974.

The New World he discovered then was not just a conventional geographical expression. It was a new world.

The California wine boom was in full swing. The two wines that were to win the famous Paris tasting in 1976 (a Chardonnay from Château Montelena, and a Cabernet Sauvignon from Stag's Leap Wine Cellars) had been made the year before. The year 1974 was a great one for Cabernet in California, but it was the third mediocre one in a row for the wines of Bordeaux, whose inflated market had collapsed. More than 50,000 acres of vines a year were being planted in the state. "California, Here I Come" was climbing fast on the wine world's Hit Parade, and Angelo, too, was seduced by that siren song.

"People were real pros there," he says. "Most of them were in wine by choice, not just because they had inherited a vineyard. They had capital. They invested. They experimented."

Angelo's eyes and ears were barely big enough to take in everything, and he did more than one double take. The wine maker at the Robert Mondavi Winery, the leading one in Napa Valley, was a woman, Zelma Long.

"It wasn't just the fact that she was a woman," Angelo recalls. "She was also so young to be in such an important position."

Of course, it was sixty-one-year-old Robert Mondavi himself, with his dynamism, drive, and restless experimentation, who made the greatest impression on him. But the older man was no less impressed by the thirty-four-year-old visitor from his ancestral land.

"Angelo hasn't changed a bit since then," says Mondavi now. "He was just like he is today: honest, hard-working, and very determined, with an idea a minute." After reflecting awhile, he finally comes up with what he hopes will do for a difference. "He's more famous now," he says with a smile.

Mondavi, whose father emigrated to the United States in 1903 from the central Italian region of the Marches, is certainly the most prestigious figure of Italian origin in the California wine world. But the particular Piedmontese contribution has been more important than is generally realized.

Ernest and Julio Gallo's father arrived in California in 1905, via Argentina, from his native Fossano, less than twenty miles from Alba. The winery his sons founded in 1933 is the largest in the world today, producing almost 8,000 bottles for every one that bears the Gaja label. A very different figure, Pietro Carlo Rossi, emigrated to California in 1875 from Dogliani, in the Langhe, with his head full of utopian ideas about work and community derived from English writers like Robert Owen and John Ruskin—ideas that led to the founding in 1881 of the Italian Swiss Colony at Asti, in Sonoma County. The experiment soon failed, but the winery became one of the most important in California.

Angelo is not uncritical of California. He knows that there are no enological utopias. "There have been some pretty wild swings in the style of the wines," he says. "Sometimes the exasperated use of technology has verged on terrorism."

But the experience was decisive. Using French varieties and wine-making methods, California showed that you could beat the French at their own game—or at least play in the same league. They weren't bound by Tradition.

Angelo had had enough of Tradition. "California gave me the courage to go ahead with some ideas I'd been thinking about," he says.

STROLLING THROUGH Sorì San Lorenzo at the end of May, when the vineyard was in full bloom, an attentive observer's eye might have been caught by a small block of vines where none of the inflorescences had opened yet. Closer inspection would have revealed that those vines were indeed different from all the others. The leaves, for instance, were a darker green and felt rougher when you touched them. Their sinuses, or indentations, were deeper—so deep, in fact, that the lobes overlapped slightly. Nor did the shoots look quite the same as those elsewhere in the vineyard. They were less exuberant and their internodes—the spaces between the joints—were shorter.

Even an amateur ampelographer would have recognized that among the vines of San Lorenzo there was Cabernet Sauvignon.

In 1973 the tops of the Nebbiolo vines in those few rows were cut off and Cabernet was grafted onto their rootstocks. With only the saint himself in the audience, the rehearsal had begun.

"The wine we made that first year was nothing special," Angelo recalls. Only a demijohn was made, a few gallons. The winery wasn't really equipped for microvinification, the making of tiny batches of wine. "What did impress us, though, was how well the vines had adapted to the soil and climate. The vegetation was perfectly balanced."

A couple of years later, just under five acres of Nebbiolo vines on the south-facing slope of the Bricco were ripped up. The land was left fallow until 1978, when Cabernet Sauvignon was planted. The performance was public now.

A *bricco* is a hilltop, but this was *il* Bricco, *the* Hill, much as Beacon Hill used to be in Boston. You can't drive in or out of the village, which it dominates, without passing by it.

"My father had suggested planting the Cabernet in a secondary vineyard," says Angelo, "but I didn't want to penalize it. I didn't want to sneak it in through the back door."

When word got around about the doings on the Bricco, the village was stunned. "Everybody was gossiping about it," says Angelo Lembo. "One grower even told me that he was ashamed of what we were doing." He wasn't the only one who felt that way. You'd think that Angelo had planted marijuana, or even worse. "Scandalous," "sinful," and "mad" were definitions of his deed that people still remember.

Even Angelo's father had a hard time accepting what had happened. Passing by the vineyard, the top rows of which are just a few steps off the dirt drive that connects his house with the road, he would often shake his head and mutter, *"Darmagi!"* "What a pity!" "What a shame!"

When Angelo bottled his first Cabernet Sauvignon, the 1982 vintage, he took devilish delight in calling the wine Darmagi. He thereby enlarged the world's vocabulary of the Piedmontese dialect, which until then had been limited to Punt e mes ("a point and a half"), the name of a well-known vermouth.

Looking back now on all the ado, Angelo doesn't pretend that it was about nothing.

"It was as if a Burgundian grower had ripped up Pinot Noir vines from a major vineyard in Vosne-Romanée or Gevrey-Chambertin and planted some outsider there, some non-traditional vine."

A foreign vine had taken away a native's job. Planting it was a betrayal of Tradition.

Scratch a tradition and you'll find a successful innovation that's been around a while: sometimes a very short while indeed, as in the case of the dry still wine called Barbaresco. There are always traditions prior to Tradition, and varietal vicissitudes are a fascinating part of the history of wine.

Cabernet Sauvignon originally owed its prestige to its predominant presence in the great vineyards of the Médoc and Graves regions of Bordeaux, but it seems that, under the name of Biturica, it had been taken there by the ancient Romans. And its predominance was a relatively recent phenomenon, dating back only to the first quarter of the nineteenth century as far as a great estate like Château Latour is concerned. At that time, all the top Médoc estates still had grapes, including white ones, in their vineyards that would be considered most untraditional today. It was not until the middle of the nineteenth century that Cabernet Sauvignon became firmly established as the undisputed number-one variety.

As an Italian producer, Angelo had a more problematic relationship with Tradition than his colleagues in France or the New World. Italian traditions were parochial, and as long on rhetoric as they were short on rewards.

France had traditions that defined for the whole world what fine wines were all about. Why would anyone want to challenge them? In the New World, with no traditions strongly associated with local or national pride, producers had a free hand. Even though Penfolds had been founded in 1844, fifteen years before the Gaja winery, Max Schubert, the winemaker who created Grange Hermitage, went to Bordeaux, studied how things were done there during the 1949 vintage, and put what he had learned into practice upon his return to Australia. The only reason he decided to use Shiraz, as the Australians call the French variety Syrah, instead of Cabernet Sauvignon for his Grange was that the latter was in very short supply in Australia at that time.

Angelo may have been the first to plant Cabernet in Barbaresco itself, but as far as the cultivation of this and other "foreign" varieties in Piedmont and in Italy as a whole is concerned, he did not lack predecessors. Indeed, the tradition behind him was a most distinguished one.

Less than ten miles from Barbaresco, at Costigliole, Marquis Filippo Asinari di San Marzano, a foreign minister of the Kingdom of Sardinia and holder of high offices under Napoleon, planted Syrah vines as early as 1808. In 1822 he obtained cuttings of Cabernet Sauvignon and other vines from the four Bordeaux chateaux that in 1855 were to be classified as first growths—Haut-Brion, Lafite, Latour, and Margaux—as well as Sauvignon and Sémillon from Château Suduiraut, one of the great Sauternes estates. In his correspondence with the Sardinian consul in Bordeaux there is a letter dated November 18, 1825, containing the replies to twelve detailed questions concerning viticulture and wine making at Château Lafite. Asinari saw no contradiction between his interest in foreign varieties and his passionate dedication to a traditional one such as Nebbiolo, which at that time was still widely cultivated around Asti.

The marquis of San Marzano was only one of a number of cosmopolitan viticulturists. In 1820, Count Manfredo Bertone di Sambuy planted Cabernet Sauvignon near the site of the battle of Marengo. He had been struck during his travels by the similarity of the soil of the Médoc to that on his estate. At Rocchetta Tanaro, just beyond Asti on the same river that flows past Barbaresco, Marquis Leopoldo Incisa della Rocchetta created one of Italy's most impressive ampelographical collections. His 1869 catalogue, which listed the 376 different varieties that he was cultivating at the time, described Cabernet Sauvignon as "one of the best" and highly recommended it to growers.

It was another great Piedmontese ampelographer, Count Giuseppe di Rovasenda, who best expressed the spirit of this viticultural tradition. "Though grape varieties may have a nationality of origin, and even that is usually uncertain," he wrote, "they have none as far as cultivation is concerned."

The cultivation of foreign varieties was not limited to growers of noble birth. In 1835 the Burdin brothers of Chambéry, in Savoie, which at that time was still part of the Kingdom of Sardinia, established a vine nursery in Turin, and French varieties were subsequently introduced into Piedmont on a rather large scale.

Interesting experiments were also carried out. Toward the end of the nineteenth century, the school of viticulture and enology in Alba that Angelo and Guido were later to attend was growing Cabernet and blending it with Dolcetto in the proportion of one-fourth to three-fourths. The results were reported as being "very encouraging."

The cultivation of Cabernet Sauvignon was also by no means limited to Piedmont. In his book on foreign varieties in Italy, published in 1903, Salvatore Mondini pointed out that it was being grown in forty-five out of the country's sixty-nine provinces. There was even Cabernet Sauvignon in a number of vineyards around Rome, for instance. One of them, planted in 1881 and making "excellent wines which have made quite a name for themselves," was located in what is now one of the capital's most fashionable residential sections, Parioli.

Mondini emphasized the promising use to which Cabernet was being put in Tuscany. "It has been observed," he wrote, "that even the best Tuscan wines improve notably if Cabernet is added in small quantities. . . . Especially worthy of note are the results obtained by blending Cabernet with Sangiovese." Three-quarters of a century later, two new Tuscan wines had become leaders of the Italian wine revolution: Sassicaia and Tignanello. Behind their creation there was not only a Cabernet connection, but a Piedmontese one as well.

Sassicaia made its debut on the international scene in 1978, when its 1972 vintage swept a blind tasting of Cabernet Sauvignons from around the world that was sponsored by the British periodical *Decanter*. The wine was made by Marquis Mario Incisa della Rocchetta, a Piedmontese and great-nephew of Leopoldo Incisa. His interest in fine Cabernet Sauvignon had been aroused by the one of his relatives the Salviatis made before the Second World War just a short distance up the Tyhrrenian coast from Sassicaia itself. Symbolically enough, the cuttings with which the Salviatis had planted their own vineyard in the 1880s came from count di Sambuy's vineyard near Marengo, the first recorded plantation of Cabernet Sauvignon in Italy in modern times. The roots of Sassicaia were deeply Piedmontese.

Tignanello was created at the Antinori winery by another Piedmontese, winemaker Giacomo Tachis, who revived the nineteenth-century practice of blending a small amount of Cabernet Sauvignon with Sangiovese

"More than anything else," says Angelo, "planting Cabernet

[98]

Sauvignon was part of a desire to experiment, to measure one-self against the highest international standards. As far as quantity is concerned, it will never be more than a minor variety around here.''

Cabernet Sauvignon was also part of a marketing strategy. An outsider in Barbaresco, it was an insider in markets abroad: an ambassador who spoke the right foreign languages. To be sure, Angelo wanted to win, but sports, not war, was his metaphor. Cabernet was never intended to take Nebbiolo's place as the star of the Gaja team, but rather to run interference for it, especially when the game was away. Though Darmagi is very expensive indeed, Angelo always prices it slightly lower than his standard-bearers, the single-vineyard Barbarescos.

People who thought that Angelo had lost his head for Cabernet didn't know their man. He might flirt with the foreign variety, but he would never betray Nebbiolo. After all, he had certainly been around, footloose and fancy free, in Italy and abroad. But the most eligible bachelor in all of Barbaresco had married a hometown girl.

Is Cabernet Sauvignon living happily ever after on the Bricco, like Angelo and Lucia? As the vines begin to come of age, Darmagi has begun to receive flattering reviews and to do well in tastings in which the company is more than respectable. The '88 even makes Guido's honor roll, and he's one of the hardest markers his wines ever have to face. ''We're getting there,'' he says, which for Rivella is almost a rave.

''We'll see,'' says Angelo cautiously. His face is straight, but there's a smile on the way. ''If by the time I retire the wine isn't up to their standards, my daughters can rip up the vines and I'll be the one to say, *'Darmagi!'* ''

July 14, 1989

ALLONS, *enfants de la patrie,*
Le jour de gloire est arrivé!

It's the bicentennial of the French Revolution and Federico is whistling *La Marseillaise*. "I don't know about the day of glory," he quips as he glances at the clear blue sky, "but it sure is a glorious day."

Sauntering through the vines of San Lorenzo, he stops every now and then, bends over a cluster and gazes at great length. This roaming of his seems random. Is there method, or is it madness?

"I'm gathering intelligence," he says.

The defense department is at it again, fearlessly fighting invisible foes. Other eyes that stare where Federico has gazed see nothing. If the enemy is there, the camouflage is perfect. Ears are no help, either. "Do you hear those ferocious soldiers roaring in the countryside?" *La Marseillaise* asks the citizens of France. But nothing is stirring in the silent *sorì*. Perhaps the rarely sung second stanza of the national anthem that Federico was whistling just ten days ago is right. Perhaps "the foe's haughty host in dread silence reposes."

Federico pulls a magnifying glass out of his pocket and at last it comes into view. But what does this sign tell him about the enemy?

"This is no sign," he says with a snort. "This *is* the enemy!"

"Aux armes, citoyens, formez vos bataillons!" There, on a grape, lies a microscopic transparent egg. They will have to spray.

To an outsider, it sounds like Federico is planning a slaughter of innocents. Perhaps intelligence has bungled. Or is defense now just a euphemism for infanticide?

Federico is no pacifist, but neither is he trigger-happy with the spray gun. His briefing explains it all.

"If you don't do it now," he says, "you'll have to spray in a month, or even later, with anti-rot products that go straight into the cellar. The egg was laid by the *tignola* moth. When it hatches, the newborn caterpillar will break the skin to get at the juice."

When Federico says "break the skin," you can hear the knell in the tone of his voice and you know for whom the bell tolls. Cabernet Sauvignon, with its thicker skin, is virtually unaffected, but Nebbiolo is a sitting duck. As Cavazza noted eighty years ago, Nebbiolo is the *tignola*'s favorite. "You could say this insect is a real gourmet," he wrote.

Federico walks up a few rows and over to a little white plastic box. "It's a trap," he says. "I put it here in the middle of the vineyard about a month ago. The inside is smeared with a sticky substance and there's a capsule which emits a pheromone."

Pheromones are odorous substances secreted by an individual that stimulate a behavioral response in another member of the same species. They are molecular messengers, like hormones, but borne by the air instead of the bloodstream. Among insects, the message may have to do with the search for food or defense against enemies, but, as with humans, it is usually a matter of mating. Pheromones can be powerful. The great French entomologist, Henri Fabre, whom Charles Darwin called "the incomparable observer," reported in the last century the almost seven-mile flight, upwind, of a male moth in response to the scent of a female.

The male moths are the first to emerge from the pupal state and fly. Attracted by the pheromone emanating from the trap, they get stuck on the sticky surface, allowing Federico to monitor their number daily. If the peak is high, he gets ready for action. A sudden drop in numbers indicates that the females have begun to emerge and emit their own pheromones. Mating will take place, the females will lay their eggs, and eight days after the peak number of males is reached in the trap the caterpillars will start to hatch.

"Some people spray as a matter of course after eight days," Federico says. "But it's essential to count the eggs after five or six days because atmospheric conditions can modify the situation. The wind, for example, can prevent mating."

He examines one hundred clusters at random. If he finds eggs on more than ten to fifteen percent of them, he'll spray.

"It also depends on the vineyard," he says. "Some are more susceptible to rot than others."

Tolerance of limited losses is important. "Growers of table grapes aim at one hundred percent protection. Appearance is all. Some of them spray seven or eight times a season." The price of this policy of unconditional surrender is getting on the classic pesticide treadmill: increasingly frequent applications of ever larger doses as insects build up resistance.

Federico will time his attack in order to catch the caterpillars just after they have hatched, when they are most vulnerable to his chosen weapon and before they can launch their own assault on the grapes. This time he'll be engaged in biological instead of chemical warfare.

"*Benign* biological warfare," he says.

Federico's weapon is *Bacillus thuringiensis,* a bacterium that paralyzes the caterpillar's digestive apparatus, but is innocuous for humans, animals, and most useful insects. He mixes in one percent of sugar to make the solution more appetizing and will spray in the early evening because direct sunlight lessens its effectiveness.

Angelo first saw baiting traps at Montpellier in the early sixties. "Just think," he says. "In Italy at that time we were spraying according to the calendar, and using lead arsenate to boot."

Federico shudders.

"Lead arsenate is a class-one insecticide!" he exclaims. "Like DDT. Those molecules are practically nondegradable. Any victory won with that weapon was bound to be Pyrrhic."

The chemicals used in disease and pest control are classified according to their toxicity, with class one the most toxic and class four the least. Federico uses only class four chemicals that have specific targets and are rapidly degraded. His goal is to preserve the vineyard's biological equilibrium, spraying as little as possible, varying the sprays he does use and avoiding what he calls "blanket bombing," which disrupts the equilibrium by destroying a pest's natural predators.

"Look what happened with the red spider and the cicada almost twenty years ago," he says. "Guido often talks about it. They thought they'd never be able to make great wines again."

Federico wipes his forehead.

"It was at the beginning of the seventies. At the end of July, when it got really hot, there was a massive invasion of red spiders and little cicadas. They started to overrun the vineyards. Nobody'd ever seen anything like it!"

It turned out that a new spray used in the spring against peronospora had not only killed the insects' natural predators, but had also increased the vine's vigor and softened its leaves. The red spider, which had formerly attacked trees and bushes, shifted its attention to the more delectable food. When they stopped using the spray, the problem disappeared.

"That's it," says Federico. "The red spider becomes a threat to the vineyard only if we goof up."

The *tignola* threat is not the result of environmental damage. The moth was a familiar foe long before modern sprays existed. Fantini describes peasants hunting the caterpillars at night with lanterns and killing them "with pins and tweezers."

"It always adapts," says Federico. "And it's too strong for potential predators." He speaks with grudging admiration of an enemy whom he has defeated in many a battle, but who always survives to fight another day.

But the *tignola* is only the latest of Federico's concerns. He and his men have not been idle during the past month. This is the sixth time they've been at Sorì San Lorenzo since June 12, for either defensive measures or the usual domestic drudgery.

Federico is always fiddling with leaves, removing a few here and there, rearranging others. "Fussing with the foliage," says the casual observer. "Canopy management," retorts the insider, using a recent entry in the vocabulary of viticulture.

It's partly a question of productivity. "A shaded leaf is a parasite," Federico growls. "It consumes, but it doesn't produce." He's exasperated by lazy leaves that fail to perform their photosynthetic labors. But defense is involved as well.

"It's not so much the quantity of leaves," he says, "as how they are arranged on the wires." If the shoots are not positioned vertically and the leaves get tangled, air doesn't circulate, humidity is created, and fungus diseases thrive. Sprays will not penetrate. You'll also get vegetal aromas in your wine.

Federico separates a tangle of leaves and positions the shoots upward.

"Look at them now, with each leaf taking the sun," he says.

He looks like a fastidious hairdresser as he holds the shoots in place. Form and function go hand in hand here.

"People talk about the microclimate of a valley or a slope," he says. "But the ultimate microclimate is that of the individual leaf or grape. If you manage two adjacent vines differently, their microclimates will be as different as if they were miles apart. One will ripen its grapes, the other won't. Rot will attack one, but not the other."

He pauses and removes a couple of leaves.

"When I was in California, I noticed that most growers didn't use vertical trellising as we do. The foliage was just draped over a wire. They weren't so concerned about the structure of the vine. They seem to get ripe grapes without having to really exert themselves, but we have to work at it. And with their drier climate, they don't have to worry so much about humidity."

At the beginning of the month the vineyard crew topped the vines for the second time. The tips of the shoots were cut off to slow down vegetative growth temporarily and direct nourishment toward the growing clusters of grapes.

"Only three or four growers in Barbaresco top," says Federico, "and in Serralunga it created a big stir. Everyone said the grapes wouldn't ripen. They're thinking of the past, when peasants used to top so drastically and remove so many leaves that it was detrimental." Once again, balance is all.

"Last year we topped a bit earlier there. Next year, we'll do it a few days later. It takes about five years to get to know a vineyard."

Four days ago, it rained three-fifths of an inch. "Thank God!"

exclaims Federico. "It wasn't much, but it brought a little relief. The vines were beginning to suffer." Since those providential April showers ten weeks earlier, there had been less than one and a half inches of rain. Federico is getting ready to face a drought emergency. Tomorrow they'll till the soil. "Very shallow," he says. "Just enough to enable the soil to absorb more water if it happens to rain and to get rid of the weeds. The vines can't stand any competition right now."

Federico throws up his arms.

"There's vintage charts again for you!" he exclaims. "Look at what's been happening over in Govone."

Govone is not even five miles away. It has hailed there three times since the beginning of the month, with three times as much rainfall in less than two weeks as in two and a half months at Sorì San Lorenzo.

Federico fondles a leaf. "The color's perfect," he says. "A nice medium green. Not too bright."

Federico keeps gazing at the leaf, but he's not looking for *tignola* eggs anymore. He's contemplative.

"Just think what's going on inside here right now," he says. "It's awesome."

Photosynthesis is the most important chemical reaction in the world. Without it, we would have no food and no fuel: neither Pétrus nor petroleum, which, like coal and natural gas, derives from plant residues originating in photosynthesis that took place in earlier geological epochs.

Federico's leaf is using the energy of sunlight to convert inorganic substances—carbon dioxide, which is 0.03 percent of the air around us, and water—into organic compounds, mainly carbohydrates. One reason grapes are great for wine is that the vine conveniently produces its carbohydrates in the form of sugar instead of starch, and glucose and fructose at that. These sugars are directly fermentable by yeast, whereas sucrose, table sugar, is not.

The chlorophyll that traps solar energy and thus enables the leaf to do its job is contained in chloroplasts within the cells. Carbon dioxide diffuses into them through the stomata, of which there are about 70,000 per square inch of leaf. In this way, plants convert some 400 billion tons of atmospheric carbon dioxide every year.

The stomata open when they are struck by light in the morning and close when the light recedes into darkness in the evening. They will also close and thereby "shut down" the vine if there is excessive heat or lack of water, which is why grapes may fail to ripen properly in very hot and dry years.

Federico snaps out of his trance-like state and whistles the last notes of the *La Marseillaise*.

"There will be fireworks all over France," he says. "It should be quite a show."

But for the mind with an eye that can see, what's happening in the leaf right now is no less pyrotechnic than the display they'll be watching in Paris tonight.

July 23, 1989

O N AN AFTERNOON like this, in the stillness of a summer Sunday, the mind is lulled into an illusion of timelessness. But memory knows better. The scene is always shifting. Halfway back through the calendar, on a January day, the Bricco was an island floating in a sea of fog.

Angelo is walking down his drive, between the Darmagi vineyard on the left and Chardonnay vines, planted a few years later, on the right.

"The Nebbiolo that used to be here," he says, nodding toward the Chardonnay, "never ripened properly. This wasn't the right exposition for it, so we had no qualms about ripping it up."

Angelo is on his way to see one of his workers, Giuseppe Botto, who is known to everyone as Geppe. He lives in a house just down the Bricco, where the drive makes an almost hairpin turn to the right.

"Geppe represents a very important step I took back in the sixties," says Angelo. "At that time we had five or six workers, all of them from Barbaresco, but only one was full-time. The others had their own vineyards to tend, so they worked only a couple of days a week for us. And, of course, they were always busy at harvest time."

All the workers were friends of Luigi Cavallo's, who wanted things to stay that way. He suggested that Angelo take on more part-time locals. But Angelo had long-term plans. There were all the new vineyards, such as the Bricco itself and Masuè, and others that would soon be purchased. He started to look around out of town.

"It was a tricky situation," he says.

There is affection in Angelo's voice as he talks about Geppe. Geppe was the first. He came to Barbaresco from the village of Dogliani in 1965.

When you look up Dogliani on a map and measure the distance from Barbaresco, it's only fifteen miles if you disregard all the twists and turns in the road. But miles are equal only in map makers' minds. In the Langhe they're longer. Dogliani was not only on the other side of Alba; it was all the way on the other side of the Barolo district. There were even differences in the vocabulary and pronunciation of the dialect. In Dogliani, a small farmer's vineyard was his *autín;* in Barbaresco, his *vignót.* Over there, "Gaja" was pronounced pretty much as in Italian, while in Barbaresco it sounded more like the name of the Spanish painter Goya. Dogliani was distant, and Geppe an "immigrant" from fifteen miles away.

"He had a hard time integrating here," Angelo recalls. "They made things rough for him." There was never any lack of excuses for Cavallo to start screaming. Dogliani is Dolcetto country, and Geppe had no experience with the ways of Nebbiolo. "He had to do things exactly the way Gino did them, right down to the most minute details. And once he managed to do them that way, he had to do them just as fast. Otherwise, Gino would get furious."

Seventy now, his face beaten by the weather, Geppe opens the door to another world. In the penumbral silence of the living room, only the television testifies that the time is the present. Here and there are relics of a past by now remote: a print of the Madonna, a faded photo of kin.

Angelo sits down and asks how things are going. He mentions the matter that has brought him here. As Geppe starts to talk, one yearns to know more about him.

[108]

"The only things that get him out of the house when he's not working," says Guido, "are his vegetable garden and Sunday Mass."

"He suffers if he has to pair off in the vineyard with talkative younger workers," says Federico. "He'll mutter two or three words at most in a whole morning. Even having to *listen* to others is painful to him."

During the Second World War, Geppe was sent off to fight in the Soviet Union. His feet were badly frostbitten. The rest one can only imagine.

In Dogliani, Geppe's most illustrious fellow citizen had been Luigi Einaudi, who in 1948 became the first president Italy elected under its new republican constitution. In 1893 Einaudi published a study of the distribution of landed property in Dogliani, which he considered typical of the Langhe as a whole. He pointed out that the changes brought about there by the French Revolution were not as dramatic as they were in France, where much larger estates had existed. When Dogliani's already small properties were sold they were usually broken up into such tiny lots that even the smallest farmers had a chance to become landowners. "You could say," Einaudi wrote, "that in Dogliani almost every family is bound to the land by the bond of ownership."

Things seemed too good to be true. And, of course, they weren't.

Geppe lives in slow motion. Pauses fill the air. Angelo listens, respectful of silence and the gravity of simple words.

A parliamentary investigation of the state of Italian agriculture reported that in 1880 97 percent of the land in the Alba area was worked by small owners, but noted that, paradoxically, the situation was detrimental to civil progress. Self-sufficiency was the peasant's only goal, and there were few sacrifices he would not make, few deprivations he would not endure, in order to attain it. Hygiene was neglected; toilets and baths were unknown. Luckily, the almost total absence of windowpanes assured a change of air, at least in the warmer months. During the winter, according to the report, the usage of plugging windows with straw and manure was widespread.

The bill that led to the obligatory attendance of elementary school had been introduced in Parliament by a citizen of Alba, Michele Coppino, but peasants in the Langhe were reluctant to comply. "They are more concerned about the cultivation of their fields," the report observed, "than they are about the cultivation of the minds of their children."

The language of statistics is stark, but eloquent. One out of four children born in the Alba area at the end of the nineteenth century died before the age of one, and more than one out of three before the age of ten. The rejection rate of local draftees was high, with the prevalence of hernias—the result of boys straining to carry heavy loads up steep slopes—one of the main reasons.

Agronomists of the period refer to peasants as "angry deforest- ers," chopping down trees to make land available for annual crops. The cultivation of vines increased many times over, but selling the grapes was another matter. The peasant needed a buyer, and often the only way of finding one was to load the grapes onto a cart, hitch it to an ox or a horse, and set off to join the crowd of small growers at the market in Alba. There he would have to bargain for many hours, and sometimes even around the clock, with crafty brokers who always wound up paying next to nothing.

Geppe's words come out in clumps. It appears that there will be problems with taxes and his pension if he continues to work full-time.

Many peasants who acquired property were unable to hold on to it. "The by now too long string of years unfavorable to viticul- ture has dried up the savings accumulated by the small owners," Einaudi observed, "and obliges them to borrow money at exorbi- tant interest rates." In 1888, 30 people emigrated abroad from Dogliani alone.

For those who had no land and did not emigrate, the prospects were grim. Sharecropping was a possibility for a few. Another was an almost medieval form of employment called *servitù*—work in exchange for room, board, and pocket money. Beppe Fenoglio's short novel, *La Malora,* is narrated by a young *servo* living with a sharecropper whose only concern is to save up enough to buy a piece of land of his own. The boy is always hungry. "Lunch and dinner were almost always dried corn mush. To give it a bit of flavor, we took turns rubbing it with an anchovy hanging from a string tied to a beam. Even when the anchovy no longer had even the semblance of one, we went on rubbing it for several days."

Angelo sits in the twilight of a world that has all but receded into history. He nods. He understands.

"Why don't you stay on," he suggests, "and work as much or as little as you choose." He pauses at length and looks around the room. "The house is yours for as long as you wish to remain here."

He gets up and walks to the door.

"Think it over," he says as he shakes Geppe's hand.

On his way back home, Angelo stops just after the drive makes its turn.

"It's a miracle," he says.

Angelo is facing the top of the Darmagi vineyard, but the object of his wonder is a humble plot of land between the Cabernet vines and the drive: Geppe's vegetable garden.

"I don't see how he does it in this poor soil."

Angelo seems ready to kneel. From the tomatoes to the lettuce, the sweet peppers and the beans, everything is splendid.

Foodways have histories no less complex than the ways of wine. What could be more Italian than the tomato? And yet it did not reach Italy from South America until the middle of the sixteenth century and was not widely cultivated for another two hundred years. The corn mush called *polenta* that Fenoglio writes about in *La Malora* is as much a rite as a food in the Langhe, but corn is another plant that Italy owes to Columbus, as are kidney beans and Capsicum peppers, both sweet and hot.

"Just think of all the work and patience it takes!" Angelo exclaims. "Geppe's always gardening. He collects rabbit drippings to provide organic matter. But there's more to it than that." He smiles. "Geppe talks to these plants. He gets them to do what he wants."

Angelo is deep in reverie, or is it reverence? The scene is certainly suggestive. This Bricco is no banal spot, with all its bonds of brotherhood. Cabernet and Capsicum: companions of the soil, though destined for different dining rooms. Who knows if Geppe tells the vine the things he tells the vegetable.

[111]

Suddenly Angelo is on the move again. Watching him stride up his hill, it's easy to forget that even the boss of the Bricco is the descendant of an immigrant.

The boss laughs. He has tried to trace his family tree beyond his great-grandfather, but unsuccessfully. The man who founded the winery back in 1859 was not from Barbaresco.

"It seems he just appeared from out of nowhere," says Angelo. "Probably from the Roero."

The Roero district is just across the Tanaro, a few miles away. But in those days, in the mind of the peasant, the river was a border. The Roero was in "Piedmont," more distant even than Dogliani.

Eyes have to readjust to seeing Angelo in fast motion again. He's already back at his house. Down the slope off to the right, sharing the south with the Cabernet, are two acres of Nebbiolo. The Bricco is bigger than you'd think. There's world enough and time here even for the natives. It all makes you wonder. How many Wampanoag Amerindians live on Beacon Hill in Boston?

August 10, 1989

ℋE'S DONE IT AGAIN," Federico says.

The saint has delivered the goods. As usual on his feast day, the grapes on his vines are changing color. It's their first flush of ripeness: the *invaiatura,* what the French call the *véraison.*

Who knows if tonight falling stars, those "tears of Saint Lawrence" traditionally associated with this day, will provide a heavenly sight to match this earthly one: liquid light in the sky above, blushing bunches below.

All is quiet on the front southwest of the village, but Federico is here all the same, paying his respects to a special saint on this, his special day.

"Last year at this time," he says, "only a grape here and there had started to turn. Now the *invaiatura* is almost over. The whole process usually takes about ten days at San Lorenzo, so ripening is more than a week ahead of last year."

Had it not been repudiated, his metaphorical airplane would be starting its descent. The vine shifts its metabolic gears from the promotion of growth to that of ripening. The most evident sign is the change of color that occurs in the grapes, as it does in many

[113]

fruits and vegetables. (All Capsicum peppers, for instance, change color. The green ones have simply been picked before they are ripe because they are easier to transport and store.)

The color changes because the membrane surrounding the chloroplast weakens and enzymes destroy the green, which is so intense that it masks other pigments already present. Acid decreases and sugar increases. Aroma begins to develop.

As the vegetative growth of the vine comes to a halt, the shoots start to lignify, to turn to wood.

"Most people don't realize that the canes also have to mature," says Federico, "if you want to have a crop the following year." One of the factors behind the excellent 1978 vintage in Barbaresco was the failure of so many shoots to mature during the poor growing season of the previous year and the small crop that was the result. The ripening of the shoots is called the *agostamento,* "Augusting," after the month in which it usually takes place. But Federico remembers shoots in another vineyard that were still green in the middle of September 1984.

Federico and his men have had relatively little to do at San Lorenzo during the past month. The vines were sprayed with copper sulfate. The shallow tillage proved to be providential. The very next day it rained a few drops, just one-fourth of an inch, and it hasn't rained since.

They were here at Masuè at the end of July, though, thinning out the Merlot crop. There had been Nebbiolo vines on that part of the slope before the Merlot was planted in 1985, but the grapes had never ripened properly because the soil is much deeper there than in the *sorì.*

Removing clusters of grapes—what the French sometimes call the "green harvest"—is a means of reducing a crop that a grower considers too large to yield the quality of grapes he wants. It was done a couple of times at San Lorenzo in the late sixties when the vines were younger and they weren't pruning quite as short as they do now.

"Since the weather was poor in those years," Angelo says, "the wines were nothing to cheer about. But we did get earlier ripening than in the plots where the crop wasn't thinned."

It is also a practice that, like short pruning, has provoked resistance on the part of workers. Angelo "can still hear Luigi Rama snickering."

Federico has had more recent experiences.

"Last year I sent a couple of men to remove clusters in another vineyard," he says. "They tied up the shoots and cleaned the ground under the vines to keep the humidity down, but they didn't cut off a single bunch." He plucks a few leaves. "I understand how they feel. They come from families that have experienced real hunger. For them, crop thinning is a waste verging on sin."

Federico thins out a crop whenever necessary, but he is puzzled by what's been happening on the great estates of Bordeaux, where it has become a routine practice.

"It sounds as if there were some kind of competition to see who can get the biggest headlines in the wine press," he says, chuckling.

In fact, you hear of unbelievable viticultural violence. You read of ruthless reduction, of countless bunches strewing the ground like bodies on a battlefield. Massacres in the Médoc and Graves, a Little Bighorn near Libourne!

"You even read reports of half the crop being removed," says Federico. "A crop like that must be pretty monstrous before the thinning!" He gestures down a row of Sorì San Lorenzo. "Can you imagine how bare this vineyard would look if we removed half the clusters? Something is wrong there. Crop thinning should be an exceptional measure, not a routine one. You shouldn't have to do that if you have weak vines and prune properly."

Federico gazes toward the slope of Fasèt, squinting in the blinding sun.

"Bordeaux must have a health problem."

His pronouncement is portentous. He mumbles something once again about clones and rising yields. About vines too healthy for their own good, or at least for the good of the grapes. It all sounds foreboding, but he says no more.

The issue of yields is one of the most delicate and controversial in all of winedom. Two things are certain. One is that if the yield is too large, the grapes will not provide the concentration one expects in a fine wine. The other is that yields are rising just about everywhere. The 1986 crop in Bordeaux, for instance, was one-third larger than the record harvest of 1982, which in turn was of a totally different order than those of the fifties, not to speak of one like 1961, which was small even by the standards of those days.

Experts do not agree on the limit. It probably depends on the vintage, the vineyard, and the variety. White wines seem to suffer less than reds from higher yields, as does Cabernet Sauvignon with respect to Pinot Noir. But though quantification may be an interesting topic of debate among producers and critics, it isn't necessary for understanding the issue. You can *taste* the yield in your glass.

The regulations for Barbaresco and Barolo allow eighty quintals of grapes per hectare—a little over three tons of grapes per acre—which means a maximum of fifty-six hectoliters of wine. Most top producers consider forty hectoliters per hectare a more suitable figure for fine wine.

"We certainly don't get that around here," Federico says.

He removes a few leaves from a vine.

"But beyond a certain point, lower yields might even have negative consequences. The vine dumps everything into fewer bunches. You have to see *what* it dumps, for example, in drought conditions."

When it is so dry and hot that the vine suffers from stress, it defends itself by absorbing larger quantities of potassium, which increases precipitation of the grape's tartaric acid in the form of tartrate crystals, cream of tartar. If excessive, this phenomenon can create problems for the wine maker.

In any case, drought and heat are topics that are hard to avoid. "Winters with little or no snow," says Federico. "Summers when it's hot like this and it doesn't rain. Let's hope it isn't a permanent greenhouse effect."

Federico's worries are being expressed by many growers around here. But their concern may be somewhat mitigated by the knowledge that there have been equally worrisome periods in the past.

Fantini sounded the opposite alarm in the middle of the nineteenth century's last decade. "From 1883 on there have been only three years—'87, '92, and '94—in which the grapes were completely ripe," he wrote. "It seems that there has been a change in the seasons: one that is unfavorable to the vine. Very demanding varieties like Nebbiolo will inevitably disappear if the weather conditions people have been complaining about for many years continue."

The seasons seemed topsy-turvy.

"For a number of years now serious and obscure atmospheric disturbances have almost changed the seasons around, so that after precocious hot spells in March and April, which stimulate the growth of the vine, we get a notable lowering of the temperature in May and sometimes even in June. In the last few years we have seen wild swings in the distribution of rainfall. Hailstorms, which once were rare and limited to a few areas, have become frequent and violent during this decade."

More than half a century after Fantini, a great wine scientist at the research institute in Asti, Garino-Canina, commented after the harvest in 1947 on "the weather of the last few years, with less and less rain and high summer and autumn temperatures." In Bordeaux, the closely spaced triad of seasons, 1945, 1947, and 1949, with its well-reputed vintages, has not been equalled since in terms of drought and high temperatures.

Federico pulls out his handkerchief and wipes his face. It's been hot practically ever since the middle of July. The second half of the month had an average temperature of close to eighty degrees, with highs way over ninety. "On July 22," he exclaims, "it even reached a hundred degrees here! And it's pushing ninety now."

That certainly doesn't faze Saint Lawrence. The patron saint of firefighters and cooks, his emblem is a gridiron because, according to tradition, the martyr met a fiery death at the hands of his persecutors. But Christian writers of the fourth century such as Prudentius and fellow saints Ambrose, Augustine, and Damasus emphasize, in addition to his fortitude, his humorous jibes at his executioners as he roasted on the gridiron. "It is done," he is reported to have said. "Turn it over and eat it." (Surely such a saint doesn't mind a little facetious fun in his vineyard now and then. He knows there's nothing low about high spirits, and would never sanction sanctimony. True veneration needs no veneer.)

"The weather was strange during the second half of July," Federico says. "Hot and muggy. When gray rot hears a weather report like that, it starts licking its chops."

He looks at his grapes. They're safe inside those intact skins. Federico stymied the *tignola;* he's not about to relax his guard.

"Now that the grapes have started to ripen, though, they are softer and more vulnerable," he says. "Wasps, for instance, are attracted to the sugar and might pierce the skins."

He caresses a leaf. "The vines are beginning to suffer," he says. The drought is so worrisome that the mayor of Barbaresco has ordered his fellow citizens to save water; all unessential uses, such as sprinkling lawns, are prohibited.

"They need a light shower now," Federico continues. "More than that would be detrimental, though." Excess rain would reactivate the vine's metabolism and bloat the grapes, making them even more vulnerable.

"Nebbiolo suffers from drought more than a less-vigorous vine like Barbera, which does well even in sandy soil. These vines are now walking that tightrope between starvation and survival that enables them to produce great grapes. If they can just keep their balance all the way to the harvest, it should be memorable."

The license of this poet apparently has no limit! Noble Nebbiolo is now an acrobat and, what's more, performing without the safety net of irrigation, which the regulations do not allow.

"You don't even have to imagine that tightrope," he says as he walks back up the slope. "There's a place where you can *see* it."

Has this visionary of the vineyard been seeing things again? Is there a place where, right before your eyes, metaphors really materialize?

Federico hops into his car. After a short drive he pulls up on a dirt road leading down another hillside and walks into a vineyard.

"Look at these vines," he says.

The vines have more clusters on them and only a few grapes here and there have changed color, but otherwise, to an untrained eye, they look very much like his own. And not even a magnifying glass would enable that eye to see: a tightrope is not a *tignola* egg!

Federico walks a few steps down the slope to another row of vines.

"Well?" he asks.

The vines have lost their balance and fallen off! The sight is something to see. Their leaves are skimpy, shriveled, and the palest

Angelo Gaja's father and grandfather, 1913

The winery's label at the end of the nineteenth century

The label first used in 1920. The Angelo Gaja on the label is the current Angelo's grandfather.

Labels first used in 1948, when the winery still
produced Barolo

Angelo Gaja receiving his diploma in enology (Alba, 1960)

Frederico Curtaz

Angelo Lembo

Aldo Vacco

Eugenio Gamba and stacks of rough-hewn staves

Camille Gauthier splitting an oak log

Giovanni Gaja

Angelo and Lucia Gaja

Guido Rivella

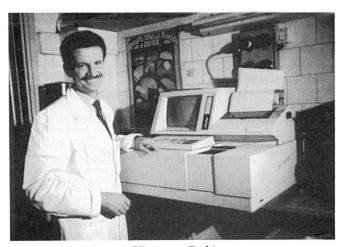

Vincenzo Gerbi

Angelo Gaja

Luigi "Gino" Cavallo

Giuseppe "Geppe" Botto

Sorì San Lorenzo (1989)

The village of Barbaresco

of greens. The shoots are stunted, as are the grapes. The vines are suffering from starvation.

"Severe hydric stress," says Federico.

The vines that he has shown are all on a ridge, the slightly convex spine that runs the length of the slope, but they belong to different owners. "The soil is very shallow on the ridge because of erosion," he explains. "Here they've left a cover crop of grass, whereas in the first vineyard they've tilled the soil. That's what makes the difference."

Beware the snake in the grass! In the spring of 1988, grass was a knight in shining armor and saved the structure of the soil. But there's no splendor in this grass, nor glory in these grapes. It's just a thirsty thief, robbing the vines of precious moisture.

Federico takes another few steps, this time across the slope. There is grass growing here, too, but the vines haven't lost their balance.

"These belong to the same grower as the wilted ones," he says. "But the soil is different. It's deeper here because the terrain is concave, so it can take a cover crop. He should manage these two sections in different ways."

Grass steals water from the vine, but it can also increase absorption.

"In a particularly dry season in the Langhe recently," Federico says, "it turned out that the vineyards with a cover crop most of the year fared better because the structure of the soil had been improved. It's all a question of timing. In the years from 1980 through 1985, when there was sufficient moisture, you could easily keep the grass right through the growing season. But in summers like last year and this one, with terribly little rain, you should cut it at the beginning of the hot season."

Grass is important for other reasons, too. It provides a reliable source of food for the natural predators of harmful insects. And without grass as a competitor, certain obnoxious weeds grow rampantly. On the whole, in a viticultural vote on grass the ayes would have it. But it all depends, and balance is all.

Federico is so sensitive to grass that he can probably hear it grow. Grass can play the roles of hero and villain with equal aplomb. It's up to the director of the vineyard drama to ensure a happy ending.

On the way back, Federico sums up the present situation.

"If San Lorenzo had a cover crop right now," he says, "the vines would be as parched as the ones that have fallen off. They would have lost their balance, too." Whether or not they make it to the end depends mostly, of course, on the vagaries of the weather. The capriciousness of nature—Govone flooded, Barbaresco dry—is anything but comforting. Especially ominous was a hailstorm that Federico doesn't talk much about: one that hit the Asti area on July 22 and destroyed all the crops on his parents' farm.

Despite the drought, the vines of San Lorenzo have a lot going for them. There's the retentive side of the soil. The hopes of the vintage are riding on that fine silt and especially on that clay. It is in drought years that within a region like the Médoc the vineyards on heavier soil, such as those of Saint-Estèphe, often produce better wines than the usually more highly esteemed ones from the lighter soil of Margaux.

Then there's the age of the vines. Their roots plunge deeper into the subsoil than those of younger ones and can supply the vine with moisture that has seeped into the limestone.

"You should see those roots!" Federico exclaims as he gets out of the car. "They slip through the minute fissures in the limestone, like sheets of paper that have been carefully inserted. When we pull out dead vines, we find roots that are at least twelve feet long."

Federico walks over to what looks like a little birdhouse. It's his "weather station." Inside is a machine that records the temperature and amount of rainfall on a graph. He removes a long sheet of paper and starts to pore over it.

"There have been regular differences of twenty-five to thirty degrees between day and night temperatures." He beams.

Cool nights mean reduced respiration: less of the sugar produced by photosynthesis is burned for the vine's growth and more is deposited in the grapes. They mean the preservation of aroma and malic acid, which can be burned off too drastically, as is typically the case with wine from hot climates. And they mean tougher skins, with more color.

Last, but certainly not least, there is Federico's steadying hand, which he waves as he takes his leave.

The vines of San Lorenzo have never been more saintly than they are on this feast day. There is no straighter or narrower path to viticultural virtue than the tightrope they're walking now. And though they may be making a virtue of necessity, they seem to be as steadfast as the saint himself. These are not vines to vacillate.

September 22, 1989, A.M.

 *T*WENTY-ONE-POINT-FIVE," says a voice among the vines.

A ray of light strikes the film of grape juice on the objective of an instrument called a refractometer. Because the juice is denser than the air through which the light has been travelling, the ray changes direction and casts a shadow. Peering through the eye-piece, Guido reads off the number indicated by the shadow line.

"Just over nineteen."

Guido wanders through the vineyard picking here and there. He squeezes a little juice onto the refractometer and holds it up to the light.

"Twenty-three," he says.

The numbers that Guido keeps calling out are part of a scale named after the man who devised it, a nineteenth-century Austrian called Babo. It's Brix ("bricks") or Balling in the United States, Baumé in France, and Öchsle in Germany, but what they all indicate is how much sugar the grape contains. The more sugar there is, the denser the juice and the greater the refraction of the light. The difference in the shadow is the sugar.

Guido picks grapes at random as he rambles through the rows.

One here: "Twenty-two and a half." Another there: "Twenty-one." As the French philosopher and mathematician Blaise Pascal wrote in the seventeenth century: "Are there ever two grapes alike in a cluster?" Guido wants to get a representative sample of his heterogeneous raw material. He's been checking here on and off since the beginning of the month.

Each grape has its place in the vineyard pecking order according to the location of its vine, the position of its cluster on the vine, its own position on the cluster. The nearer a grape is to the top of its cluster and the nearer the cluster is to the trunk of the vine, the more sugar it will contain. Afternoon readings on the refractometer are slightly higher than those taken in the morning because the vine respires water during the day, but not at night.

Guido examines a cluster where a few grapes are missing. "A bird has been here," he says. "Look at the clay its feet have left."

The weather from August 10 to almost the end of the month was just about as hot as the second half of July. Then on August 27, a windstorm struck the area. Saint Lawrence must have interceded with the hail that hit Barbaresco here and there, for it spared his vineyard.

"But vines were knocked down all over," says Guido. "It took us two days to get them all back up. Vineyards like Pajoré, which is higher up and more exposed, suffered much more than San Lorenzo."

In the first week of September there was a very light but persistent rain.

"Just a sprinkling," says Guido with a smile. "But it brought relief to the vines at a critical moment."

With the storm, the heat wave came to an end.

"The beginning of September seemed more like October. Fog down below and a chill in the air. Fall weather. We were all wearing sweaters early in the morning."

Ripening was slowed a bit. But for over two weeks now the days have been warm and sunny.

"The vines were so far ahead of schedule," Guido says, "that it's still a precocious year."

Guido gazes at a cluster. He's literally sizing it up.

"I was just thinking back to 1979, ten years ago. We made a

[123]

lovely wine, which was balanced from the start. The grapes were healthy, but the bunches were quite a bit larger because it rained more that year." He pauses. "They were normal, though. These are tiny."

Drought makes the difference. Even with the same number of buds left on the vine at pruning, the yield can vary by one-third or more, according to how much water the vine gets. Since the middle of July, just one inch of rain has fallen on Sorì San Lorenzo.

Raising the cluster with his hand, Guido shows it off—precious jewels on display.

"They're so velvety you want to stroke them. That almost silvery look is the bloom."

He plucks a grape. "Crush this in your hand," he says.

The skin is thick and so is the juice. There isn't much of it, but your hand feels sticky right away.

"See how the color is already coming out? The grapes are good."

Guido doesn't take words any more lightly than he does his job. Good means good—a strong word in his vocabulary. A noble word, not déclassé by hype. A word of genuine and generous praise.

The tightrope walker has made it.

Guido marvels at the string of good vintages they've had. "Let's knock on wood, though," he says, "and hope it doesn't mean we'll soon get another run like we had in the seventies." He pauses to taste a grape. "Those years did have the merit of convincing a lot of growers that they had planted the wrong variety in the wrong spot. There were people who had Nebbiolo in absurd places. It's in poor years that you see the limits of a site." He gestures toward the valley at the bottom of the hill. "In years like this, you could grow Nebbiolo even down there."

The look in his eye is suddenly faraway.

"Some of those harvests back in the seventies were tragic," he says. "The only choice was between bringing in unripe grapes or waiting and having them rot on you."

A harvest can break your heart. On September 21 more than a hundred years ago, in 1884, Domizio Cavazza gave a talk on that year's harvest to an audience gathered at the school of viticulture and enology in Alba, of which he was director at the time. "This year the harvest is a real disaster," he began his talk, which he called "an Iliad of grapevine maladies."

The peronospora crisis was at its height, and the disease was virulent. Many buds didn't even open because the wood hadn't ripened during the previous growing season. "Obstinate drought was followed by obstinate cold and rain," according to Cavazza. Fertilization at flowering was poor. There was severe damage from hail, oidium, and the *tignola* larva.

If Guido were to return to his old school today and give a talk on the same topic, his tone would be different indeed. The weather has been good. Federico and his crew have accomplished their defensive mission. Guido can freely choose when to harvest.

The date of a given harvest may be chosen for reasons that seem rather surprising.

The 1775 vintage at renowned Schloss Johannisberg in the Rheingau district of Germany has gone down in history because of both the extraordinary wine that is said to have been made that year and the anecdote behind it. The grapes were already ripe that fall, but the manager had to get permission to begin the harvest from the owner, the abbot of Fulda, who lived a week's ride away. The courier sent to get instructions took so long that by the time he got back with the go-ahead the grapes were all rotten. But the rot was the noble one, *Edelfäule* in German, and a wine of legendary lusciousness was made.

Almost two centuries later, across the Atlantic near the shore of the Pacific, the owner and wine maker of Mayacamas Vineyards made another famous late-harvested wine: a dry Zinfandel with 17.5 degrees of alcohol. In 1968 he had grapes that were completely ripe, but all his fermentation tanks were full. With no room in the cellar, he had to wait before he could harvest the grapes, with the sugar meter ticking away. It can be as banal as that.

Guido laughs. "I know all about that," he says. "I used to do a real juggling act around here myself."

Guido has a choice that couldn't be freer.

"Even if it rained for a few days now," he says, "the skins are in such great shape that there wouldn't be any danger of rot."

Since the weather is so unpredictable in the fall, the traditional temptation has been to play it safe and harvest before the grapes are fully ripe. "All Those Good Reasons for Harvesting Early" is the title of an amusing piece by Émile Peynaud. "The weather forecast is bad. I'd better harvest before it's too late," says a grower. "The forecast is good," he says the following year. "I'd better take advantage of it while it lasts." But the weather isn't the only excuse. "The foreign workers I hired will be here tomorrow." "Château X is starting tomorrow and I've always started the same day." The list goes on and on.

But the grower's fear of rain is anything but unwarranted, even when the weather is splendid. The 1964 vintage in France seemed headed for winedom's Hall of Fame. In August the French Minister of Agriculture announced that it was going to be a marvelous *millésime*. And indeed it was, for instance, in Pomerol and Saint-Émilion, where the most important grape is the early ripening Merlot. What happened in the Médoc, which is Cabernet Sauvignon country, could best be understood by tasting, one after the other, the wines made by two great peers from Pauillac: Latour and Mouton-Rothschild.

The weather was fine until October 8, when the heavens opened and it poured for two weeks. Latour had finished picking by then and made a splendid wine, but Mouton-Rothschild made a wretched one because it was waiting for extra ripeness and got caught.

Guido has a choice. What will it be?

"Ah!" he exclaims. "If only we knew more! There are so many factors to consider."

Mainly, though, it seems to be a matter of choosing the moment of optimum balance among a few crucial elements.

"Way back in the old days growers just looked at the grapes and tasted them. Then they started to measure the sugar. For a long time, that was the only criterion." Guido chuckles. "If sugar was all you needed, we could do this job with beets—and they're a lot easier to grow!"

Coarse, overly alcoholic wines used to be common in places where growers were paid for their grapes according to the amount of sugar they contained: the more sugar, the more money. In Italy, unbottled wine, with which the shopkeeper would fill the customer's container, used to be sold according to the alcoholic degree. No fussing over grape variety, site, or producer: alcohol was all.

Guido wanders down the slope. Pick, squeeze, stare. A grape from the top of a cluster near the trunk; one from the bottom of a cluster farther out on the cane.

"It was in the sixties that wine makers started to pay more attention to acidity," he says, "and recently more attention has been given to the ripeness of the skin and the phenol compounds it contains." He stops to wipe his hands. "But in the end, as the sugar increases, the other indices usually tag along."

The name of the Nebbiolo grape supposedly derives from the fog, the *nebbia,* which supposedly accompanies the harvest. According to a just-published book on Italian wine, "it is usually harvested at the end of October and sometimes well into November, when the Langhe hills are wreathed in thick, eerie fog." But the latest harvest at Sorì San Lorenzo since Guido has been at the winery was October 17, 1978. (It is always the first of the Gaja Nebbiolo vineyards to be harvested.)

"It's hard to generalize," he says. "I remember my father telling me that in 1949 the peasants went to the Fontanafredda winery on September 28 to be paid for their Nebbiolo grapes. This meant that they had harvested them at least ten days earlier, in the middle of September. And those really late harvests in the past can be explained to some extent by viticultural practices. The way they poured on copper sulfate, for instance, slowed down all the physiological processes of the vine."

The concept of ripeness is not a simple one. Sometimes less is more. In 1978, after damp and cold had characterized much of the growing season, a glorious fall seemed as if it would never end. Angelo and Guido decided to delay the harvest at Sorì Tildìn and wound up waiting until November 20.

"We were really just showing off more than anything else," Guido confesses. "It was a challenge to those old-timers who were always saying that grapes weren't what they used to be, that they had always harvested after All Saints' Day, and so forth. We wanted to be able to say, 'Come and see for yourselves!' And, of course, we wanted to get everything possible out of the grapes."

It was quite a feat.

"We even had to put up a sign saying that the grapes hadn't been picked yet so that people wouldn't think they were just hanging there after the harvest and thus were up for grabs."

Even though it was just a youthful peccadillo, Guido is repentant.

"The grapes were way overripe, of course. It's been called a great wine, but it's still tough and unyielding after over ten years. If ten people taste it, eight of them will make a grimace."

Guido has noticed that the earlier batches of grapes harvested at Sorì San Lorenzo produce more supple wines, with deeper color and a finer bouquet, than the later ones. The skin is firmer. They have more malic acid, which will later be converted by the malolactic fermentation to the softer lactic acid and can be a factor of suppleness.

"In the past, we lacked the knowledge and maybe even the courage to harvest earlier," he says. "If the weather's good, you feel that it's a shame not to wait just a little bit longer."

He turns around and starts back up the hill. "I've got a date with a load of grapes," he says with a grin.

BACK AT THE WINERY, a load of Barbera has just arrived. Guido goes over to confer with Federico before dashing down the steps to the cellar.

The vines of San Lorenzo had barely initiated their descent when others were already approaching the runway. Guido began sampling for the most precocious varieties just after the middle of August. The Sauvignon from a locality called Bernino touched down on September 5, and since then the control tower run by Guido has been doing its juggling act with all the requests to land.

No alarm sounds at the winery when the harvest begins, but the alert is permanent. There's excitement in the air, and a touch of tension, too. The courtyard swarms with traffic. New faces appear on the scene; new voices are heard. The harvest needs extra hands. There is constant conferring in the courtyard, and the sky is a magnet for eyes that scrutinize hopefully. Sometimes it seems there's fog, but it's only the Turkish bath moving outdoors as the harvesting equipment is scrupulously steamed.

Guido can't make decisions in a void. He has to take into account various vineyards and the availability of harvesters. But even if the air traffic were to get a bit congested, Sorì San Lorenzo would never have to circle. Its only competition for precedence could come from Sorì Tildìn and Costa Russi, and they are always harvested later.

Federico reports the latest news, fresh from his huddle with Guido, as he hops into his car. Tomorrow's the day for San Lorenzo!

"That is, if that guy lets us," he says, nodding in the direction of Angelo's office. "If he got it into his head that they'd be the better for it, he'd leave those grapes on the vine until Christmas."

Federico's car pulls out of the courtyard.

"We'll start at 7:30 in the morning," he yells. "If there's no dew."

September 22, 1989, P.M.

"ABRACADABRA!" is what you expect to hear. "*Ciao!*" is what they shout.

As Guido pulls up in front of his hilltop house just a couple of miles south of Barbaresco, three figures are standing around a blazing fire at the end of the drive, stirring two steaming caldrons.

"That's Barbera," says Guido's wife, Maria Grazia, pointing to one of them. "The other one's Dolcetto."

Maria Grazia's helpers are the Rivella's two children: Silvia, who is still in kindergarten, and Enrico, who attends elementary school. She herself works as a nurse at the hospital in Alba. With all the cleaning and cooking she does, where does she find the time to make *cognà?* These ladies of the Langhe hardly know what leisure is.

The house is surrounded by fruit trees, flowers, and a lawn. There's a vegetable garden, too. "Don't look at the garden," Guido says. "We've practically abandoned it this year." He laughs. "If only I could get Geppe over here to give me a hand!"

Guido goes into the house to get a sweater. It was hot most of the day, but now it's cooling off fast.

"That's good for the grapes," he says. "It keeps them healthy." '

With the cranes at the Gaja winery rising up above the village along with its ancient tower, Barbaresco shimmers in the last full light of the equinox. Has the southbound sun already crossed the celestial equator? Are these the last rays of summer or the first ones of fall?

Guido comes back with two bottles of wine: a Dolcetto for later, a Chardonnay for now. "It's still covered a bit by the wood," he says as he takes a sip and sits down by the table on the patio, "but it'll find its balance."

Like Angelo, he leads a double life with respect to wine. At the winery he's meticulously critical, even carping; at home he's casual and relaxed. Wine here is just one thread tightly woven into the fabric of family life.

Every year, as harvest time approaches, Guido dons his diving gear and plunges deep into the sea of stress. But now it seems he's surfaced for the moment.

He laughs.

"Sure," he says, "if all our vines were in one big vineyard and we worked with just a couple of varieties, it would be a lot easier. But when the harvest is like this and things go smoothly, it's not so bad. You can even relax after work."

He glances up at the sky.

"It's when it rains that the going gets rough. Unfortunately, you can't just give the grapes a raincheck and reschedule the game when it suits you."

Such worries now seem far away. The setting sun is celebrating this mellow moment of transition with a display of subtle fireworks. In the midst of hills glazed with golden hues, Barbaresco is burnished bronze.

"Weather like this does wonders for your spirits," he says. "After all, a whole year's work is on the line now. When you see grapes like those at San Lorenzo you feel it's all been worthwhile."

Guido's smile is teasing.

"You know, with good grapes this job is a lot more interesting. You can make two kinds of wine: a good one or a poor one. With poor grapes, there's no suspense."

The Bible of wine making has yet to be written, as Guido is fond of saying, but that's certainly gospel. As the great manager of

Château Latour, Lamothe, wrote in 1816, "When Nature fails to provide the ingredients of good wine, man cannot compensate for the deficiency. He will never achieve anything greater than mediocrity."

What will Guido achieve with Sorì San Lorenzo 1989? The transformation of grapes into wine is still a metamorphosis fraught with all kinds of mysteries, one of the great wonders of the world.

"It all depends how you look at it," says Guido. "Wine making isn't all that mysterious." He nods towards Maria Grazia, who is now busily at work in the kitchen. "The wine maker's job is a lot like the cook's. Of course, a cook can try out things every day, while we get a crack at it only once a year. And a cook doesn't have to wait years to judge the results, as we sometimes do. But in the kitchen as in the cellar, things like taste, color, and texture derive from chemical properties that you can influence to the extent that you understand them. Heat speeds up chemical reactions; cold slows them down. The cook has technology like the stove and the refrigerator; the winemaker has his."

Guido pauses. His expression is dreamy. Is he having visions of himself as a custom-tailored chef? There's already a famous restaurant called Guido in nearby Costigliole, but Michelin stars could also fall on a restaurant run by Rivella!

"Just think what you can do with the same piece of meat!" he exclaims. "You can roast it or grill it, braise it or boil it. Leave it whole or cut it up. Cook it a few minutes more or less. Add a pinch of salt or not. And you've only scratched the surface! It's the same with wine. It's all in the details."

Guido is off and running about details: from how you crush the grapes, to when and how you bottle the wine.

"Details you can taste," he says. "Take the same wine, put it in two different containers, and—presto! You have two different wines."

Details can dazzle. They can also make you dizzy. But another sip of Chardonnay and Guido is on his way to further considerations.

"In the end, of course, even the greatest chef is no better than the quality of his raw materials. He can cover up defects with a heavy sauce, just as you can mask the shortcomings of a wine with a lot of new oak or a little residual sugar, but that'll never be great cooking. Like the chef, the wine maker should exalt his ingredients, the characteristics of the grapes he gets in a given year from a given vineyard. My job is to get the best out of the grape."

Guido reaches out to a bowl of grapes on the table and plucks one off the bunch. He squeezes out most of the juice with his fingers.

"Chew on this," he says. His face lights up at a grimace. "You see? The solid parts of the grape contain most of the substances that give red wine flavor and structure, but also a lot of bitter and astringent stuff. The challenge is to get everything out that will enhance the wine and leave the rest behind."

Maria Grazia sticks her head out the kitchen door. Dinner will soon be ready.

There are many other kinds of food and drink that involve processes similar to those that take place during the creation of wine: bread, beer, many cheeses, yogurt, even sauerkraut. They are all the result of fermentation, a kind of controlled spoilage.

"What a wine maker has to do," says Guido, "is encourage certain processes and discourage others. But to get the best out of the grape, you have to risk getting the worst."

He pauses pensively and sniffs his Chardonnay.

"Young people would find it hard to believe how much wine making has changed since I was a kid," he says. "And it's not just the new varieties that some of us are working with now. Sure, great wines were made here in the past, but only when the right conditions occurred by chance. Now we understand the processes better and have the technology to control them to a certain extent. Everything used to be fate, like certain diseases that now we can prevent or cure."

Guido is saying much the same thing about the wine making of earlier times that Socrates said about cookery more than 2,000 years ago. In Plato's dialogue *Gorgias,* Socrates observes that cookery "is content to record what normally occurs." It doesn't know "the reasons which dictate its actions" and therefore "is no more than a knack acquired by routine." Guido's conception of wine making is also similar to the Socratic idea of philosophizing, based on dialogue. The philosopher-teacher is like a midwife. His job is to assist the birth of ideas that are already present in embryonic form in the mind of the interlocutor. The wine maker is the midwife at the birth of wine.

Guido talks not only with the quiet confidence that comes with experience—this is his twentieth harvest at the winery—but also with the humility that is its companion. There is passion, too, in what he says.

He has never worshipped the twin idols of nature and technology. The fantasy of total control doesn't attract him: "a food-processing mentality," he says. "It's the death of wine." Guido wouldn't harm a fly, much less commit enocide. But he has tasted too many defective wines to have any truck with fuzzy and facile notions of letting nature do the wine making all alone. In the cellar, as in the vineyard, nature is never to be ignored, but always to be nurtured.

Despite the coolness of the air, Guido has more than warmed to his subject. But a novice who has yet to take his vinous vows might be getting impatient by now. What, he might wonder, is this thing called wine, and how is it actually made?

According to one dictionary, wine is "the fermented juice of grapes," and fermentation is the "conversion of sugar to carbon dioxide and alcohol by yeasts." Making wine is simple enough—so simple, in fact, that all it took was Prohibition to turn tens of thousands of Americans into wine makers.

Before Prohibition began in 1920, an annual average of 13,500 railroad carloads of wine grapes were shipped east from California. By 1926 the number had practically quintupled. In a railroad freight depot, federal agents discovered numerous barrels with large red stickers on the head of each. The stickers read:

Warning! The contents of this barrel is unfermented grape juice. Do not add yeast and do not keep barrel in a warm place or the contents will ferment and become wine.

The sticker was a brief course in wine making. All you need to make wine is grape juice, yeast, and a warm place. It's as easy as that.

Guido laughs. "That's a pretty good first-year course," he says. The second-year course would teach you a few things of secondary importance. If the carbon dioxide escapes, you have a still wine; if it remains in the wine, this yields a sparkling one. When the juice of red grapes is fermented with the skins, the wine will be red; when the juice of white grapes is fermented, or that of red grapes without the skins, it will be white.

"That's the basics," Guido says. But as he starts to explain exactly how the grapes from Sorì San Lorenzo will be transformed into wine, he becomes hard to follow. He goes into the house and comes back with a book that's more than 1,000 pages long.

So wine making is simple, eh? Biology! Chemistry! Equations! Not to mention all the jargon. What do glycolisis and decarboxylation have to do with the fermented juice of grapes? He also uses terms that a layman has heard before, but only dimly understands. Oxidation and reduction. SO_2 and CO_2. And then, of course, pH: "the negative logarithm of the hydrogen ion concentration expressed in moles per liter." Do you have to have a Ph.D. to understand pH?

One thing is clear—fermentation is the key to the complex creation of wine. Actually, for Sorì San Lorenzo 1989, there will be two of them, each carried out by creatures so small that even a magnifying glass fails to make them visible.

"Enology is a microbiological science," Guido says. He talks of yeast and of bacteria, of genera and of species. Have you ever heard of *Schizosaccharomyces pombe?* Of *Leuconostoc mesenteroides?* Unless you went to M.I.T., you'd best forget enology!

Guido's wink is reassuring.

"That stuff makes the job sound more complicated than it is," he confides. "There isn't really all that much for me to do. I just keep an eye on things. I see to it that the yeasts do a proper job and that the bacteria behave themselves."

So Guido is just a supervisor of invisible subordinates! Even Santa Claus and his helpers seem plausible by comparison. But as shadows lengthen and dusk is about to fall, Guido is transfigured. The fabulous foreman's eyes flash and sparkle as he conjures up the world of his microscopic workers, and the spellbinding tale he tells no longer seems tall at all. They've been on the job together now for almost twenty years. Could it be that he talks to them as Angelo Lembo talks to his vines and Geppe to his vegetables?

[135]

He moralizes: there are "good" yeasts who do this and "bad" ones who do that. He sympathizes: "They did the best they could in those conditions." But there is also fear in this crepuscular confession of his. He knows what can happen when those workers get out of hand: yeast going on strike, bacteria on a binge.

Listening to him talk, it's hard to believe that in a country and a region where wine has been made immemorially, neither of Guido's native tongues has a satisfactory name for what he is. Wine making was traditionally an agricultural activity like any other and not thought to require any special skill. A peasant made wine as he planted potatoes or harvested hay. He was a peasant who performed those tasks.

Names are not all, but neither are they nothing. Officially, Guido is now an *enotecnico,* an enotechnician! A word that you will never speak trippingly on your tongue. A word that sticks in your craw. There's a movement underway in the profession to have it changed to "enologist," but does that sound so much better? Both words are Greek to Italians as well as to English-speakers. They offend both eye and ear of whoever loves words and wine. Is a writer a logotechnician? Should he be a logologist?

The most felicitous name—colloquial, comprehensive, and graced with the dignity of its doing—is found in the English language. But not in eno-English. Guido is a *wine maker,* and that's all there is to that.

But though English fills the gap with a workmanlike word, there are magical moments like this—with the coals all aglow under the cauldrons of *cognà* and the sun's last beams bewitching Barbaresco—when one wistfully wishes for something more. A name commensurate with the wonder of wine and consonant with Guido's enchanted, elfin look. In a less prosaic world, in the wonderland of wine, he would be acknowledged as the wizard he really is. Just as Charles Ludwige Dodgson lives on as Lewis Carroll and Frances Ethel Gumm is forever Judy Garland, somewhere, over the rainbow, Guido Rivella is the Wonderful Wizard of Wine.

September 23, 1989

FEDERICO NODS. It's official.

"There's no dew," he announces to the group standing in the courtyard of the winery. "We'll leave in a few minutes."

If there were dew he would wait a couple of hours.

"Actually," he says, "it's more of a psychological barrier than anything else. A few drops wouldn't make any real difference in the wine." But what harvesting hand wouldn't hesitate at the sight of dewy-eyed grapes?

Most of the faces are familiar. There are those of the year-round vineyard crew: Piero's, for example. "It's my twenty-sixth harvest here," he says.

There are others whom one has seen about the village: somebody's wife, somebody else's husband, a girl who lives down the road. But some are total strangers.

Federico's parents are here. They will soon be moving into a house overlooking the Gaja vineyard in Serralunga and working for the winery.

His mother is wearing a beret, but she has also brought a ventilated straw hat. "It's better to be prepared for everything," she says. There's an autumnal chill in the air, but summer may just be playing it cool and biding its time until later.

"Cheer up!" says Federico to a lightly clad neophyte hand as the harvesters leave the courtyard. "These shivers augur well."

The top of Sorì San Lorenzo is just a few minutes by foot from the winery. You walk down to the beginning of via Torino and turn right at number one toward the place a sign indicates as Secondine. After a hundred yards or so you'll see a gate on your left and you're there. To get to the bottom of the slope without going through the vineyard itself, you continue straight on from Luigi Cavallo's house down the road that leads to the valley between the Masuè slope and the backside of Fasèt and on to the Tanaro.

The leaves on some of the vines are just starting to show a slight change of color. "Where they're still the same green," says Federico, "the soil is somewhat deeper. They get a bit more nourishment. But in any case, the vines have reached the end of the line."

For his vintage verse, Federico has chosen a terrestrial metaphor to replace the earlier aerial one. "Okay," he says with a grin. "But don't get me wrong. This isn't a crash landing. Let's just say they're running low on fuel."

Sometimes, in special circumstances, Federico gives detailed harvesting instructions to the workers. When ripening is very uneven—which can happen, for instance, if flowering was protracted—they make more than one pass through the vineyard. At the beginning of the month they went through the Chardonnay on the Bricco, eliminating the bunches here and there where rot had appeared.

"We could have harvested the whole vineyard right then," says Federico, "but Guido thought a few more days would do it good. The rot had to be removed, though, to prevent it from spreading."

All he tells them today is to be careful when they start picking near the bottom of the slope. The soil is a little deeper there. The vines grow with a bit less sun and a bit more humidity.

"Nuances," he says. "But you can pick the upper and middle sections with your eyes closed."

With the very first clusters already being clipped, the harvest is under way. But the sound of the shears is not what was heard at pruning. The full foliage of fall softens what was sharp in the bare and wintry *son*: autumnal acoustics make for mellowness.

The harvesting here is all accomplished by hand. The only machine in sight is the tractor that will haul the grapes away.

"You'd better watch your tongue!" warns Federico. "You talk to Angelo about mechanical harvesting at the risk of your life."

There are arguments in favor of harvesting by machine, especially on flat land. In hot climates it enables you to harvest in the cool of the night. It gets the job done quicker and more economically.

But to harvest with machines you have to train the vines for their convenience. And machines are notoriously heavy-handed. The Nebbiolo grape, which clings tenaciously to its stem, would be shaken to death.

"Mechanical harvesting would be a big step backward," says Angelo almost angrily. It's a topic that makes this Taurus see red. "After all the time and effort we've spent training workers to select grapes carefully and handle them gently!"

Angelo draws the quality line and dares a harvesting machine to cross it.

"Machines don't think," he says with a snort. "How can they select grapes?

To pick also means to select.

Federico clips a bunch with slightly shrivelled grapes. "You have to distinguish between two kinds of shrivelling," he explains. One is caused by the sun and the grapes are sweet, like this one." He plucks a grape off the bunch and tastes it. "You get the other kind if the shoot has been damaged. The grapes are sour. You shouldn't pick those."

Angelo Lembo points out a couple of slightly moldy grapes on a cluster. "I remember my first harvest here," he says. "Angelo kept telling us to pick only ripe and healthy grapes. 'With rotten grapes you'll make rotten wine,' he would say." He removes the affected grapes and puts the rest of the cluster into the container. "Most growers around here don't do this," he remarks. "Some even say the rot makes the wine taste better!"

A harvester in the next row yells through the vines. "Putting

[139]

rotten grapes in with good ones is like mixing the sacred and the profane."

The containers are made of plastic.

"Sure," says Federico, "they're less picturesque than the wicker ones used in the past, but they're a lot more hygienic. It's impossible to really sterilize wicker."

The containers used for harvesting white grapes are even shallower than those here at Sorì San Lorenzo.

"White grapes are fair-skinned," says Federico. "They bruise more easily."

When grapes are piled too high, those on the bottom get crushed and that can be the beginning of the end. Guido's "bad" yeasts are there on the grapes, just waiting for the starting shot—a ruptured skin—to get to work on the juice. The birth of wine is fraught with danger without the midwife to assist, and you don't want the labor that is fermentation to begin before the grapes get to the winery.

"And that's not all," Federico adds. "There's the danger of oxidation."

The relationship between wine and oxygen is complex. Wine needs oxygen, but it can also be severely damaged by it. The hand that caresses can also slap, or even hold a dagger, and it is never more of a danger than at the beginning and at the end: at harvest time and when the wine is bottled.

The perils of parturition are increased by heat, which is why pre-harvest shivers are a comforting sign.

Federico's parents are like kids in a candy shop. "We'd heard about these grapes before," his father exclaims, "but you have to see them to believe it!" His mother grins and nods.

The workers move slowly down the slope in the section of the *sorì* called *la punta*. This part is always harvested first and will be fermented and aged separately, as will the other section, *sotto il cortile*. Guido and Angelo will decide later whether to blend the two.

Would the wine be different if the vineyard were harvested differently? The question provides food for vinous thought.

In one of his nonfiction works, the great French novelist Stendhal described a dinner that took place in Burgundy in 1837.

Practically the only topic of conversation throughout the entire evening was how the famous Clos de Vougeot should be harvested: transversally—across the vineyard—or from the top of the slope to the bottom. Served at the dinner were the vintages of 1832 and 1834, which were examples of the two systems. (Stendhal remarked wryly how the talk was far more lively and entertaining than the dreary political dogmatism that usually constituted dinner-table conversation in the provinces.)

La punta, "the tip," is a triangular section of which the hypotenuse is the former Strada Montà that led up to the village from the ferry landing on the Tanaro. It is more subject to erosion than *sotto il cortile,* "under the courtyard"; the soil is slightly shallower and there is a bit less clay, so that it drains a little more and retains a little less. In 1987, a year with substantial rainfall, *la punta* produced a more concentrated wine, and Sorì San Lorenzo '87 was made entirely with grapes from that section.

"But in a year like this," says Federico, *"sotto il cortile* may even come out better."

The Italian language has a saying about the difficulty of translating from one language to another. *Traduttore, traditore:* "translator, traitor." A translator is bound to betray the original. The vine, however, as Colette observed, is a most faithful translator, catching all the nuances of the soil and transferring them to the grapes. As vine after vine is picked, you can see the slight variations in cluster and grape size even within a vineyard with relatively homogeneous soil.

In the first vineyard that the Gaja winery harvested this year, a plot of Sauvignon at Bernino, there's a spot where the soil is considerably deeper because of the earth that got piled up there when the site was being prepared for planting. The vines in that spot are more vigorous than the surrounding ones; the grapes ripen more slowly. When the vineyard was harvested on September 5, the grapes from those vines were still greenish in appearance and had the characteristic grassy taste of Sauvignon. The grapes from the other vines in the vineyard were yellow and had a more complex flavor. There are famous vineyards, such as Clos de Vougeot itself, where the growing conditions are so heterogeneous that only a portion of the whole merits the prestigious status. But even vineyards much smaller than the 125 acres of the Clos are only more or less homogeneous.

"Ah!" exclaims Federico, with a mixture of awe and exasperation. "If he could, Angelo would pick and vinify each row separately!"

He pauses as he removes a couple of leaves that have fallen into the container along with the grapes.

"But differences among grapes stem from the vines themselves as well as the soil."

He takes a few steps down the row.

"Look at these two vines. On this one there's a cluster with a touch of rot." He cuts off the affected grapes. "The soil is the same, as is the management. But this vine has slightly tighter clusters than the one right next to it here. Air doesn't circulate as well among the grapes, so if, say, a wasp perforates a skin, rot might develop from the atmospheric humidity alone. These two vines belong to different clones."

Federico is caught; now he has to explain! Why all the fuss about clones?

"Clone" may sound ominous, but it's just a slip of a word. It comes from the Greek for "twig," a cutting used for planting or grafting. The denotation is clear and innocent enough: "a group of genetically identical organisms descended asexually from a single common ancestor." It's the connotations that can be creepy.

Like gardeners everywhere, vine growers have long observed that a given plant may be more or less vigorous than others, more or less resistant to this or that disease. In the past, when they planted a vineyard, growers selected cuttings from those plants they considered best, a procedure known as massal selection.

Clonal selection differs in many ways from this traditional method, as you can see in the University of Turin's experimental vineyard at La Morra, in the Barolo district. Planted there are representatives of more than forty different clones of Nebbiolo. The vines come from varied sites as far away as the Valtellina, near the Swiss border in the region of Lombardy.

The differences stare even a layman in the face. The clusters differ in size and compactness. There is more or less foliage. The internodes vary. (It's important to have shorter ones if you want to plant more densely, because the vine simply takes up less space.)

Each clone is planted on two different rootstocks. Every year certain data are recorded: the date of budding, flowering, and the *invaiatura;* the percentage of fertilization at flowering; the diameter of the trunk—in other words, its vigor; its resistance to rot; and so forth. A separate wine is made from each clone and the results are compared. At the end of the selection process certain clones are made available to growers.

The differences between clones of the same variety can be enormous. One can be up to three times as productive as another; the difference in the average sugar content of the grapes on vines growing right next to each other can be as much as two degrees in terms of alcohol; components such as tannin and coloring matter can vary by a factor of two. Sometimes a clone selected solely on the basis of one characteristic can cause problems, as happened in Bordeaux. After rot had turned the 1968 vintage into a disaster, between 1970 and 1975 authorities allowed growers in the region to plant only a single, rot-resistant clone of Cabernet Sauvignon, which proved to be nearly impossible to ripen.

Clonal selection began in Germany in the late nineteenth century, in France in the 1920s, and in Italy in the 1960s. The original goal of the process was to make healthy vines available to growers. Most vines in France before the Second World War, for instance, suffered so severely from viral disease that their productivity had drastically declined. The only fly in the enological ointment is that the rigorous elimination during the selection process of any vine with a hint of disease and the use of heat therapy to kill viruses have led to an increasing predominance of vigorous, highly productive vines in the vineyards of the world.

"You need vines that suit your goals," says Federico. "If your goal is to produce great wine, planting those clones is like buying a Ferrari to drive on the narrow, winding and crowded streets of a medieval town."

The warmth of the sun is just starting to make itself felt and a gentle breeze is blowing. A worker makes his way up the slope to retrieve something he forgot.

"When's Gaja going to install a sky lift here?" he shouts, feigning near-fatal fatigue.

The mood is merry; laughter ripples through the rows.

The first load of grapes is ready to go. The tractor starts to move slowly down the alley.

"There they go!" a worker says. "San Lorenzo '89 is packing its bags and moving to the cellar."

Federico grins and flashes the V sign. He must feel as a dedicated teacher does when a favorite student graduates. They'll meet again some day, but the relationship will never be the same.

The tractor pauses at the bottom of the slope before starting off down the road. "We'll be at the winery in less than ten minutes," the young driver says.

Not so many years ago, on hot afternoons, a cartload of grapes from an outlying vineyard being drawn slowly toward the winery by an ox was like a defenseless stagecoach in the Wild West. All sorts of enological outlaws—"bad" yeast, oxygen, bacteria—were lying in wait to pounce on those grapes of gold.

The road is already curving and climbing up the hill. The grapes are still cool from the low temperature last night.

The tractor passes below the Bricco and the Darmagi vineyard. It moves on to via Torino, through the "square" and past the town hall. At number thirty-six it turns off and honks in front of the huge red door.

Folding and rumbling as it goes, the door rolls slowly back. The tractor moves forward.

In the final moment before the process begins, the mind imagines the magical metamorphosis of the grapes into a glass of Sorì San Lorenzo 1989. But it will be at least three years and many transformations later before bottles start to appear in wine shops around the world.

The only other product of Barbaresco soil comparable in price and renown is the white truffle, produced free by nature, which you can dig up, wipe off, and eat.

September 23–October 4, 1989

NO SOONER has the vineyard crew handed over the grapes to him than Guido does what Federico strove mightily for almost four months to prevent: he breaks their skins! A machine on the first level of the cellar does the job.

What is the meaning of this maiming?

Guido has a workaday explanation. He's just opening the door for his workers so they can get into the grapes and on with the job of making wine. But there's also a more romantic way of putting it. Like boy and girl, yeast and sugar—the sweet heart of fermentation—have to meet before nature can take its course. In any case, the grapes are crushed.

Guido winces. His grimace calls for a gloss. He's as sensitive to the nuances of wine making words as he is to those of wine itself. Crushing suggests violence, and nonviolence is an essential part of the wine maker's creed: "one of his very first commandments."

"It's like squeezing an orange," Guido says. "If you press too hard you get bitter substances from the peel in your juice."

For want of a better term, the machine that's humming away in the cellar is called a stemmer-crusher. It consists of a perforated horizontal drum with a shaft running through it to which a series of paddles is attached. The shaft and drum rotate in opposite directions at speeds that can be regulated, and the paddles rub the clusters against the drum. The grapes pass through the holes and into a tube that conveys them to the fermentation tank on the floor below; the stems are ejected. In the mind of the manufacturer, the drum is the stemmer, and underneath is the crusher part of the machine: adjustable rollers that squeeze the grapes as they pass through.

The traditional crusher was the bare human foot. You just got into the vat with the grapes—vats used to be much smaller—and trod them. It may have been inefficient, but it was a long time before machines developed a touch that was anywhere near as light.

Writing about his trip through Europe in 1861, Agoston Haraszthy, founder of California's oldest premium winery, Buena Vista, recounted that he had met a German grower who made excellent wine. The man had all the latest technology, but no longer used his expensive new crusher. The rollers crushed not only the grapes, but the stems as well, making the wine bitter, so he had gone back to the traditional method. Twenty years later, Ottavi confirmed that, although they had made progress, manufacturers were "still not able to construct crushers that can perform the task as well as the bare human foot."

Guido nods. "Unfortunately," he says, "manufacturers have not always been sensitive to the distinction between real progress and mere efficiency."

He still remembers the model that the winery purchased in the thirties: "the first one in Barbaresco," according to Giovanni Gaja. It crushed first and then destemmed.

"It did the job with rollers," Guido says with a shudder. "It was a real grinder." He gestures like Jack the Ripper as he describes the gory details. "Stems would get caught between the rollers. Everything got squashed, sometimes even the seeds."

Six machines later, he feels that manufacturers are finally getting there. "They're waking up to the fact that this is a very delicate operation, one which has a significant impact on the quality of the wine." Refinements have been introduced, such as the use of less abrasive materials like Teflon.

[146]

Guido regulates the drums to rotate as slowly as possible. "That way," he says, "the effect is something like the one you got when stemming was done by hand and the clusters were rubbed over a grid."

No matter what the problem is in wine making, there's no grape like Nebbiolo when it comes to exacerbating it. Nebbiolo needs special handling, so Guido welcomes it to the cellar with his kid gloves already on.

"Some French wine people came to visit us last year," he says. "They couldn't get over how difficult Nebbiolo is right from this very first phase." A knowing look spreads across his face. "Of course, they were used to working with Cabernet Sauvignon."

Of all the graduating grapes each year, Cabernet Sauvignon is everyone's choice for "most likely to succeed." It knows how to win friends and influence people in all walks of wine life. For Guido in the cellar, as for Federico in the vineyard, whenever Cabernet comes up the adjective is always "easy."

Nebbiolo has a thinner skin than Cabernet, but is harder to detach from its pedicel, the small stalk connecting it to the peduncle, which attaches the cluster to the shoot. A thin skin and a high index of detachment are a problematic combination for the stemmer. The drum has to rotate faster for Nebbiolo than for thick-skinned Cabernet, which could take the extra battering more easily.

"In fact," says Guido, "we never turn on the rollers of the crusher underneath. Most of the grapes get split in the stemmer and it's actually a good thing if whole ones get through. That makes for a more supple wine."

Unlike crushing, stemming is not mentioned in the oldest texts on wine making. Crushing is an obvious necessity, but nothing obliges you to stem.

Stems contain about one-fourth of all the tannin on a given cluster, but no sugar. While they increase the amount of tannin in wine, they actually lower the acidity. They also add herbaceous, "stalky" flavors and have a negative influence on color because pigment sticks to them.

In the past, there were very practical reasons to stem. Stems could be quite painful to the bare foot. Although they account for only about 5 percent of the weight of a vat of grapes, they constitute close to one-third of the volume. Stemmed grapes took up less space, not a small consideration for peasant growers. But there were also good reasons not to stem. Stems keep the crushed grapes from becoming too compact during the fermentation, for example, making them easier to handle and allowing air to circulate.

It was only fairly recently that stemming became a standard practice in Barbaresco. Ottavi stated that "they do not destem in the Langhe," while Garino-Canina noted in his important study of Barbaresco, published after the First World War, that producers fermented with from one-half to two-thirds of the stems.

Today, taste is the main consideration for the best producers. Peynaud is categorical. "If it's not good to eat, it won't be good to drink," is his maxim. Anyone who has chewed on stems understands why he insists on their exclusion, but undoubtedly much depends on the variety. It's hard to see how stems could enhance Cabernet Sauvignon, not to speak of Nebbiolo. Tannin is to Barbaresco what coals are to Newcastle. But stems have their advocates among producers working with less tannic varieties such as Pinot Noir, Zinfandel, and even Merlot. In his book on Bordeaux, Robert Parker reports that a great château like Pétrus, with its almost 100 percent Merlot wine, uses up to 30 percent of the stems. And when making Dolcetto, a grape that yields a supple wine, Guido has experimented with adding them. But when "To stem or not to stem?" refers to Nebbiolo, he's anything but a Hamlet. After all, what he really needs to stem is that tide of tannin!

GUIDO FILLS A PITCHER with juice as it comes out of the stemmer-crusher and takes it upstairs to his lab.

"I need a little must," he says, calling the aspirant wine by its technical name.

He pours the pale-pink liquid into two tall beakers. He wants to know more about its composition. But as he goes about his task, his mercurial metamorphoses never cease to amaze. It's a string of surprises. With all his varied guises, one hardly recognizes Guido anymore.

He starts out as a reassuring doctor. After all, it's just a prenatal checkup. Turn your back for a second and a meticulous accountant is ascertaining the liquid's assets: "Let's see how much sugar it's got." Then, all of a sudden, a tough police detective starts to grill the pallid rosé. Could this be a throwback to the poor vintages of the seventies, when many a must was suspect?

Guido picks up an instrument that looks like a long thermometer with a weighted bulb at one end and sticks it into the must, where it floats upright. As he observes the scale on the stem, his face lights up. You expect him to shout "Eureka!" That's what Archimedes is reported to have done as he raced home naked from a public bath in Syracuse after discovering the principle that enables Guido to find what he's looking for.

King Hieron II, Archimedes' friend, had ordered a crown of gold for himself, but suspected that the artist had cheated him by mixing alloys with the precious metal. Lying in his bath, Archimedes got the idea that a body immersed in a fluid is buoyed up by a force equal to that of the liquid it displaces. He had only to take a quantity of pure gold equal in weight to that of the crown and then see if the amount of water it displaced was equal to the amount displaced by the crown. If it wasn't the crown was not pure gold, as indeed it turned out to be the case.

Guido's instrument is called a hydrometer, and he is measuring the density of the must, which is indicated by the number at the intersection of the graduated stem with the surface of the liquid. The higher the hydrometer floats, the denser the must.

"It's 1.104," says Guido. Water has a density of 1.000. The difference between the two figures being mostly attributable to the sugar, he now has a good idea of how much the must contains.

Diabetics are probably the only people as concerned as wine makers are about sugar levels. The amount of sugar in the must gives Guido a good indication of how much alcohol the finished wine will contain and how hard the yeasts will have to work in order to accomplish their task. It will also enable him to check if the fermentation is proceeding regularly. As the sugar is converted into alcohol, which is less dense than water, the density of the must should decrease steadily.

The hydrometer reading is more accurate than sampling in the vineyard with a refractometer, but is less reliable than the reading

Guido will soon have with must taken from the tank after all the grapes have been crushed. An even more accurate figure will be the one in grams of sugar per liter obtained by chemical analysis.

If you don't have a hydrometer handy the next time you make wine, you might try the method suggested by the famous eighteenth-century French encyclopedia edited by Diderot. "A must is considered sufficiently rich in sugar to make a very strong wine," you read there, "when a fresh egg floats on its surface." (If an egg is very old, it will float even in water.)

Guido puts down the hydrometer and sticks the electrodes of a small, boxlike machine into the other beaker. He turns it on and reads a number off the scale.

"It's 2.99," he says.

That's the pH of the must. The term means "hydrogen power" and was coined in 1909 by the Danish chemist S. P. L. Sørenson. The pH scale of 0 to 14 indicates the acid or alkaline strength of a medium. Pure water is neutral and therefore has a pH of 7. A figure below the midpoint on the scale means that the medium is acid, and the lower the pH is, the more so. Upwards of 7, the higher the pH, the more alkaline the medium is. Most foods are at least slightly acid—egg whites and baking soda being rare exceptions—and, at around 2 on the pH scale, lemon juice is very much so; soaps and detergents are alkaline, with household ammonia close to 12. Wine is almost always between 3 and 4. The pH of must or wine is not the same as its total acidity. The later refers to the *amount* of acid, but acids vary in strength: tartaric is stronger than malic, which in turn is stronger than lactic.

Wine makers check the pH of their must and wine as carefully as people on a strict diet check their weight. Many important processes in wine making are influenced by pH, which thus acts indirectly as well as directly on the sensations you get when tasting. What appears to the layman to be a small difference in pH can make a big difference in a wine.

Must usually contains everything that microbial metabolisms need: glucose, fructose, nitrogen in various forms, the vitamin-B complex. It's a savory feast at which all sorts of unsavory characters would love to gorge—a feast not only for yeast, but also for bacteria.

"The pH is like security at a reception for VIPs," says Guido. "It shouldn't be lax, because you don't want anyone to crash the affair. But it shouldn't be so zealous that it harasses the guests. If I had a must with pH lower than 2.90, or higher than 3.30, I'd be worried."

Yeasts are much more fit than most bacteria to survive in the world of must and wine. Bacteria prefer neutral or even slightly alkaline environments, and none of the ones that are pathogenic for human beings can tolerate a pH anywhere nearly as low as that of must. A few species can multiply at a much lower pH, however, and spoil wine.

The pH is also crucial for color. The pigments in young red wine are extremely sensitive to it. You can observe this phenomenon by taking any red fruit or vegetable that contains the same kind of pigment—red cabbage, for example, or the peel of a red apple, but not a beet—and adding a small amount of baking powder. With its alkaline pH, it will turn gray overnight.

"It's always tricky with pH," Guido says.

One reason is the heterogeneity of the grape itself. The area immediately surrounding the seeds contains more acidity and sugar than the one just below the skin. If the grapes have been only lightly crushed—in a proper nonviolent way—and the must is taken as it comes out of the crusher, there will be little juice from the center of the grapes.

"If you take the pH right away," he continues, "you get one figure. An hour later it's already another."

Part of the problem is the phenomenon of salification, whereby tartaric acid precipitates out of the wine in the form of cream of tartar.

"Look here," he says. "You can see the crystals on the pH meter and the hydrometer. The phenomenon is unpredictable, but there's no doubt it's been increasing lately."

Guido is worried about the link between high tartaric acid levels and the heavy use of potassium fertilizer that experts were recommending a while back.

"It's okay when you get normal rainfall, but in drought conditions those fertilizers can be a real time bomb."

The must Guido is analyzing now has the rare combination of

high sugar content and low pH that is typical of Barbaresco. The birth of Sorì San Lorenzo 1989 will be a natural one. Elsewhere in the world, wine makers often adjust the must. In Burgundy and Bordeaux, for instance, it is common practice to boost the sugar content to increase the alcohol in the finished wine, a procedure known as chaptalization, after Jean Antoine Chaptal, a French chemist and minister under Napoleon. Musts are frequently acidified in hot climates and chemically de-acidified in cold ones.

"The figures are pretty much like last year," says Guido. "A bit less sugar and slightly higher total acidity." That's just what he wanted. Still, he tries to find a few nits to pick.

"There was the drought. The heat. The storm at the beginning of the month," he says. "You never know."

But his smile stretches from wall to wall of his lab. If this must isn't the most, it comes pretty close.

"IT MAKES ME FEEL like a criminal," Guido says as he glances around with mock furtiveness.

He's adjusting the dispenser that adds sulfur dioxide—SO_2— to the grapes as they come out of the crusher and alluding to the "contains sulfites" warning that appears on every bottle of wine sold in the United States. The modest amount of sulfur dioxide used by competent winemakers nowadays is harmful only to the few people actually allergic to it.

"At least I have partners in this crime," he whispers with a wink. "The yeasts!"

Yeasts produce SO_2 in the normal course of fermentation—a fact known since 1894 but practically forgotten until the beginning of the 1960s. At that time a German producer declared a wine of his to be without SO_2, but a government laboratory discovered that it contained a significant amount. When taken to court, the producer maintained his innocence and was finally acquitted when a leading enologist testified that the sulfur dioxide could have been the work of yeasts. Even as a totally "natural" product, wine "contains sulfites" and their elimination is a wine making will-o'-the-wisp.

Along with pH, SO_2 constitutes the nucleus of Guido's security team. The use of sulfur to protect wine from bacterial spoilage and oxidation goes back at least as far as the late fifteenth century. René Pijassou, the great historian of the wines of Bordeaux, once confessed that, when going over the account books kept by certain estates in the eighteenth century, he had long been puzzled by the item "matches," which were bought every year in large quantities. He finally discovered that the reference was to the so-called "Dutch matches"—wicks dipped in sulfur—that were burned in barrels to make them aseptic before wine was stored in them.

It was only at the end of the nineteenth and the beginning of the twentieth century that the technique of adding sulfur to crushed grapes before the start of fermentation was introduced into wine making. This innovation, one of the most important in the history of wine, was due to the Swiss scientist Hermann Müller-Thurgau. (As people who generally look at the positive side of things, wine lovers may prefer to remember him for his fundamental contributions to enology rather than for the dull grape—a cross between the Riesling and Silvaner varieties—that bears his name.) By 1919 Garino-Canina, the eminent researcher at the institute in Asti, was writing that "sulfur dioxide is for wine making what copper sulfate is for viticulture."

In addition to protecting wine against oxygen and bacteria, SO_2 acts as a solvent on the pigments contained in the skins of the grapes. Extracting color is one of the problematic aspects of making wine with Nebbiolo. Cabernet Sauvignon, of course, is . . .

"Easy!" exclaims Guido. "In fact, I've made Cabernet without SO_2, because I don't have problems with the color. The only time SO_2 is absolutely essential is at bottling. But you don't want to throw out the quality baby with the sulfur-dioxide bath! I prefer wines made with minimal amounts. They're cleaner, with fewer off odors and flavors. When I was growing up, we didn't use any SO_2 in our cellar at Montestefano. Sometimes the wine turned out okay, and sometimes it didn't. It was just a matter of chance."

Part of Guido's job as the foreman of fermentation is to make sure that only the "good" yeasts are assigned to the task. The problem is that they are vastly outnumbered at the moment of crushing by the "bad" ones. Some of the latter are real troublemakers, though most are merely messy.

[153]

"They dirty while they ferment," he says. "They produce a lot of stuff that you don't want in your wine, especially VA."

VA stands for "volatile acidity." A volatile acid is one that evaporates readily at normal temperatures: one you can smell, as opposed to fixed acids like tartaric and malic, which you can't. The volatile acid of wine is acetic acid—the acid of vinegar—and its formation is frequently accompanied by that of ethyl acetate, familiar as the smell of nail-polish remover and model-airplane glue.

"Sulfur dioxide inhibits the bad yeasts," Guido explains, "and gives the good ones time to increase their numbers until there are enough of them to do the job. It takes a while, which is why fermentation doesn't get started right away. The good yeasts don't exactly like SO_2 either, but they aren't too put off by a moderate amount."

He's adding 3 grams per quintal (about 220 pounds) of grapes right after they come out of the stemmer. "If I add it in the tank, there may already be so many bad yeasts around that I'd have a hard time controlling them."

Guido is not only a staunch defender of SO_2, but also a severe critic of its abuse.

"There are people who always dump in the same amount—far too much—because that's what they were told to do by salesmen who just want to sell as much of the stuff as possible. It becomes a habit, like salting your food before you've even tasted it. Now that we know how SO_2 works, permitted levels are still too high." Excessive SO_2 causes a prickle in your nose when you sniff.

The amount Guido uses depends on a number of factors. A crucial one is pH: the lower it is, the less SO_2 you need to add.

"Security, yes!" he exclaims. "Overkill, no!" A given amount of SO_2 at pH 3.5 merely slows down the fermentation a bit, while at 2.8 it will prevent it from taking place at all.

SO_2 is able to do its security job only if it does not combine with elements of the wine itself. Free SO_2 blocks oxygen, which otherwise would oxidize the wine; combined SO_2 is like a security guard whose hands and feet are tied. A fraction of the free SO_2 also has an antiseptic effect, and the lower the wine's pH, the larger that fraction is.

There seems to be no end to the secrets of SO_2.

"When you have grapes like these," Guido says, "it's practically optional. But in years when rot is rampant, like 1972 and 1973, it's impossible to make wine without SO_2. You have to use it to block the oxidase enzymes, like you use penicillin to stop an infection."

Oxidase enzymes?

Guido's grin is a signal not to worry. He's not going to lapse into enologese. But a wine lover has to know something about enzymes!

Enzymes are proteins that catalyze practically all the numerous and complex biochemical reactions in plants and animals. They speed up the reactions, which otherwise would take place so slowly that they could hardly be measured, by as much as a billion times without changing their nature or being changed themselves. Enzymes are the ultimate specialists—each works on only one kind of reaction in one substance. Every living cell contains numerous different kinds of them.

You can't even digest food unless it's broken down by enzymes. Take the common case of lactose intolerance, for example. Lactose, or milk sugar, has to be broken down by the lactase enzyme into the simpler sugars glucose and galactose before it can be absorbed and used by the body. Otherwise, it passes through the small intestine into the colon, where it may be fermented by bacteria, producing gas. The level of lactase enzymes reaches its peak in the human intestine shortly after birth and declines sharply thereafter. In fact, they are absent in the vast majority of adults in the world, though most Westerners are exceptions.

As for the oxidase enzymes that cause Guido to send an SOS to SO_2 when there's rot around, you can get some idea of their effect on vulnerable grapes by observing how some fruits turn brown when you peel them and by comparing the smell of a freshly cut apple with one that has been exposed to oxygen for a couple of hours.

Guido has finished "Operation SO_2," but he hasn't forgotten that warning label.

"You'll find more sulfites on the salads in supermarkets and fast-food restaurants," he says. "And the irony is that the amount of sulfur dioxide used in wine making has never been as low as it is now. When I started to work, it was common to use three times as much."

GUIDO'S AT THE GRAPES AGAIN, but you'll never guess what he's doing now. He's adding food for the yeast!

"It's just a dietary supplement," he specifies. "If they aren't properly fed, they'll do a poor job and might even stop working altogether."

Yeasts have precise nutritional requirements that are usually satisfied by what they find in the must. But nutrients can be depleted as fermentation proceeds, and the dutiful dietician is taking no chances. Yeast cells need easily assimilable nitrogenous matter in order to reproduce, so on the menu today is ammonium phosphate. The portions being served are so minute that only they will notice it's there: eight grams per quintal of grapes.

"I could also add cultured yeasts to get things going quicker," says Guido, "but I want to give our native ones a chance to do the job."

Didn't yeasts use to be just good or bad? Guido doesn't even pause to explain the new distinction.

"Sure," he says, "I could play it safe. If you bungle the fermentation you can't recoup anything. . . ."

As Guido goes on, the grapes continue to flow from the stemmer into the stainless steel confines of tank number twenty-six on the floor below. Suddenly the novice realizes that they have all disappeared.

So much for his initiation into the mysteries of must becoming wine! But why should these grapes suddenly be forbidden fruit for the eyes of a neophyte? Could what is called fermentation be an occult occasion? Perhaps it's the grapes' rite of passage as they pass from vine to wine. There's the rite of spring, after all, so this could be the rite of fall!

Guido insists there's nothing to hide. "Just climb up to the top of the tank," he says, "and see what's going on."

Yet the view from above sheds little light on the dark doings below. The grapes are there all right, but there's no sign of wine.

"DON'T WORRY," says Guido as he fills a bucket with must from a tank where fermentation is already under way. He takes it back to his lab and pours it—skins, seeds, and all—into a large glass cylinder.

"This will be a visible version of what will soon be happening down there in tank twenty-six."

Guido has provided a front-row seat at what he calls "the greatest show on earth."

What the spectator sees is mostly the CO_2—carbon dioxide, or carbonic acid gas—that carbonates your Coke and sparkles your champagne. Small bubbles rise from the bottom, gathering speed as they go. They latch onto particles of solid matter and propel them toward the surface.

"There are about thirty different chemical reactions involved in fermentation," Guido explains. "You get alcohol only at the end, but CO_2 is produced by the next-to-last reaction, when pyruvic acid is broken down by the carboxylase enzyme into CO_2 and acetaldehyde."

Soon a thick layer of pomace—the solid parts of the grape—is floating on top of the must.

"That's what we call the cap," he says.

The pressure of the gas is so great that the pomace is compressed and about a third of it is pushed up out of the liquid. Seeds and other solid matter have fallen to the bottom of the cylinder. Between these two layers is the turbid must. Most of the turbulence is near the cap.

The amount of CO_2 produced during fermentation is prodigious. When champagne is made, the bubbles come from a second fermentation induced in the bottle by adding a small amount of sugar and yeast to previously fermented still wine. The CO_2 produced, which remains in the bottle, creates so much pressure that if you let the cork pop out, it can reach speeds of up to sixty miles per hour. The second fermentation produces barely more than one degree of alcohol and a bottle of champagne contains only three-fourths of a liter. The amount of carbon dioxide produced in a large tank of fermenting must that will result in a wine like Sorì San Lorenzo 1989, with close to fourteen degrees of alcohol, boggles the mind.

As the fermentation proceeds, the pace becomes frenetic. You see why older Italian treatises on wine making often use the word *bollire,* "to boil." And, indeed, "fermentation" derives from *fervere,* Latin for "to boil." Etymology enlightens: the must is effervescent because the fermenters are so fervent!

It's all due to the yeasts. They are the stars of the fermentation show. But you only see the action; the performers are lying low!

ALDO VACCA parks in front of the Department of Microbiology and Food Sciences of the University of Turin. The CN license plates on his car stand out in the sea of TOs.

"Here in Turin," Aldo chuckles, "they say that CN stands for *capiscono niente.* People from the province of Cuneo used to be considered real country bumpkins." *Capiscono niente:* "They don't understand nothin'."

Aldo knows his way around Turin. He graduated from the university with a degree in agricultural science before going off to study for a term at the University of California at Davis. Now he has brought Guido's pH meter to be calibrated by their microbiologist friend, Vincenzo Gerbi.

Crammed into close quarters, Gerbi's laboratory is located in a dingy basement. Impish Aldo is implacable.

"At Davis," he whispers, "not even a janitor would work in a place like this."

But the lab is humming with activity amidst books, periodicals, test tubes, and chromatography equipment, which breaks wine down into its aroma and flavor components and indicates their levels on a graph. There are even a small wine press and demijohns for experimental vinification.

Gerbi is in his late thirties. In his white lab coat, with his neatly trimmed moustache and his measured, precise gestures, he is the very image of the scientist—an image that has yet to find its rightful place in our collective imagery of wine. From Pasteur to the present, the great advances in our understanding of wine have all come from science.

"It's funny," Gerbi says. "Many people still associate science and technology with things like additives and all kinds of unnatural goings-on, when they actually enable us to make purer wines than ever before."

The talk turns to fermentation. Gerbi explains the major discoveries since Pasteur's time. Enthusiasm and detachment interweave in his words. As he talks about yeast, he notices that eager eyes have been ogling the electron microscope on the table next to him.

"Just a minute," he says. He calls over an assistant and asks her to prepare a slide with a drop of must taken from one of the demijohns. When the slide is ready, he puts it under the microscope.

"You have to adjust it here," he explains.

At long last, magnified 740 times, there it is: the erstwhile phantom of fermentation, a single yeast cell.

This sight was first beheld, though rather more dimly, more than three centuries ago in Delft, Holland, by an amateur lens grinder, Anton van Leeuwenhoek. Observing a drop of fermenting malt through a simple homemade lens in 1680, he described what he saw as "very little animalcules." They were to a mite "as a honeybee is to a horse" and their circumference was "not as great as the thickness of a mite's hair."

At the end of his novel *The Great Gatsby,* F. Scott Fitzgerald evokes the pristine Long Island "that flowered once for Dutch sailors' eyes" and speculates that "for a transitory enchanted moment man must have held his breath . . . face to face for the last time in history with something commensurate to his capacity for wonder." But the world that those sailors' fellow countrymen discovered later in the same century—the world of microorganisms—is surely no less breathtaking and wonderful. For winedom's faithful, the vision of a yeast cell reproducing in must is a revelation. Those who have had it can truly bear witness to the miracle that is the birth of wine.

The role of yeast in fermentation was not definitively demonstrated until Pasteur and the birth of microbiology nearly two centuries later. And at the very end of the nineteenth century, a German chemist, Eduard Buchner, took our understanding of the phenomenon one step further when he discovered that fermentation is actually carried out by enzymes secreted by yeast.

You can enter the microworld of yeast only through a powerful microscope. Once you're there, get out your rulers and measuring tapes. Measure an inch. Now divide that into 25,640 equal parts. Each one is a millionth of a meter: a micrometer or micron, the unit of measurement in the land of the infinitely small.

"This cell is about five microns by four," says Gerbi. Reproducing by a process called budding, or fission, it seems to be blowing a bubble. A small swelling at the edge of the cell gradually grows larger. When it is the same size as the genitor, it will split off by constricting at its base and begin budding itself. The parent cell, which retains a scar from each fission, produces only a few dozen buds and then dies.

"In optimal conditions," Gerbi continues, "the generation of a new cell takes about two hours." Starting with just one cell, after only forty-eight hours you'll have 16,777,216 of them. At the height of fermentation, there are about 5 million in a single drop of must.

The division of all living things into two kingdoms, animal and vegetable, remained satisfactory until the study of microorganisms developed in the nineteenth century. Then, for a while, it would have been hard to play twenty questions with yeasts in mind. They were obviously not mineral, but how could you have stated whether they were animal or vegetable when scientists themselves did not agree how to classify them?

Yeasts are now considered part of the vegetable kingdom, so it is to the collaboration of two utterly dissimilar vegetal virtuosos— the sprawling grapevine and the single-cell yeast—that we owe the creation of wine.

Observing the yeast cell under the microscope while Gerbi comments is an eye opener for the wine lover and another blow to his enocentricity. Like vines, yeasts do not work for wine. They, too, are interested only in reproduction, with cells instead of seeds as their concern.

Yeasts ferment sugar to obtain the energy necessary for reproduction. Alcohol is simply a by-product, and a lethal one at that. For these tiniest of teetotalers, alcohol is toxic. When it reaches a certain degree, the yeasts are poisoned by their own pollution and cease reproducing. They are not willing wine makers. In fact, they do not produce alcohol at all unless they are deprived of oxygen: whence Pasteur's definition of fermentation as "life without air." When adequate oxygen is available in aerobic conditions, they break down sugar all the way to water and carbon dioxide, thereby extracting more energy from the fuel and multiplying faster.

The production of commercial yeast such as baker's or brewer's involves forced aeration. The yeast cells themselves are the primary product, and the medium in which they grow—water, some form of sugar, and nitrogenous substances—is discarded after the cells have been centrifuged out. In wine making, the medium is the final consumer product, and it is the yeast cells that are eventually discarded.

Gerbi smiles. "You see," he says, "even though yeasts are one of the simplest forms of life, they are very complex."

The cell under the microscope is oval-shaped.

"Genus: *Saccharomyces*," says Gerbi. Greek wine lovers will recognize it at once as "the sugar fungus," and even English-speakers will see the etymological connection with the sugar substitute saccharine. "Species: *cerevisiae*." Of all the entries in the Who's Who of yeast (there are about 500 species, and close to 100 of them have been found on grapes, in must, or in wine) this is the only one that you need spend much time on: *Saccharomyces cerevisiae*.

When fermentation occurs without any human intervention except crushing, it is always started by "bad" yeasts. The most important of these are the apiculates, so-called because the cells are pointed at both ends. In spontaneous fermentation, the species that most often plays the role of the villain is *Kloeckera apiculata*. The apiculate gang and other enological outlaws not only produce undesirable substances like acetic acid, but they never even finish the job because they can't take more than four degrees of alcohol. As the level of alcohol in the must approaches that level, they stop fermenting.

If the performance is still following the standard script, it is at this point that the hero takes over the show. The production of alcohol causes a natural selection of yeasts to take place. The fittest fermenter survives to become the master of the must, transforming the remaining sugar. Although now and then there may be another contender for the role, *Saccharomyces cerevisiae* is the protagonist of almost all fermentative dramas. It has the stamina to keep performing until the curtain of dryness falls and all the sugar has been converted into alcohol.

"But spontaneous fermentation hardly takes place anymore," says Gerbi, "except in the most primitive kind of wine making."

Müller–Thurgau's insight that the apiculate yeast could and should be excluded from fermentation from the beginning by using SO_2 opened a new era of vinification. The level of acetic acid in wines of earlier times, for instance, was far higher than would be tolerated by wine lovers today. Although nowadays bacteria are usually the culprits when VA is high, apiculate yeast used to share the blame.

Saccharomyces cerevisiae may be the wine lover's yeast, but if you've seen one, haven't you seen them all? A glance from Gerbi sets you straight. Even the most casual observer of the motley mob called *Homo sapiens* shouldn't be too surprised by the almost infinite diversity that a single species can encompass.

"Yeasts have evolved over a very long period of time," says Gerbi, "and, like all plants, have mutated to adapt to different conditions. Countless strains have developed. Those from southern regions, for example, are generally able to produce more alcohol than others because the average must there is richer in sugar."

A given strain's resistance to alcohol is called its fermentative power, and it varies greatly within the species. Until 1984, when the standard yeast classification was last revised, one strain with the capacity to tolerate exceptionally high levels of alcohol was actually considered a separate species: *Saccharomyces bayanus*. During the fermentation of a given wine, different strains of *Saccharomyces cerevisiae* may take over at various points as the alcohol level increases.

"Take a certain amount of must," Gerbi continues, "divide it into two equal parts, and ferment it with two different strains of *Saccharomyces cerevisiae*. The fermentations will start and end at different times. It's a question of fermentative vigor, of how fast it multiplies."

As you watch the spectacle of the fermenting cell, one question inevitably comes to mind. Where do yeasts come from and how do they get into the must?

The standard answer is that they exist all around us and are transported to ripening grapes by insects, birds, and the wind. This is true for many species, but *Saccharomyces cerevisiae* poses a problem for scientists who study the ecology of yeast.

"There's quite a bit of controversy," says Gerbi.

An Italian microbiologist recently studied ripe grapes on the vine in Umbria for two years in a row and failed to find a single cell of *Saccharomyces cerevisiae* on them. A control study conducted a couple of years later examined 2,160 ripe grapes picked at random, and only on one was *Saccharomyces cerevisiae* found. The hypothesis was put forth that the species is strictly a cellar yeast, since it is predominant in musts with more than four degrees of alcohol, but practically absent on grapes still on the vine.

It may happen that *Saccharomyces cerevisiae* is entirely absent in small quantities of grapes, but there are always a few cells in larger quantities, and these suffice. Wine makers have long noted that fermentation gets under way more easily in large containers than in small ones. They also know that the first load of grapes every harvest is the slowest to start fermenting. Many prepare a starter culture with the ripest grapes three or four days before the harvest begins and have a certain amount of must already fermenting to inoculate the first vat. Contaminated by the yeasts produced during the first fermentation, equipment and workers' hands inoculate successive loads.

"In the past," says Gerbi, "even in difficult years, fermentations went more smoothly. Recently, yeasts have had more trouble converting all the sugar into alcohol. Many new products used in the vineyard against rot also inhibit yeasts." He grins. "After all, yeasts are fungi. Weedkillers and pesticides have lowered the natural yeast population and have affected *Saccharomyces cerevisiae* more than the tougher apiculates. The microflora that we now take to the cellar with the grapes is certainly inferior to what it was only ten years ago. Even increased cleanliness in the cellar has been unfavorable to yeast."

Gerbi pauses. The subject is indeed complex.

"In order to avoid problems with fermentation," he says finally, "more and more wine makers even in Europe are using cultured yeast strains. In the New World, where yeast strains have not evolved over so many centuries, it's been the standard practice for a long time."

In 1876 the great German doctor and microbiologist Robert Koch isolated the bacterium that causes the disease called anthrax and grew it in pure culture. Five years later, at the Carlsberg brewery in Copenhagen, Emil Hansen first isolated and grew a pure culture of yeasts for brewing beer. Wine makers eventually followed the brewer's example.

Cultured yeast strains are clones—all cells are descended from a single ancestor and are identical to it. These clones are to wine making what their vineyard counterparts are to viticulture.

"The trouble with cultured yeasts," says Gerbi, "is that the market is dominated by a few big companies. They make only a few strains, which tend to be the vigorous ones, at the expense of those with characteristics more important for quality. Each strain affects the wine differently."

Clonal selection. Vigor. The direction seems to be the same in both cellar and vineyard.

Gerbi looks at his watch and nods at the microscope.

Another cell is now splitting off. Who knows what kind of personal mark it and its billions of fellow fermenters back in the demijohn are leaving on the wine?

"Yeasts can't turn mediocre grapes into great wine," Gerbi says, "but they can add complexity. We still have a lot to learn."

Vast tracts of the microworld have yet to be explored. Even when one looks through a powerful microscope, there's more to yeasts than meets the eye.

"IT'S RUSH HOUR, all right," says Aldo as he slows to a crawl. "I figured we'd hit some heavy traffic."

Up ahead, as far as the eye can see, traffic is at a standstill. Drivers have turned off their engines and are socializing in the street.

The street is Turin Street, but it's not a street in Turin. The citizens of Barbaresco seem to enjoy the evening traffic jams that occur every fall as members of the cooperative winery wait in line with their tractors to have their grapes weighed and the sugar content determined.

"Maybe all this traffic makes us villagers feel less provincial," Aldo suggests wryly.

At the Gaja winery the fermentation floor of the cellar is still all lit up. Guido is there talking to Albino Morando, a friend and researcher. Morando has the mind of a scientist and the hands of a farmer. He can lecture learnedly on manure, but he's also slung it. The peasant-professor smiles as eager eyes gaze questioningly at tank number twenty-six.

Guido opens a valve and an unwary nose is met by a blast of acrid CO_2. But by now, even a novice understands what that signifies. The grapes of San Lorenzo are well on their way to wine! It's a sight that must be seen.

The view from the top of the tank has changed. Buoyed by the CO_2, the cap is so close you want to reach out and touch it. And the furiously foaming must is anything but mute. Those native yeasts are certainly hard at work, but they must be making whoopee as well as making wine!

Guido tells Morando of a professor at the University of California at Davis whom he met a few years ago.

"We were talking about fermentation and he insisted that, in order to avoid problems, you should get it going right away with a cultured strain. 'Make a beeline for alcohol,' he said."

Guido looks indignant.

"But yeasts don't produce just alcohol!" he exclaims.

"Thank God they don't!" Morando says brusquely. "If they did, we'd have weak vodka instead of wine."

"Yeah," Guido says. "Yeasts aren't factory workers turning out a standardized product. They're artisans! Getting the sugar converted to alcohol as quickly as possible discourages all those secondary processes that make for individuality and complexity."

[165]

Guido is almost as ebullient as the must inside the tank.

"Getting there is half the fun!" he proclaims. "The wine maker who makes a beeline for alcohol is like a hasty tourist. You know, the kind who dashes off in a taxi to have a quick look at a couple of the most famous monuments instead of wandering around leisurely. There's more to Rome than the Colosseum and St. Peter's!"

Morando nods in agreement.

"Yeasts contribute all kinds of other stuff to wine," he says. "And with each strain it's different. If the conditions are identical, a given strain will transform a given must into a wine that's different from one produced by any other strain."

Peter Vinding-Diers, a Danish wine maker working at Château Rahoul in the Graves district of Bordeaux, got a lot of publicity in the wine press because of experiments he carried out during the 1985 and 1986 vintages. He drew off must from the same vat into three casks and inoculated each one with a different strain of *Saccharomyces cerevisiae*. One had been isolated at Rahoul and the other two at estates in Margaux and Pauillac. The result was three wines that were easily distinguishable when tasted "blind."

How is it possible that the minute quantities of certain substances produced by yeasts can make such a difference in wine?

The components of wine that are quantitatively most important are not the ones that give it distinction. Like the human body, wine is mostly water, which no more distinguishes one wine from another than it does a Michelangelo or an Einstein from your neighbor, Mr. Jones. Alcohol—usually from twelve to fourteen percent of a fine red wine—contributes more to a wine's character, but Château Laplonk may have the same alcoholic degree as Château Latour.

"Threshold" is the term that indicates the minimum level of an odor or taste that an average person can detect.

Ethyl alcohol, for example, is slightly sweet, but when it is gradually added to pure water most people won't perceive it at all until it reaches a concentration of more than 11 percent. The threshold of table salt is only 0.2 percent, and that of acetic acid is 0.012 percent. Put another way, if you had an Olympic-sized swimming pool, you would have to add 50 gallons of ethyl alcohol before it would be perceived upon tasting, while one-tenth of one drop of isobutyl methoxy pyrazine—IMP, the compound that gives bell peppers their characteristic flavor—would suffice.

Minute quantities of some substances can dominate a wine's odor. A chlorinated compound called 2,4,6-trichloroanisole is one of the most common causes of "corked" wine. Its threshold is 10 ppt, or parts per trillion. If you have a solution that is 999,999,999,990 parts pure water and 10 parts of compound, you can taste the latter. Since analyses of corked wines have shown they contain from 20 to 370 ppt, it's no wonder there's no mistaking them.

But taste involves more than threshold levels. There are those of preference and aversion as well. Just as almost any substance can be sickening if the quantity is large enough, even those usually considered negative can add appealing complexity to a wine if the quantity is small enough.

If you've ever smelled a rotten egg, you no doubt remember the odor even if you don't know the name of the chemical compound that caused the stench: hydrogen sulfide, H_2S. Yet H_2S is a component of the classic grilled-nut flavor that sends lovers of white Burgundy into ecstasy.

A bit of acetic acid gives a wine's bouquet a lift; more makes it smell like vinegar. The right amount of IMP gives Sauvignon its proper varietal character; more makes it herbaceously aggressive. Even some of the really sinister denizens of the microworld— spoilage yeasts like the infamous *Brettanomyces,* for instance—can add a bit of complexity if their touch is *very* light.

Threshold itself is a statistical fiction. It may vary enormously between two people, as is notoriously the case with sulfur dioxide. It evolves in the same person over the years, but it can also change in a matter of weeks.

Preference and aversion are, of course, relative, too. One person's stench is another's delight. Take a cheese like Camembert. Everyone will agree it's insipid when freshly made and repulsive when overripe. But as the cheese ripens and the amount of ammonia increases, individuals will shout "Now!" at very different points.

The myriad components called "secondary" are what give wine its distinctive character. Most of them come from the grape itself.

That's why to make the "best" wine in the world you need the "best" grapes. But they also come from a number of other sources, including how a given strain of yeast metabolizes what it finds in the must.

"Yeasts have their vices as well as their virtues," Guido chuckles. "Take hydrogen sulfide, for example."

Yeasts produce H_2S through the decomposition of various sulfur compounds present in the must. But different strains vary greatly in the amount they produce. In fact, about one percent of them don't produce any at all. At the other extreme, there are strains that produce up to four or five milligrams per liter—enough to make a glass of wine stink like a sewer.

"When yeasts are stressed," says Morando, "they produce more stuff like acetic acid and hydrogen sulfide."

Yeasts let the wine maker know when their working conditions are poor. If it's too hot or cold, if there's too much SO_2 or not enough to eat, they protest.

When the nitrogenous matter in the must is used up, yeasts break down amino acids to get at the nitrogen, and hydrogen sulfide is a byproduct. One strain that works just fine at 68 degrees Fahrenheit produces two monstrous grams of acetic acid at 50 degrees.

"That's not protest!" exclaims Guido. "It's sabotage!"

But if that happens, he admits, it's also the wine maker's fault for giving his yeasts the cold shoulder. "If you care about your wine, you have to coddle your yeast."

He's pleased the native yeasts are working so well on Sorì San Lorenzo '89. "Those cultured strains are mercenaries," he says, deadpan. "They'll work for anybody."

It's not a question of chauvinism, but of birthright. Yeasts that have evolved in a particular place contribute to a wine's uniqueness, to its identity.

Guido uses a cultured-yeast strain whenever there are factors such as rot that make it imperative to get the fermentation going as quickly as possible. But otherwise, he gives the native ones a couple of days to see if they can do the job.

"Sure," he says, "it would be safer not to. But to get the best out of the grapes you have to take risks now and then."

The specter of spoilage still haunts the house of wine. The dictates of Davis are taken as dogma. And the siren of nature attracts the heretics with her seductively simple song.

"It's easy to let nature do whatever she wants," Guido says, "and equally easy to tyrannize her with technology. What's hard is steering a course between Scylla and Charybdis."

The strait of wine making is like the Strait of Messina, between the island of Sicily and mainland Italy. He's determined to navigate his Nebbiolo between the rock of spoilage and the whirlpool of dispossession—dispossession of the wine's potential.

Guido may now be a navigator, but don't think he's at sea when it comes to fermentation. He's got his feet on the ground. Except, of course, when he's performing on the high wire. There's a tightrope in the cellar as well as in the vineyard. Could the greatest show on earth be without one?

THE DIGITAL THERMOMETER on tank number twenty-six indicates 28 degrees Centigrade—just over 82 degrees Fahrenheit—and the red light is on. The automatic cooling system has gone into action.

Of all the factors that regulate the course of fermentation, temperature is the most important. It was Müller-Thurgau who codified the basic law: at higher temperatures, the fermentation starts and is over sooner, but less alcohol is produced and there are fewer yeast cells at the end.

"The ideal fermentation is steady," says Guido, "but not too fast. If it's slower, it's more balanced. You get purer flavors, a nicer bouquet, and more complexity. When it's too fast, it's as if the yeasts were too busy producing alcohol to produce anything else."

The temperature can also be too low.

"If you ferment in small casks and the cellar is cool, the problem is how to raise the temperature enough to get things going."

But it's the high temperatures that worry wine makers most nowadays. The problem used to be restricted to hot climates, but with the increasing use of large fermentation vats, it became more widespread: the larger the container, the less heat is dispersed. Only about 40 percent of the energy released during fermentation is used by the yeasts for reproduction; the rest is given off as heat. An increase of one degree centigrade causes a 10 percent increase in the speed of fermentation, which is twice as fast at 30 degrees Centigrade as at 20.

But heat stresses yeasts. They produce more acetic acid, find it harder to tolerate alcohol, and are less able to assimilate nutrients. When, in Cole Porter's words, "it's too darn hot," they simply stop reproducing. The fermentation gets stuck, creating a dangerous situation. Without its protective cover of CO_2, the wine is exposed to oxygen and vulnerable to attack by bacteria that transform alcohol into acetic acid.

In a sense, wine is just a passing phase between must and vinegar. The word "vinegar" itself comes from the French *vin aigre*, "sour wine." Since modern wine making has virtually eliminated the problem of vinegary wines, it's easy to forget the proportions it reached in the past.

"The most common ailment is the acetification of wine," Fantini wrote. "Some convert their wine into vinegar, which is perhaps the only way to attenuate the damage. Others mix it with sound wines and thus spoil the little good wine they have in their cellar." In an article titled "The Storage of Wine," Garino-Canina wrote in 1934 that more than 25 million gallons of spoiled wine a year were produced in Italy, with acetification the main cause.

Angelo frequently points out while eating in small restaurants in the Langhe that there is too much vinegar on the salad.

"It's an old tradition around here," he says. "It goes back to the time when peasants didn't have much oil, which was too expensive. But they sure had plenty of vinegar!"

When Guido started to work at the winery, fermentation took place in three huge vats. The smallest had a capacity of 3,000 gallons, the largest 8,500. Made of cement and built into the wall of the windowless cellar, the tanks were as insulated as they could be. During the great vintage of 1971—with grapes that were practically groaning under their load of sugar—the fermentation was galloping out of hand because of the heat. Angelo rented a minibus that sped load after load of ice from the slaughterhouse in Alba to the winery.

Guido shudders as he recollects.

"The blocks weighed about fifty pounds each! And we had to

carry them in jute sacks on our shoulders down to the cellar. We wrapped a long hose around the ice and pumped the wine through to cool it off."

Even a famous estate like Château Lafite had not always been successful in dealing with the problem. In 1895, Ulysse Gayon, director of the enological research center in Bordeaux, happened to be staying there. When he realized what was happening in the cellar, he advised Baron de Rothschild to order ice from Bordeaux, and the blocks were dumped straight into the vats. The wine may have been a little diluted, but it was saved. In 1921, Lafite wasn't so lucky, and it found itself temporarily in the vinegar, rather than the wine, business because of the scorching fall. So when the fall of 1928 turned out to be very hot, they pasteurized the wine in order to avoid spoilage problems. But the Bordeaux merchants who had bought the vintage in advance took legal action against the château and returned the wine.

The first cooling systems were developed by French growers in torrid Algeria during the 1880s, but they were simply modifications of systems that had long been used in the brewing industry: another instance of wine's indebtedness to beer. Henri Woltner of Château La Mission Haut-Brion had enamel-covered steel tanks installed as early as 1926, but it was not until the early sixties—with Haut-Brion and Latour leading the way, and to the accompaniment of mumbling and grumbling about "turning wineries into dairies"—that stainless-steel tanks began to spread throughout Bordeaux and the rest of the wine world.

In 1973 the new cellar at the Gaja winery was completed. If the temperature started to climb too high, the windows could be opened and the cellar would be cooled off. And new vats were installed right underneath them the following year.

Although they are beginning to show their age and look a bit old-fashioned in comparison with younger tanks like number twenty-six, there is still beauty in the eye of their most frequent beholder. Guido bangs on the tank with his knuckles. "Listen to that!" he exclaims. The sound of metal only three centimeters thick is music to his ears. It means heat dispersal. He'll never forget that these vats took the heat off him when they took it out of the must!

"They changed my life," he says. "From 1974 on, fermentation was a whole new ball game."

With the latest tanks, Guido can regulate the temperature with the flick of a switch. But he knows the lessons of history: Once a revolution has overthrown an oppressive regime, it may well impose its own form of tyranny.

"A lot of people go to the other extreme and control the temperature too rigidly," he says. "We shouldn't put a straitjacket on fermentation."

Across from number twenty-six are other stainless-steel tanks that seem to be identical to it. But if you look carefully you'll see that they are a little taller and thinner; the bottoms are flat instead of funnel-shaped. They were the winery's first temperature-controlled tanks, bought in 1983 to make the first wine from the Chardonnay vines that had been planted in 1979. High temperatures are even more harmful to whites than to reds.

"Those tanks are fine for whites," says Guido. "But number twenty-six and the others in this row, which we bought in 1985, are better for reds. They make it easier to manage the cap."

The relationship between the solid and liquid parts of the grapes is the most problematic aspect of making red wine. Left to itself, the pomace floats on top of the liquid and the surface dries out. The pressure of the CO_2 from below makes it compact.

"My mother-in-law had an open, cone-shaped vat," Guido says, "and one fall the cap got stuck in the upper part. It went two days without being broken up. When we tried to push a stick through it, it wouldn't go. The cap was as hard as a brick!"

The greater ratio between the width and the height of tank twenty-six and its mates means that the cap is more spread out and thus thinner. There's more surface contact with the must. A cylinder running up the middle effectively disperses the CO_2, preventing the cap from being compacted by the pressure of the gas.

Guido grins.

"With that hole in the middle, the cap looks like a big doughnut."

He presses a button.

"I'm going to pump over," he says.

[172]

The must is pumped from the bottom of the tank through a hose and over the cap. To spread the must evenly and gently—to make pumping over as nonviolent as possible—Guido devised a pipe with holes that sprays while revolving near the top of the tank.

The job used to be done by hand. Must was drawn off into a bucket and then carried up a ladder to the top of the vat and poured over the cap.

"Just think," says Guido. "Not only was there hard physical labor involved, but whoever held the hose while the must was coming out of the vat had to breathe all that CO_2!"

Pumping over helps keep the temperature from climbing too high and makes it uniform throughout the tank. For, unlike one of white, a tank of fermenting red wine does not have a uniform temperature. It can be as much as 50 degrees Fahrenheit hotter right under the cap than at the bottom.

The heterogeneity of red-wine fermentation was first studied systematically by the Tuscan Polacci, who began his experiments in 1867 with specially made small glass fermentation tanks similar to the cylinder Guido used for his "visible version." He noted that the main force of fermentation was located near the cap, "while the liquid underneath remains almost in the state of must."

Pumping over also aerates the wine, making it easier for the yeast to multiply. As fermentation gets under way, Guido pumps over for an hour twice a day to build up his work force.

Aeration is not much of a problem when fermentation takes place, as it did in older times, in small, open casks. In that case, the cap is managed by punching it down periodically with a stick or similar tool, a process that lets in air. But in the winery's large, closed fermentation vats the system used was what is known as "submerged cap." A grille placed across the vat kept the cap submerged and prevented it from drying out. The submerged cap remained compact, however, and oxygen could not penetrate.

In great years the fermentative task facing the yeasts is always difficult: riper grapes mean more alcohol. When working conditions are poor in addition, they may go on strike and the fermentation gets stuck, which is what happened in 1961.

"What do you expect?" says Guido, who always looks at things from the yeasts' point of view. "With all that sugar, loads of SO_2, and no aeration. And nutrients weren't added in those days, either. The yeasts did the best they could in those conditions."

Finally, by mixing the liquid and solid parts of the grapes, pumping over does something similar to what a coffee percolator or the rotating drum of a washing machine does, although more gently. It helps the process of extraction.

"*MAGARI!*" exclaims Guido. "*Magari!*"

Magari! is an Italian exclamation that has no one-word English equivalent. You would have to translate it as "Would that it were so!" or "If only it were true!"

Guido is referring to the definition of wine that you find in most dictionaries: "the fermented juice of grapes." Could it be that the people who write those definitions don't know how *red* wine is made? But perhaps, in the end, the definition is only a well-meaning attempt to spare whoever consults it the harsh truth about extraction. Perhaps it's just a white lie.

The difference between red and white wine is in part a question of grape variety. No matter how skillful a wine maker one is, one can't make a red wine out of Chardonnay or Riesling. But one can make a white wine out of any red grape, except the now-uncommon varieties the French call *teinturiers,* which have red pulp and were used in the past to "dye" or "tint" red wines considered too pale. All you have to do is to press the grapes, as in white winemaking, instead of crushing them, and ferment the juice without the skins and seeds. That would be "the fermented juice of grapes."

Far more of the most famous white wine in the world, Champagne, is made from the two red grapes allowed by the regulations—Pinot Noir and Pinot Meunier—than from the lone white one, Chardonnay. That's why a Champagne made solely with Chardonnay is called *blanc de blancs:* a white *(blanc)* wine from white *(blancs)* grapes.

The making of red wine involves extraction of substances from the skins and seeds of the grapes. Though many writers refer to the process as maceration, it's actually infusion—the product to be

[174]

consumed is the liquid, not the solid. Like tea and coffee, red wine is an infusion.

When you make tea or coffee, you extract substances from solids into water. The quality of your cup will depend, of course, in part on that of your raw material. Coffee beans and tea leaves differ, just as grapes do; some contain more and better things than others. But it also depends on how you manage the extractive process.

If you make tea with water that has not reached the boil, for instance, the leaves rise to the surface of the pot; if the water has been boiled for too long, they fall to the bottom. In neither case does otpimal extraction occur because there is too little exchange between the solids and the liquid. But when the water has just started to boil vigorously, there is a lot of air in it and most of the leaves circulate up and down.

Temperature affects extraction. If the water cools off, its extractive power is diminished: thus the tradition of heating the pot. The duration of the infusion is important, too. Color is extracted more quickly than flavor, whence the accusation by British connoisseurs that Americans "drink tea with their eyes" and remove the leaves too soon. You can also wait too long before removing them, with excessive tannin and astringent tea as the result.

Extraction in the making of coffee involves similar considerations. It also depends on the fineness of the grind. When you make coffee with a filter, for example, the grind has to be fine because the solid and the liquid are in contact for a very short time. If you filter with a coarse grind, you'll have underextraction and weak coffee.

Though the latest presses keep it to a minimum, some extraction is inevitable even in the making of white wine. And a brief period of contact with the skins is actually becoming common for fine white wines in order to extract more flavor and aroma.

"You shouldn't even talk about white wine in the same breath as a red one like San Lorenzo here!" Guido exclaims. "They're like night and day! War and peace!"

Guido didn't experience the air raids of World War II, but he still knows that a red alert indicates that an attack is imminent. But at the Gaja winery, the red alert actually goes on only when Nebbiolo is approaching.

"There's a war going on in there!" Guido exclaimed enigmatically while pointing to tank twenty-six a couple of days after the grapes from Sorì San Lorenzo had been crushed. "A war between tannins and anthocyanins!"

Could Guido be suffering from combat fatigue? With Nebbiolo, after all, extraction means extra action!

Both anthocyanins and tannins belong to a class of organic compounds called phenols. About 65 percent of a grape's phenolic compounds are contained in the seeds, 22 percent in the stems, 12 percent in the skins, and 1 percent in the pulp.

Just as the bubbles produced by CO_2 were the most obvious sign of fermentation, the reddening of the must is the signature of extraction. The color comes from the anthocyanins in the skins of the grapes. They are the pigments responsible for most red, purple, and blue colors in flowers and vegetables, as well as fruits such as apples, plums, cherries, and many berries. Grapes need a lot of sunshine to produce them abundantly, which is why you can tell a great deal about a vintage from the color of the wine.

Tannin has been used since prehistory to tan animal hides. It combines with the proteins on their surface, converting gelatin into insoluble, non-putrefying leather.

The most dramatic chapter in Guido's wine making memoirs will undoubtedly be "The Taming of the Tannin." Lions, shrews, and wild frontiers are nothing in comparison with his bugaboo.

"Tannic wines like Barbaresco are penalized when tasted without food," he and Angelo are always saying. When you drink them with a meal, not only do oils and other fats lubricate your mouth, but the tannin combines with proteins in meats and sauces. The same phenomenon occurs when you add milk to your tea. The tannin of the tea combines with the protein of the milk instead of with the mucoproteins in your mouth and the tea tastes less astringent.

If Nebbiolo is long on tannin, it's short on anthocyanins.

"In a year like this," says Guido, "Nebbiolo will have at most five hundred milligrams per liter, and an average of half that, whereas Barbera and Cabernet will average between six hundred and seven hundred. And Nebbiolo's have a different molecular structure: they're less stable and easy to lose.

His expression suddenly brightens. "If Nebbiolo had Barbera's or Cabernet's anthocyanins, that would make all the difference." But he snaps back to reality with a shrug. "Some apples are redder than others, that's all."

The challenge is to extract as much color as possible without getting too much tannin in the process. In the war between tannins and anthocyanins, Guido seems to side with the latter. And his tactic sounds simple enough: take the color and run before the tannin takes over.

Anthocyanins are water-soluble, while tannin is extracted by alcohol. (In making tea, *boiling* water does the job.) Thus, the first forty-eight hours or so after crushing—when the yeast cells have not yet started to produce alcohol—are crucial to the outcome of the war.

"That's another reason we pumped over so much at the beginning," Guido says. "To extract as much color as possible. If we did that in the presence of alcohol, we'd get oodles of tannin. SO_2 is also important because it extracts color, but not tannin."

Guido has also done a lot of experimenting with heat. The warmer the must, the more soluble anthocyanins are. If he increases the temperature while there's still no alcohol, as he can with the new fermentation tanks, he gets a lot of color without tannin. But he's still cautious about the results.

"You have to see the long-term effects of the temperature on the wine," he says. "You don't want it to develop cooked flavors. And you have to see if the color remains stable."

Guido has even been experimenting with removing seeds that collect in the funnel-shaped bottom of the tank. When alcohol works on the seeds for a long time, it extracts bitter and astringent tannins. He hopes that removing some of them will have the same kind of effect as destemming.

Although you usually read that the skins also contain a lot of tannin, some experts maintain that, strictly speaking, those of noble grape varieties contain none at all.

"Ah!" Guido exclaims. "If only we knew more about the phenolic compounds in the grape: exactly where they're located, how they're extracted during vinification, and how they combine. If only we could master extraction as we've mastered the malolactic fermentation, about which we knew very little not so long ago! One thing is certain, though. Phenolic compounds—polyphenols—constitute the new frontier of enology.''

But no one knows better than Guido that the new frontier is still wild and woolly.

When he was in California a few years ago, he talked with one of the world's leading experts on polyphenols, V. E. Singleton, of the University of California at Davis.

"He told me that superior wines are supple when they have from 1,200 to 1,400 milligrams of polyphenols per liter. But our Barbarescos usually have over 2,000. And one with as much as 2,800 might be balanced and another with 1,800 astringent.''

It's not only the *quantity* of tannin that's important, but also the *quality*. The great enologist Jean Ribéreau-Gayon made a distinction between coarse, aggressive tannins and "noble" ones. According to him, they differ because the former are resistant to polymerization while the latter polymerize and become velvety.

A polymer is a compound consisting of many—sometimes millions—of identical linked units, each of which is a relatively simple molecule called a monomer. As wine ages, more and more monomers grow out of their individualism. Joining the union, they polymerize to the cry of *e pluribus unum!*

Polymerization is central to what the ageing of wine is all about: to why wine looks, smells, and tastes different as it grows older. And, it seems, the more the merrier. The more components that take part in the process, the richer and more complex the wine will be.

As they combine with one another, the ex-monomeric tannins cease combining with the mucoproteins in your mouth. They feel smooth instead of astringent because they no longer "tan" your tongue. Those that stubbornly remain monomers are harsh to the bitter end.

In the long run, some polymers become so heavy that they fall out of the wine and form a deposit. Others may revert to aggressivity. Or so it seems.

Guido smiles wryly.

"I was at the research institute in Asti just the other day," he says, "talking to Rocco di Stefano. He's been investigating phenolic compounds. 'We know everything about monomers,' he told me, 'and nothing about polymers!' "

Although Guido has spent a lifetime grappling with tannin, he learned nothing about it at school.

"We hardly studied it at all," he says. "It wasn't considered problematic. Everyone simply assumed that the more tannin you had, the longer the wine would age."

But isn't that true? Won't Barbaresco age less well if it is less aggressively tannic than in the past?

No one really understands why some wines age better than others. Tannin and acidity are important, of course. Wines that are very low in both of them will not age. But more is not necessarily better.

Bordeaux, which has received more critical attention in these matters than Barbaresco, furnishes some classic examples. Two historic pairs of vintages—1899–1900 and 1928–1929—are instructive. All four years were considered outstanding from the start, but 1900 and 1929 were drinkable when still young, while 1899 and 1928 were tough. Many people thought that the former would fade rather fast and that the latter would win out in the long run. The consensus of expert opinion, however, is that such has not been the case at all.

Guido's tactics during fermentation may seem anti-tannin, but they can only be understood in the broader context of strategy. He doesn't want to eliminate the tannin, but only prevent it from dominating the wine. He needs tannin for flavor and structure. He also needs it for color.

Anthocyanins provide only the initial color of red wine. The color of a young Dolcetto, for example, is much more intense than that of a young Nebbiolo because the grape contains more anthocyanins. But it doesn't last. As wine ages, its color depends more and more on tannin, of which Dolcetto contains very little. Cabernet Sauvignon, of course, is rich in both, which is one of the reasons it's always at the top of the class.

"The color of Nebbiolo," says Guido, "depends on the marriage between anthocyanins and tannin. We have to find a way to keep it stable."

From strategist to marriage counsellor: Guido's work, alas, is

[179]

never done. The extractive war cannot be won. Every fall the red alarm goes on again and the fighting breaks out anew. Guido is always licking his wine making wounds. After all, even though making red wine and making tea both involve extraction, a war in a winery is not just a tempest in a teapot! But he sees red if you suggest he wave a white flag. He's as courageous as they come. And his badge of courage is the color you know.

FERMENTATION ENDS when all the fermentable sugar in the must has been converted into alcohol, but extraction ends when the wine maker decides to drain the wine off the pomace. The duration of the second process has varied greatly throughout the modern history of wine. Émile Peynaud cites documents from the mid–nineteenth century showing that at Château Mouton d'Armailhacq (now Mouton Baronne Philippe) extraction lasted only five or six days, while at neighboring Château Lafite it went on for a month.

Before Guido took over as wine maker, Luigi Rama would leave the wine with its skins and seeds for a month or more. That was the Tradition. And in a great year like 1978, even Guido succumbed to the temptation of a "macho" infusion, as he says, mockingly thumping his chest.

"We were trying to demonstrate something," he says. "We wanted to extract everything from such great grapes."

Thinking back, he would gladly have left more in the skins and, especially, the seeds. He talks more approvingly of the '79, which was drained off after twelve days.

Twelve days of extraction—the duration of a balanced fermentation itself—would be satisfactory for most wine makers in the Langhe today, but you still encounter old-timers who shake their heads and tell you how things used to be.

But the tradition before the Tradition turns out once again to be quite different. According to Fantini, "The fermentation usually lasts eight days. When it is over, the wine is drained off into barrels." Ottavi was sharply critical of "wines that are left with their pomace for twenty or thirty days," finding them "rough, coarse, and fit only for a cheap tavern." And Cavazza, the father of modern

Barbaresco, gives the 1905 vintage as an example of an "average fermentation" at the cooperative winery. It lasted eleven and a half days, from the morning of September 29 to the afternoon of October 9, after which the wine was immediately drained off into barrels.

"If you hear stories about lengthy infusions in the past," says Guido, "you have to remember that grape growers also had other crops to look after. They had to sow wheat in the fall, so often the wine had to wait a while before they had time to drain it off. And frequently there weren't enough barrels in the cellar. The wine was simply left in the vat until some container became available for it."

The *duration* of the process is only one of the variables affecting extraction, and not the most important.

"If the wines of the past tended to be hard and coarse," says Guido, it was mainly because of the high temperature during fermentation and all that vigorous punching down. Punching down let in air, but it also extracted gobs of tannin. Look at the difference between our 1982 Barbaresco and the '85. In 1982, we still punched down some. With the latest tanks and the fact that the cap doesn't become so compact, we haven't had to do it anymore. The '82 has great potential, but it's still hard. The '85 is another thing."

He's decided. He'll drain Sorì San Lorenzo '89 off as soon as the fermentation is over.

"THAT'S IT," says Guido as he reads the scale on his hydrometer.

Even a novice noticed the signs that the party at number twenty-six was coming to an end. There was less and less CO_2. The cap started to sink. The temperature was dropping.

Guido has been following the decline and fall of fermentation with regular readings of his hydrometer. As sugar is converted into alcohol, the density of the must decreases until it is less than that of water. Now all the sugar has disappeared.

"Actually" Guido says, "the wine never achieves absolute dryness. There always remains about one gram per liter of pentose, which yeasts don't ferment. But that's below the threshold of perception, so the wine tastes perfectly dry."

[181]

Pentose? Like the Pentagon, it must have something to do with five.

"It's a sugar with a molecule that has five carbon atoms instead of the six that hexose sugars such as glucose and fructose have."

Even though you may not be familiar with the difference, not to worry: those yeast cells are!

SORÌ SAN LORENZO 1989 has been racked off its pomace and into a large, twenty-year-old barrel made of Slovenian oak. Now the pomace is being pumped out of tank number twenty-six and conveyed to the press, which is on a platform on the same floor. Some of the liquid remaining in it—the press wine—will be pressed out and sold off in bulk.

"In the past," says Guido, "without today's equipment, if all went well, five and even ten men did in a whole day what two now do in an hour or so. And removing the pomace was a real drama when we were working with those cement vats."

Guido's thinning hair no longer stands on its few remaining ends, but his expression leaves no doubt that in his younger days the experience was hair-raising.

"Just think!" he exclaims. "The largest vat contained 8,500 gallons. When the wine had been racked and it was time to remove the pomace, there was always a moment of suspense. If it was nice and compact, you could manage. But if it was mushy, watch out! Even with three people holding the door to the vat, there was little you could do with two tons of the stuff pressing to get out. When he knew he had to rack the wine from one of those vats, Rama would turn pale and break out into a cold sweat the day before!"

*G*UIDO HAS BECOME A PAINTER, and an abstract one
at that!

Perhaps he's getting ready for a show. Several works have recently appeared on the wall of his office. At first glance, they look
identical, with the same yellow spots on the same blue background,
but closer inspection reveals that the intensity of the spots varies
from painting to painting: subtle shadings of an obsessive style!

Guido dances down to his lab.

"Come see the artist at work," he says.

He takes a sheet of blue paper, draws a line across it about an
inch from the bottom, and marks it at approximately one inch
intervals. Then he puts a drop of clear liquid on the first mark and
a drop of red wine from a different one of several beakers on each
of the other marks. The artist is painting with wine!

"Now it has to dry," he says.

The first drop that Guido put on the chromatography paper was
a solution containing malic acid; the others were samples of new
wines, including Sorì San Lorenzo. The acids contained in each
wine move up the paper at different rates according to their molecular weight and appear as yellow spots in the following order from

the base line: tartaric, malic, lactic, citric. The malic acid standard in the first column shows the level to which that acid has moved, and the intensity of the yellow spots at the same level in the other columns indicates the amount in the various samples.

Guido is checking the progress of the malolactic fermentation— the MLF—during which malic acid is decomposed, just as sugar is decomposed during the alcoholic fermentation. Not only is the total *quantity* of acid in the wine reduced—a third of it goes with the wind as CO_2,—but its *quality* is changed as well. Harsh malic acid is replaced by lactic, which is only half as strong. Since it reduces the wine's acidity, the malolactic fermentation is also referred to as biological de-acidification.

"For whites," says Guido, "it all depends. Some grapes and styles need that extra acidity. But for reds, it's essential. There's a lot of synergy between acid—especially malic acid—and tannin. They intensify each other's harshness. This fermentation makes the wine more supple. It enables you to enjoy richer wines, with more tannin."

The wine changes in other ways, too. The aroma becomes less grapey and more vinous, the flavor more complex. The fermenters leave their metabolic mark, just as they do during alcoholic fermentation.

"Not all the changes are positive," says Guido. "Citric acid is also fermented, which results in a little additional VA. And since the pH goes up, the color is a bit less vivid. But on the whole, the wine improves greatly."

The wine has been fermenting again for about a month now, but it's only been the slightest of simmers compared to the boisterous boil of a month earlier. Malolactic fermentation can even go unnoticed, and in the past it was just assumed to be the tail end of the alcoholic fermentation.

The MLF takes place spontaneously, but, as with the primary fermentation, the wine maker can facilitate matters.

"There shouldn't be too much sulfur dioxide," Guido says. "That's another reason for going easy on it." In fact, he hasn't added any since the grapes were crushed. "And, the temperature should be over 60 degrees Fahrenheit."

That was no problem when the wine was drained off its pomace on October 4. The barrel is in the part of the old cellar nearest the fermentation tanks, where many wines were still boiling away and producing heat. A lot of steam was still being used there to clean the tanks. The weather itself didn't turn cold until the very beginning of November. And Guido put the wine in a barrel rather than in a metal tank precisely because it would retain heat from its alcoholic fermentation much longer there.

In times past, in regions like Bordeaux and Burgundy, the malolactic fermentation was often inhibited because the wines were racked off after the first fermentation into small casks in cold cellars. It would often start up in the spring when the weather got warmer. Peasants used to say that the wine would start "working" again when the sap began to rise in the vine.

Guido goes over his mental list.

"There have to be enough nutrients," he continues. "And the pH shouldn't be less than three-point-two."

More than a strict supervisor, Guido sounds like a solicitous host making sure that important guests have everything they need. He wants the job to be done as thoroughly and quickly as possible.

"As long as the malic acid is still there in the wine," he says, "it can be fermented. Once it's gone, you can have a peaceful aging process. Then it's all more a question of style than of anything else. But in the old days, wine makers never had the peace of mind that comes only with a stable wine. A biologically unstable wine is like a time bomb."

But there's certainly no reason to worry now. Everything seems to be proceeding just fine. Yeasts are working yet another wonder.

"Yeasts?"

Guido can hardly believe his ears.

"What do yeasts have to do with this? The malolactic fermentation is carried out by bacteria!"

Talk about putting your foot in your mouth! Even a neophyte should have got that one right. Perhaps the thought of *bacteria* was just too much to bear.

Most bacteria are actually respectable members of the biological community. Indeed, life on earth depends on the services they perform. And the worst bacteria from our point of view—the pathogenic ones that infect us with disease—don't develop in wine because of its low pH. But as with human beings, a few delinquents can give a bad name to an entire population.

Bacteria are even more micro than yeast. They can be as small as half a micron or less. But they can make a big difference in your food.

The next time you buy yogurt, for instance, have a close look at what's written on the container. It will probably mention *Lactobacillus bulgaricus* and *Streptococcus termophilus*. The elongated bacillus and the spherical coccus represent the two basic shapes of the bacteria that also concern the malolactic fermentation.

Like yeast, these bacteria ferment sugar to get energy for reproduction. In the case of milk, the sugar is lactose, which is why even people who can't digest milk can digest yogurt. Lactic acid and CO_2 are the waste products of their demolition job. And like yeast in the spontaneous fermentation of must, two genera perform as a relay team.

The coccus runs the first leg. As the amount of lactic acid increases, the pH decreases: the reverse of what happens in the malolactic fermentation, in which lactic acid replaces malic acid instead of sugar. When the medium gets too acid, the coccus passes the bacterial baton to the bacillus, which tolerates more acidity and reduces the pH even further by continuing the fermentation. When it's over, the yogurt will not go bad because it's too acid for spoilage bacteria. (It's also too acid for many humans, which is why most commercial yogurt has sugar added to it.)

Although everyone who's anyone in wine now takes the vinous virtues of certain bacteria for granted, such was not the case until quite recently. Microbiology was born out of concern with disease. When in 1862 Napoleon III asked Pasteur to investigate the cause of wine spoilage, the situation was critical. "There may not be a single cellar in France, be it owned by rich or poor," the emperor said, "that does not contain some wine that has gone bad."

Observing samples of spoiled wine under his microscope, Pasteur found rod-shaped organisms similar to those he had seen in sour milk and spoiled beer: what later were to be called bacteria, from the Greek for "little rod."

Pasteur established a dichotomy, according to which yeasts were the good guys who make wine, and bacteria the bad guys who spoil it. The assimilation of Pasteur's doctrine was reinforced by the crisis in the vineyard during his time due to oidium, downy mildew, and phylloxera. Concern with spoilage monopolized research; more attention was paid to the detrimental activities of microorganisms than to their beneficial ones.

The bacterial ban was on. The very mention of them evoked nightmarish visions of wee witches brewing, of a Walpurgis Night of wine. "Give 'em a micron and they'll take a meter," the eno-authorities warned. "Don't let them get their foot in the door or you'll soon have a sabbat in your cellar!" The bacteria box was worse than Pandora's, and never to be opened.

The rehabilitation of certain bacteria had a long line of distinguished advocates, beginning with Robert Koch, who observed bacteria in the dregs of wine that had undergone a sharp decrease in acidity. When the bacteria were cultivated in must and wine, they energetically decomposed malic acid. "Far from being classified as a cause of spoilage," Koch wrote, "such bacteria should be considered useful, as contributors to enhancement."

While staying at Château Lafite in 1895, Ulysse Gayon not only saved the estate's wine by advising the use of ice to slow down the runaway fermentation, but also disproved Pasteur's notion that yeasts are the only microorganisms present at the birth of wine. And the vats in which he observed bacteria make their appearance shortly after fermentation had begun were not those of some suspect, lower-class cellar. Not even at aristocratic Château Lafite was the conception immaculate!

One early investigator of the phenomenon worked much closer to Barbaresco. As early as 1914 and as nearby as the research institute in Asti, Garino-Canina noted that the malolactic fermentation occurred spontaneously in all the Piedmontese wines he had under examination. (The use of inhibiting SO_2 was not widespread at that time.) Returning to the subject in 1943, he pointed out that "the malolactic fermentation as a factor in the natural evolution of wine has not yet received the attention it deserves in the Italian enological literature." But Garino-Canina's remained a voice crying in a wine-making wilderness.

"One of the first significant things I did when I started working here," says Guido, "was to check the MLF."

But the stimulus to do so didn't come from his training at school.

"It wasn't given much attention at all," he recollects. "They just assumed it would take place at some point during the three or four years that the wine would probably spend in the barrel and weren't concerned about how or when."

His eyes begin to gleam with a hint of mischievous glee.

"But it was the bacteria, not the professors, who did the job, and *they* were very concerned about the conditions they had to work in! The results were often disastrous. Do you remember all those labels advising you to uncork your bottle of Barbaresco or Barolo several hours or even a day before drinking it? You bet! Ninety-five percent of all the stench in wines back in those days was due to incomplete malolactic fermentations that started up again in the bottle when the temperature where it was stored rose a bit. Just think of the conditions in which those bacteria had to work!"

Guido's face expresses the same horror one feels when reading accounts of factory conditions during the Industrial Revolution in England. Times for the malolactic bacteria were hard indeed.

"Think of the gobs of SO_2 that were used at bottling in those days and the lack of nutrients. The wines got cloudy and gassy because of the CO_2 produced. Is there anything worse than fizz in a red wine that's no longer young? The tannin, the acidity—including a lot of VA—and the CO_2 exalted each other."

Guido lets the effect sink in before divulging the last ghastly detail.

"And to top it all off, most people took all of that for granted as part of the wine! They didn't think anything of those off odors. That was just the way wine smelled!"

Guido's own malolactic education began during his trip to Burgundy in 1970. It was in the cellars of the well-known producer Joseph Drouhin that he not only observed the attention that was being given to the MLF— " 'la malo,' they called it, with the accent on the last syllable"—but also first saw the chromatography paper that was used to check its progress.

"My canvases," he says, nodding at his latest tests.

He translated Peynaud on the subject for himself and began to use the supply of paper that he had bought to test the wines of the 1970 vintage.

[188]

"The next spring," he says with delight dancing in his eyes, "the director of the school in Alba where I had studied came around to see me. When I showed him the chromatography paper he was amazed. He had never heard of it before! He ordered some for the school right away."

A few years later, in 1974, Angelo had a heating system installed in the cellar to facilitate the malolactic fermentation. It turned cold in the fall and they turned on the heat. It took a long time to bring the wine up to the critical temperature in the large barrels.

"You should have seen Angelo's father!" Guido exclaims. "He kept running around the cellar making sure that all the doors and windows were closed tight. He declared war on drafts and was determined to wipe them out!"

Those were inflationary times and the price of heating oil was rising fast.

The MLF was here to stay. Pasteur had failed to distinguish between malolactic bacteria and those that cause disease in wine. The former ferment malic acid and little else; the latter ferment substances like tartaric acid. When that happens, the result is what Pasteur called *tourne*—the wine "turns" flat and dull in color; the VA goes way up. Or these "bad" bacteria might ferment glycerol and produce, in addition to lots of VA, a bitter substance called acrolein.

But even this bacterial distinction is too simplistic. The behavior of malolactic bacteria themselves confirms social theories that emphasize environment and circumstances as causes of crime. Even good guys can become deviants. Temptations are not lacking, and if security is lax, if the pH is a bit too high . . .

No bacterial species is perfect, but there is one that stands head and shoulders above the others: *Leuconostoc oinos*. (*Oinos* is Greek for "wine," whence all those eno-words.)

Leuconostoc oinos is to the MLF what *Saccharomyces cerevisiae* is to the alcoholic fermentation. It is rare in nature compared to other species, but it is the most common in wine when the pH is under 3.5. And because of its tolerance of alcohol, it's frequently the only one left in the wine at the end of the primary fermentation.

The pH is doubly selective. It determines not only which species can develop in the wine, but also which components they can

[189]

ferment. For *Leuconostoc oinos,* the situation becomes problematic only when there is residual sugar. Even then, if the pH is low it will mind its malolactic business; otherwise it will go for the sugar and make a metabolic mess.

This is the paradox of the malolactic fermentation. The more acid a wine is, the harder it becomes for the process to take place, but—with bacteria toeing the malolactic line—the purer the MLF will be and the greater its impact on the taste. Red wine at its best—with low acidity—is vulnerable to bacterial attack.

When the pH starts to climb, as happens in the course of the MLF, other species may get into the act. The other two malolactic genera—*Lactobacillus* and *Pediococcus*—leave metabolic products in the wine that can be deleterious. *Pediococcus,* for instance, produces histamine and enormous amounts of diacetyl, a compound that gives butter its characteristic flavor and, in fact, is added to margarine for that reason. It is produced in smaller quantities by other bacteria, too, and up to two parts per million is usually considered an acceptable level. But if you find you'd rather spread your Chardonnay on toast than drink it, you can be sure that *Pediococcus* was there. "Dirty socks" is another trademark of this genus, while "earthy" and "dusty" wines are often the result of a visit by *Lactobacillus.*

Even more than the alcoholic fermentation, the MLF is a real whodunit. What you ultimately smell and taste in your glass will depend in part on which bacteria did it. Yogurt containers sometimes reveal the mystery, but wine labels never do.

Sorì San Lorenzo '89 started out with a pH so low (2.99) that it should have been very difficult to get the MLF going.

"But," says Guido, "yeasts also ferment some of the malic acid." By the time the alcoholic fermentation was over, about 30 percent had already disappeared and the pH was close to 3.20."

When yeast ferment malic acid, they don't replace it in part with lactic. As long as not too much is demolished, such a reduction is useful because it facilitates the malolactic fermentation. The capacity to ferment malic acid is another characteristic of *Saccharomyces cerevisiae* that varies greatly from strain to strain.

Guido has been checking the wine ever since the alcoholic fermentation ended. The intensity of the malic-acid spot on his "paintings" decreases regularly if the MLF is occurring. When it disappears, or stays at a constant low level, the process is over.

He examines his latest work of art. The acids he's looking for are in the second column. The second spot from the bottom line has disappeared, and the third is more intense than it was on the previous sheet. Mortal malic is dead; long live lactic!

But Guido is not letting his guard down yet.

"Just think of all those bacteria that are now out of work and starving! They're desperate. They may get out of hand and attack other substances in the wine."

He'll now rack the wine off to a colder place, where any bacteria not left behind will be unable to work anymore. With the sugar and malic acid now fermented, the time bomb has been defused. But it's only after his workers have gone into their end-of-season retirement that you'll finally hear Guido breathe a sigh of relief.

November 24, 1989

Sorì san lorenzo '89 is flowing out of the barrel and through a hose into one of the epoxy-lined steel tanks.

This is the second time Guido has racked the wine since the end of the alcoholic fermentation. On October 20 he drained it off the very coarse dregs—dead yeast cells, coloring matter, seeds—that still made up about 5 percent of its volume.

"Now that the wine is biologically stable," he says, "we have to work on its chemical stability."

He wants to make the salified tartaric acid (cream of tartar) precipitate by subjecting it to the cold. If it doesn't fall out in a large container in the cellar, it might do so in the bottle. The crystals are harmless, but many consumers are put off by them.

The wine is being racked into these tanks because they are much less insulating than not only the huge concrete vats, but also wooden barrels. When the wine was kept in barrels in the windowless cellar, it sometimes did not get cold enough for the tartrate to fall out.

Guido opens the windows wide so the temperature of the cellar will go down.

"People were really scandalized when we started doing this almost twenty years ago," he recalls. "They said the wine was still working, but we knew that the malolactic fermentation was over."

Nonviolence is as important as ever in this operation.

"The process should take place as slowly as possible. It should be barely as cold as necessary and no more. Between Christmas and the end of January, the temperature usually drops to a degree or two below freezing, and that's perfect. If it gets too cold, a lot of the stuff that contributes flavor and character will fall out, too. You wind up impoverishing the wine."

Generous Guido is as frugal as can be when it comes to the wealth of his wine.

February 19, 1990

$\mathcal{I}$T'S ON THE MOVE AGAIN," says Guido.

Sorì San Lorenzo '89 is now flowing out of the tank on the fermentation floor and into small casks on the lowest level of the cellar.

Once the tank is empty, Guido opens the small, porthole-like door.

"Look at this!" he exclaims.

A probing hand finds wine-stained crystals coating the sides with a layer about two-fifths of an inch thick, and the bottom with one much thicker.

"That's the tartrate," he says. "Stuff keeps falling out of the wine until it's bottled and we have to go behind it, cleaning up the mess."

Sometimes this midwife sounds like a housewife!

Three floors below, the wine is now ensconced in cozier containers.

February 1990–February 1991

*D*URING 1989, if you looked down from the rail at the end of the winery courtyard, you saw a typical construction site. To the left were a bright green crane, steel girders, and bags of cement. Stacks of lumber covered most of the remainder of the area. An observant eye might have noticed that the stacks to the right—the ones farthest from the crane—looked somewhat different from the others. The boards were smaller and uniform in length; their color varied from pale pink and cream to dull gray; they were stacked more methodically.

Now the construction site has vanished, but those stacks are still there. They are rough-hewn staves that will be used to make small casks similar to the *barriques* of Bordeaux and the *pièces* of Burgundy.

Such containers date back to ancient times, before Christ, when Alpine peoples of Celtic origin invented the craft of making barrels. By the third century A.D., when Gaul began to supply Rome with them, they had superseded the traditional, but fragile and unwieldy, earthenware amphora for the transportation of wine. We can even catch a glimpse of the transitional period on a relief in the Calvet Museum in Avignon, France, that shows slaves pulling a barge upstream on the Rhône River. On the barge are two casks, but above them on the relief is a row of amphorae.

Unlike stainless-steel tanks and scientists in lab coats, casks are an integral part of our collective wine imagery. An attentive visitor to Trajan's Column in Rome, for example, can spot a scene depicting a boat transporting three of them. A stained-glass depiction of a cooper in the process of making a cask graces the cathedral at Chartres, and the cathedral in Florence has a relief by Giotto and Andrea Pisano that portrays the drunken Noah lying next to one.

It is ironic that just as wood was ceasing to be the universal container of wine and was being steadily replaced by stainless steel for fermentation and storage and by bottles for shipping, awareness of its role in the making of fine wine was increasing rapidly among wine lovers all over the world. And, as with our awareness of grape varieties, California played a leading role in the process. In their effort to re-create the wines of Burgundy at the Hanzell Winery in Sonoma Valley, owner James D. Zellerbach and wine maker Bradford Webb ordered *pièces* from Yves Sirugue, a cooper in Nuits-St. Georges. Astonished by Hanzell's 1957 Chardonnay—a wine that tasted more like the real Burgundian McCoy than anything previously made in California—other producers followed suit.

For American consumers of fine wine it was love at first sip. They were wooed and won by wood in record time. Many Americans assumed that the flavor of oak was the flavor of Chardonnay or even Cabernet Sauvignon, and wine makers around the world began catering to that assumption. The status of the container began to rival that of the contents. The oaking of the world had begun.

"IF ALL YOU WANT is the taste of oak," Guido says, huffing as he checks a cask, "just toss some oak chips into your tank. You needn't bother with a *baric.*"

That's his Italianized spelling of *barrique.* Guido is at once indignant and amused.

"Look," he says, "these little casks are a lot more trouble to use than big ones. They're expensive and you lose a lot of wine through evaporation."

Imparting the flavor of new oak to wine is not the most important function of a small cask. But that's a consideration that tended to get lost in the Great *Baric* Controversy.

The wave of new wood struck Italy in the early eighties. More and more producers were seduced, and the orgy of oak was on. Some truly believed that a *baric* could confer nobility on common wine. But there were tricksters, too, for whom it was merely a Midas. If your wine is no good, just put it in new wood! It's really so poor they say it's a joke? Don't worry, my friend; enrich it with oak! What more could you ask of a cask than to mask mediocrity?

But the new wave of wood didn't win without a fight. Anti-*baric* barricades were erected overnight and denunciations were not long in coming. Defenders of the faith cursed the new oaken idol and railed against infidel "carpenter's wines." Troops were sent to man the trenches of Tradition. When the foe yelled "Oak 'em!" they replied with "Hokum!" and cries of "Ban the *baric!*"

Taste is far from timeless. In ancient times, it had been common to mix foreign substances with wine to cover up off-odors and flavors due to spoilage. Certain places even acquired a reputation for producing superior ones. In his *Natural History,* written in the first century A.D., Pliny the Elder observed that the best resin came from Cyprus and the finest pitch from Calabria. And, of course, vermouth itself, an Italian creation, is a flavored wine. But new wood was a new taste to Italians. Some of them rejected that taste in their wine as vehemently as the English had opposed the introduction of another "foreign" substance, hops, into their traditional ale. Hops was associated with the beer of Continental Europe, and in 1484 the city of London passed an ordinance forbidding its addition to ale. Not until the beginning of the eighteenth century was ale hopped as a matter of course and became pretty much the same thing as beer.

The adversaries of the *baric* were used to the *botte,* a big barrel (or cask—the terms are synonymous) such as the one in which Sorì San Lorenzo '89 went through its malolactic fermentation. When Guido started working at the winery, all wines were aged in *botti,* which were made with staves seven inches thick and held up to several thousand gallons of wine.

"They were used for decades," says Guido, "and repaired many times. They were hard to keep clean in the old days when there was no steam. The only qualities demanded of them were that they be neutral and not leak. They were used for the first few years with lesser wines so they wouldn't impart the taste of new wood to the more prestigious ones."

Barriques are made with staves that are less than half as thick and contain only about sixty gallons. "They have a technical justification," Guido says.

Where wine is concerned, the container—even if it's made of stainless steel—always influences its contents. It determines the wine's crucial relation with oxygen.

"And that relation should be very diplomatic," Guido says. "There are two roads a wine can take; one is reduction and the other is oxidation."

Before an embryonic expression of puzzlement can develop into a question, he nips it in the bud.

"In the absence of oxygen and in its presence," he explains. "You need to strike a balance between the two. At one extreme, reduction leads to the odor of tar for which Barbaresco and Barolo used to be famous; at the other, oxidation leads to the stale odor and taste of maderization. Whether there's too much oxygen or too little, the result is the same: astringent wine. Somewhere in between, you get a supple one. Slow oxidation is the key. With their thinner staves and higher surface-to-wine ratio, small casks dose oxygen perfectly. Our *botti* are almost like steel, which is one reason why Barbarescos in the past were not supple."

Guido pauses to take in some oxygen himself. The way he's speeding now, he needs a lot more of it than his wines do!

"Of course, you can't put just any old wine into a new *baric*. If it doesn't have a good structure and a lot of character, it'll be overwhelmed by oxygen and the taste of oak."

Although Guido doesn't worship at the altar of oak as such, as many of his colleagues do, he gladly officiates at the altar of the *baric*. That's where the marriage he has long dreamed of may finally be realized.

"A stable marriage between tannin and anthocyanins," goes his homily, "is the key to the stability of Nebbiolo's color. The *baric* strengthens their bond."

The *baric* is also ideal for the precipitation of coarse substances out of the wine. Unlike in a large container, the particles don't have far to fall.

Since the surface-to-wine ratio is much higher in a *baric* than in a large barrel, there is more extraction of aroma and flavor, as well as other substances from the wood.

"And," says Guido, "the newer a *baric* is, the more it gives. It releases about two-thirds of its extractables the first year of use, and one-fourth the second. After the third year, it has little left to give."

His face lights up.

"But a new *baric* is a whole bagful of scents and sensations!"

Sorì San Lorenzo '89 is going into casks that are 40 percent new and 60 percent one year old. He wants his wine to be "neither under- nor overwhelmed," and thinks that is a balanced mix for Nebbiolo.

When it comes to the Great *Baric* Controversy, which is still raging in Italy today, Guido is a passionate pragmatist in a crowd of ideologists.

"It's a sterile dichotomy," he says. "Evaluation must always be based on tasting and refer to particular wines. Wood can be one more form of violence to wine, but, like any seasoning, can enhance certain ones if it blends in harmoniously rather than grabbing all the attention itself."

New oak can K.O. your wine, but it's more than okay if the touch is right.

"It's like makeup and clothes," he says. "They can highlight beauty, but they can't create it if it isn't there to begin with."

Mostly, though, Guido is amused by the abstract character of the controversy.

"Hey, you know," he says, "some of us have actually been out there *doing* things and comparing this to that. When the controversy erupted in the early eighties, we'd already been experimenting for over ten years!"

TOWARD THE END of the sixties, Angelo was looking for a way to age his Barbaresco that would give it more finesse and preserve more of its fruit and color.

Strangely enough, Italians, like English-speakers, refer to "aging" wine. *Invecchiare,* they say. Most people want to grow *up,* but who wants to grow *old?* As is often the case—at least, when the topic is wine—the French know what they're talking about. *Élever,* they say. The French don't age their wines. They bring them up, as they do their children.

Angelo laughs.

"But perhaps *invecchiare* was the right term after all for most Barbarescos in the old days," he says. "They lost their color and fruit and dried out, but remained tannic and hard. They grew old without ever growing up to maturity."

Rereading his old textbook by Garoglio would not have helped Angelo in his quest, for the eminent enologist dedicates only one paragraph in 1,500 pages to the question of barrels, and the little he does have to say merely reflects the standard Italian practice of his day—Tradition. The best containers for aging fine wine are made of wood, the best wood is oak, and the best oak comes from Slovenia and Croatia in Yugoslavia. Barrels should be *botti* and should be old. French oak is mentioned only in connection with Cognac, and small, sixty-gallon casks only as containers destined for transportation.

The contrast with Ottavi, whose discussion is detailed and cosmopolitan, could hardly be more striking.

"It is not enough to have good grapes and know how to make wine," he writes. "You also need the right kind of barrel, the most important instrument in the cellar." Since Italians are always talking about the wines of Bordeaux as the ones that have enjoyed the greatest success on the international market, "let's at least learn how they are aged."

He notes that although the choice of staves may seem like a trifling matter, "it actually has the greatest importance." Italians use staves that are two and a half or three inches thick, or even more, "almost as if quality increased in proportion to thickness," whereas in Bordeaux about one inch is the norm. "The combination of sixty-gallon casks, thin staves, and new wood, which has not been encrusted with tartrates and other sedimentation, allows the slow oxidation of the wine through the pores of the wood."

Ottavi also discusses various kinds of wood that have been used for making barrels. The only acceptable ones are oak, wild chestnut, and acacia, of which oak is by far the best. "But not all oak is excellent," he warns. "The best is *Quercus pedunculata* when it grows in certain conditions of soil and climate."

Angelo had not read Ottavi, but he had been to Bordeaux as well as Burgundy. In 1969 he bought some used *barriques* from one of the greatest estates in the Médoc.

"They really ripped me off," he says. "The casks were supposed to be two years old. Fifteen would have been more like it. But I was pretty innocent in those days."

Thus began the Great *Baric* Adventure. When Guido arrived on the scene, Angelo was just shifting into high gear and refused to take anything for granted. They left no stave unturned. Casks made with all kinds of wood were ordered from both French and Italian coopers. Peach: "The wood really smelled of peach!" After all these years, Guido still seems amazed. Beech: "The wine tasted like sawdust." Angelo winces and gestures as if to spit. Cherry: "No comment!" they chant in chorus. Oak was the only one.

They hit upon the idea of using pressurized steam as a means of making the wood less aggressive and varied the length of the treatment to see what gave the best results. When Robert Mondavi heard what they were doing, he couldn't believe his ears. Those Italians were trying to get rid of some of the flavor that American consumers couldn't get enough of!

They were hoping to get rid of not only flavor, but of tannin as well. The thought of the tannins of a new *baric* taking the field along with Nebbiolo's struck terror in their hearts. Who wants to play against two teams of tannins? "One team at a time!" they said.

Angelo grins.

"When we steamed the casks, the water ran yellow. That was the gallic acid—the tannin—coming out."

Advice was sought from famous French coopers and wine makers. One day Jacques Puisais, *le pape des papilles*—the pope of the taste buds—as they call him in France, came to visit. Angelo and Guido were impressed. "He could enchant you for half an hour just talking about a glass of water," says Guido. But when asked specific questions about aging wine in small casks, Puisais would always give the same answer, imperturbably: "You have to ask the wine."

Guido's face lights up with amusement as he repeats the words. *"Il faut le demander au vin.* I thought he was putting me on. It took me quite a while to realize just how right he was."

Every wine was different, and Barbaresco was more different than others. Long experience was the only guide worth following.

"Ah, experience!" exclaims Angelo. "We bought wood that we'd been told was less tannic than others. We didn't like it at all. We simply didn't have the experience you need to taste young wine from a new cask."

There was no end of problems.

Some of the casks leaked. The wine rusted the iron hoops, which were not galvanized then as they are now.

"One day I was just going down into the cellar," Guido says, "when I heard an explosion. I rushed downstairs. Some hoops had burst and wine was pouring all over the cellar!"

He turns up his nose.

"Those casks were made out of sawn wood," he says enigmatically.

Then there were the bung plugs.

All the casks in the cellar are lying so that the bunghole is on the side—*"bonde à côté,"* says Guido, using the French term for the position. "A lot of wine evaporates as it ages in these casks, and if the bunghole were straight up, an air space would form right under it. Since the bung plugs never fit hermetically, that would allow too much oxygen to enter the wine."

He runs his finger around a bunghole.

"This is a tricky spot," he says. "It's a real breeding ground for bacteria."

Bacteria are always worrisome. Guido seems to have lost his train of thought, but it doesn't take him long to get back on track.

"We couldn't use *bonde à côté* the first year because we didn't have the proper plugs. It's a lot more work when the cask is *bonde dessus,* with the bunghole up. You have to keep filling it with wine from another container so that the air space isn't formed. I had some plugs made out of wood by a craftsman in a village near Cuneo. They were okay, but they didn't fit as tight as the silicone ones that we've been using for a while now."

Guido looks around. The casks have quite a history. Each one has the name of its maker stamped on it. As you wander down the rows, you notice that many of the names on the older ones are French. But on the newer casks, one name appears more frequently than any other, and it's Italian: Gamba.

"UNTIL ABOUT TEN YEARS AGO," says Angelo as he turns off the main road, "Gamba was just another cooper."

The name in Italy was Garbellotto, at Conegliano in the Veneto, who had built all the large barrels in the Gaja cellar. Burton Anderson wrote in *Vino* that the company's product had earned itself the accolade of "the Rolls-Royce of barrels." Yet by the late seventies, the move away from the traditional large barrel to stainless steel was already so apparent that Anderson could also write of "the Italian anti-barrel movement." Garbellotto, however, did not join the budding small cask movement.

"He had heard that French coopers were in crisis," says Angelo, "but he thought the stiffest competition would be coming from stainless steel and that wood would become too expensive. Garbellotto didn't foresee the great explosion of quality wines. The wines of his own region were mostly cheap ones for early drinking and certainly not candidates for aging in small casks. And since he stuck to his traditional supplier of staves, Slovenia, he fell behind as more and more producers demanded French oak."

Angelo pulls up in front of a building with stacks of staves on either side of the door.

"Gamba sensed which way the wind was blowing."

The "prize-winning Angelo Gamba barrel factory" is located in the nondescript town of Castell'Alfero, a few miles north of Asti. Eugenio Gamba comes to the door and accompanies Angelo inside.

Gamba is fortyish and sleepy-eyed, but it would be hard to doze in the din of his shop. He talks with pride about "the six generations of Gambas" who have run the cooperage. The business was indeed founded in 1809, but it was more than a century and a half later before it began to have anything more than strictly local fame. The turning point came in the mid-seventies.

"A fellow from Mâcon, in Burgundy, showed up one day," Gamba says. "He owned an enological supply company and had come to inquire about large barrels for some customers of his. The local coopers had little or no experience with them. He came back a couple of years later with three customers. They wanted to buy some barrels, but insisted that they be made out of French oak."

Until then, Gamba, like all his Italian colleagues, had always used Yugoslavian oak.

"At the time," he says, "I thought those French guys were just being nationalistic." He winks his eye. "You know how the French are."

Gamba went to France to find someone who would supply him with wood. One day, while he was visiting a company in Beaune that manufactures machinery for coopers, he met a well-known French colleague who agreed to sell him a shipment of staves.

"He really took me for a ride," Gamba says, tight-lipped. "It was all sawn stuff."

Gamba's amazement that an apparently intelligent human being—and an adult at that—doesn't know the difference between a split stave and one that is sawn borders on disbelief. He goes outside and comes back with two staves.

"Feel this sawn one," he says. It feels smooth as you rub your finger over it. "Now try this," he says, holding out a split one. It feels much rougher.

"But, looked at under a microscope," says Gamba, "the split surface looks smooth, while the sawn one is fuzzy. The fibers of the split wood are intact; the others aren't. That's what makes the difference and gives the split stave its superior mechanical strength."

Gamba pauses to let his words sink in. But there are secrets of split and sawn still to be revealed.

"Then there are the vascular rays, long chains of cells that grow radially from the heart of the oak to the bark. They're particularly large in oak and make the wood more elastic. In split wood, the rays run parallel to the width of the stave and form a barrier to the penetration of wine. When they are perpendicular, the wine may leak out through them."

Manifold are the mysteries of wood! There are distinctions to be made even when it's sawn.

"One way is to split the logs into four sections with a wedge and then to saw them radially, sparing the rays. The other way . . ."

Gamba turns up his nose. He looks as if he's about to gag on what he has to say.

"The other way is to saw the whole log straight across."

His contempt is total. For a cooper with a conscience, it's hard to sink lower than that.

The shipment of sawn staves made Gamba realize that dealing with the French was not going to be easy. But he was moving in the right direction. The first orders for small casks made of French oak were not long in coming, and from some of Piedmont's leading producers at that: Giacomo Bologna in 1979, and Pio Cesare in 1980. Giacomo Tachis, the creator of the Tuscan Tignanello and one of Italy's most eminent wine makers, asked him for casks made with oak from a particular district in central France.

Gamba was determined to find reliable sources of stavewood—what the French call *merrain*. From the late seventies on, he travelled more and more often to France. With what were at first his "four or five words of junior-high-school French," he went from village to village inquiring about *fendeurs*, wood splitters. His list of suppliers gradually lengthened. By 1983 he was making his first casks with "real split and properly seasoned wood." When the small cask trickle turned into a flood, he was ready.

"It's funny," Gamba says. "When I started using French oak, people thought it strange. I was considered a heretic. Now it's the new orthodoxy, and I'm making close to three thousand small casks a year."

"I remember Gamba coming around to us several times at the beginning of the eighties," Angelo says. "We ordered a few casks

[205]

from him, but they turned out to be less well made than we had hoped. We had to keep after him. Then, in 1986, we placed our first big order with him.''

Looking at a pile of rough-hewn staves on the floor of Gamba's workshop, it's hard to imagine them transformed into one of the refined objects that grace the Gaja cellar.

Gamba smiles.

''It's much easier to make a small cask than one of those big ones. The bigger they come, the harder we have to work.''

The staves are about a yard long. Gamba has them cut to a length of 91 centimeters, whereas a *barrique* from Bordeaux is 96 centimeters long and a Burgundian *pièce* is 88.

''That's the length Tachis wanted,'' he says, ''and I've stuck to it.''

Gamba's casks are thus a cross between the two classic models: more elongated than the *pièce,* but plumper in the middle than the *barrique.* Gamba runs his hand over a finished cask and winks his eye.

''That's Italian elegance for you,'' he says. ''It beats both of them.''

The sides of the staves are tapered at each end so they will fit together tightly when the cask is curved into its definitive shape. The staves are also hollowed out a bit on the sides that will form the inside of the cask and then be planed.

A worker starts to place staves upright inside an iron hoop attached to a frame. With quick and confident movements, he alternates wider and narrower ones until he has formed a circle containing twenty-eight of them.

''There might be one more or one less the next time,'' he says.

Then he slips three more ''working'' hoops over the assembled staves and rolls the cask-to-be into the main room of the workshop, where it is placed over a low fire. As the staves warm up slowly and evenly—too strong a flame would crack them—they become pliable.

The fire is fed with chips and splinters of oak.

''You can cut corners even here,'' Gamba says with a knowing look. ''There's at least one cooper in Burgundy who uses a gas flame to bend his staves.''

After a few more minutes, the process is continued over a

stronger flame, where two other men are working. Sweat streams down their faces as one of them puts a steel cable around the hoopless end of the cask. As the wood gets warmer, the other worker slowly cranks the cable tighter and tighter, pulling the staves ever closer together. When they are snug enough, four more working hoops are added and the cable is removed.

The cask has assumed its definitive shape, with the characteristic bulge called the bilge in the middle. The curvature sets as the wood cools off.

Heat not only makes the wood pliable; it also affects its chemical composition, and thus the flavors that it imparts to wine. The charring of the inside takes place over a third flame.

"Rare, medium, or well-done?" asks Gamba, ever ready to take your order. "If a customer wants a really heavy toast, we cover the cask for a few minutes." The degree of char is important. The taste of vanilla characteristic of much wine aged in new oak, for example, reaches its maximum intensity between a medium and a heavy char and then decreases.

"It's better if a cask gets at least a medium toast," Gamba says. "If the toast is too light, you run the risk of having it crack at the bunghole in cellars that are humid or subject to big jumps in temperature."

The casks are rolled off to another sector of the workshop, where the working hoops are removed and replaced by the permanent ones, made of galvanized iron. Each cask head, which is made out of seven pieces of wood held together by headless nails and has been sawed on a lathing machine into a circular shape, is inserted into the groove, or croze, cut out of either end of the cask. Rush is stuffed into the croze to make the fit airtight, a condition definitively ensured by a machine applying four hundred atmospheres of pressure. The cask is lathed with sandpaper and the final operation is performed by another hydraulic machine, which pushes the hoops into their final position.

"I don't know how coopers of old managed without these machines," Gamba remarks, "unless they were a helluva lot stronger than I am!"

The transformation of a pile of wood into a cask is now complete. Gamba is beaming as the audience voices its admiration.

"We're just workers doing our job," he says. "Not wonder-workers. The quality of these casks ultimately depends on the quality of the *merrain.*"

THE DARK BLUE BMW with the CN license plates enters the tunnel under Mont Blanc, Europe's highest mountain.

"When it comes to wood," says Angelo, "we producers really have very little firsthand knowledge."

The tunnel may have obliged Angelo to put on the brakes, but the accelerator in his mind is down to the floor.

"How can we do meaningful experiments and draw valid conclusions from experience if we aren't certain of the wood's origin and seasoning?"

Angelo's conclusion after twenty years is that, of all the myriad factors affecting the quality of a cask, seasoning is the most important. Among other things, wood must lose its moisture and certain impurities before entering the charmed circle of a cooper's hoop. A stave can spend this phase of its pre-cask career outdoors, exposed to the elements, or indoors, in a kiln.

"Don't talk to me about kilns!" Gamba says with a snort. "I've had kiln-dried staves that split when we tried to bend them. Even at best they'll have microscopic cracks where bacteria and molds thrive. When wood has been seasoned naturally, it contracts evenly and won't warp."

"There's a lot more to seasoning than just drying!" exclaims Angelo. "Sure, a kiln extracts the water from the wood, but it also inhibits all the natural processes that contribute to its biochemical evolution. When wood seasons naturally, it loses its bitter, harsh, and grassy character. A kiln means the end of the enzymes that sweeten the wood and make it aromatic. Drying wood in a kiln is like pasteurizing wine. It won't mature."

Drying wood in a kiln is much quicker than letting it season outdoors. Kiln-dried staves cost less.

"Yeah," says Angelo. "But there's the temptation to cut corners even when you season the wood naturally. After all, it ties up a lot of capital for several years if you do it properly."

That's why those stacks of staves are back there in Barbaresco.

Angelo is convinced that it's the only way to be sure the job is done properly. Now he's on his way with Gamba to visit *fendeurs* in central France.

"Most experts say that a stave seasons at the rate of about one centimeter a year," he says. "That would mean three years or so. But we'll have to experiment with that, too."

On the way, Gamba stops briefly to greet a cooper in Burgundy. While waiting to see him, he inspects a stack of staves.

"Look at this," he whispers. "Most of this stuff is sawn, with a little split wood on top."

ALL OF A SUDDEN it's almost dark. Angelo turns on his parking lights.

It's the middle of the afternoon, but the trees on either side of the narrow road are so tall and close to one another that very little light gets through. When the car comes out of the tunnel of trees, you can't see the ground anymore, so dense is the growth of saplings.

For wine lovers, Tronçais is the fairest forest in all of oakdom, and one of the most evocative names not referring to a place where wine itself is made. It's a unique sylvan *cru*. All other *merrain* is described in much broader geographical terms: administrative districts (*départements*) like Allier or former provinces like Limousin. There are other excellent oak forests in the Allier, such as Gros Bois, but none inspires the reverence that often accompanies the mention of Tronçais.

"I bet that if all the wood sold under the name of Tronçais actually came from here," says Angelo, "the whole forest would have been chopped down long ago."

Gamba nods in agreement.

"It would be more accurate," he says, "to talk about oak that's similar to Tronçais."

The Tronçais forest owes its fame to Jean-Baptiste Colbert, controller general of France under Louis XIV. Woodlands had been one of the most corruptly administered sectors of the royal domain, and by 1670 the indiscriminate felling of trees and the pasturing of animals had devastated three-fourths of Tronçais. Colbert wanted to ensure an adequate supply of timber for the naval construction essential to the country's commercial ambitions, so he undertook extensive replanting and intensified vigilance. In the present-day forest there is a stand of oaks more than three hundred years old that bears his name. Similar considerations of shipbuilding and naval power more than half a century earlier had led King James I of England to forbid the burning of wood for the manufacture of glass, a measure that led to the birth of the modern wine bottle. Coal began to be used to fuel the furnaces, and the result was stronger glass that could be plugged tightly with a cork and transported without breaking. The ways of the Lord may or may not be infinite, but it is certain that they have not neglected the aging of fine wine.

"Forests such as Tronçais are managed with the aim of producing the tallest and straightest oaks possible," says Gamba, "with no branches and thus no knots in the wood."

The principle informing such severe sylviculture is that of natural selection. After ten years or so, the seed plots issuing from the acorns of old seeder oaks become impenetrable thickets. Such extreme density forces the young oaks to grow tall and straight in order to ensure themselves a place in the sun. The weaker plants die off or are cut down as the plot is progressively thinned out. At one hundred years of age, most of the oaks that are still standing have reached their maximum height of about one hundred feet and a diameter of about one foot. A two-hundred-year-old *haute futaie*—a stand of very tall trees—has only forty to sixty trees per acre left.

"The few remaining Italian oak forests are far too sparse to produce the kind of timber you get here," says Gamba. "The trees grow outward instead of upward, which means a lot of branches and knotty wood."

Gamba is always on the lookout for new suppliers.

"*Fendeurs* are an endangered species," he says. "They're threatened with extinction. Take Bourdier over at Lurcy-Lévis, just a few miles northeast of here. When I discovered him ten years ago, he had a number of *fendeurs*. He was an artisan. Now he's got 32 workers, all the latest high-tech machinery, and sells mainly to contractors and furniture manufacturers. He has only one splitter left, and the poor guy works all alone in a little shed. That's how it is all over."

Angelo stops to get a map from a tourist information center. Gamba asks the lady at the desk if there are any *fendeurs* in the vicinity, and his face lights up when she mentions an unfamiliar name.

"He's at Vitray," she says, "a hamlet on the edge of the forest about three miles down the road."

THE RUDDINESS of Monsieur Daffy's face is set off by the utter whiteness of his moustache and his closely cropped hair. Surrounded by piles of logs and neatly stacked staves, he is splitting away in a little clearing across the dirt road from his house and workshed. The air is spicy-sweet with the smell of freshly hewn oak.

Deliberate and dignified, Daffy's speech is as trim as his body. A third-generation splitter, he has been plying his craft for more than forty years.

"Ever since I was thirteen," he says.

Referring to it as *grume*, he stands on end a log that is just over three feet long. With precise movements, he splits it first into quarters with a wedge and maul, then into rough-hewn staves with an axe and a wooden mallet.

"Over in my shed I'll remove the core and bark," he says. "And also this wood here, next to the bark. That's the sapwood. It's okay for floors, but for staves we use only the heartwood."

Daffy confirms Angelo's suspicions about much of the wood sold as Tronçais.

"An older *fendeur* from around here, like my father, would never split wood that didn't come from within a few miles of Tronçais. Nowadays we get it from all over the center of the country. The fact is, there's less and less good wood for *merrain*. Just ten years ago, I could make a cubic meter of staves from three of *grume;* now I often need six or even seven."

Working eight hours a day, he can make about one hundred fifty staves.

"And in those days," he adds, "a *fendeur* would use only the choicest part of the trunk. It would all be real *merrain.*" He shakes his head slowly. "Now many use the whole thing."

Angelo is itching to learn.

"Where does the best wood come from?" he asks.

"Well, Tronçais and Grand Bois here in the Allier," Daffy replies. "St. Palais up in the Cher, and Bertrages in the Nièvre. Watch out for forests where there's a lot of pine. The oak's never first-rate there."

"How about seasoning? How long?"

"A stave needs three years at least. Three to four is the optimum."

Gamba has been sniffing splinters of wood and chewing on them as if he were appraising fine cigars.

"Hey, taste, this!" he exclaims. "It's really sweet."

He's all excited now and ready to make his move. Monsieur Daffy wouldn't have any staves to sell him, would he?

Daffy smiles. No, he wouldn't. He has an exclusive agreement with a large cooperage firm in Bordeaux.

ANGELO HEADS NORTH and into the Cher. Not far out of Bourges, a lover of the wines of the Loire would note that national highway 140 passes along the western fringe of the Menetou-Salon appellation, with the vineyards of Quincy and Reuilly off to the left. This part of the Loire is Sauvignon country. Signs point the way to Sancerre, on the river just twenty miles to the east, and to more distant Saumur. There's no Sauvignon in Saumur, but it's the town of old man Grandet, the father of the eponymous heroine of Balzac's novel *Eugénie Grandet* and the most famous *merrain* dealer and cooper in literature.

In the village of Méry-ès-Bois, near the forest of St. Palais, Gamba guides Angelo through a labyrinth of lumber. Here and there whole trunks lie awaiting their turn. Angelo pulls up in front of a large shed.

"There he is!" Gamba exclaims. "The professor of oak himself!"

With his authoritarian, but roguish air, brisk gestures, and index finger always at the ready, Camille Gauthier wastes no time in getting the lesson going. He has a worker bring out five staves.

"Lift these up," he says, "and tell me which one is the heaviest."

Stocky, graying, and mustached, the professor beams at the answer.

"Yes, indeed!" he roars triumphantly. "That's Limousin, a *gros grain.*"

Limousin is coarse-grained because it grows rapidly. It comes from the region of that name to the southwest of the Cher, where the soil is rich and the forests are mainly *Quercus pedunculata,* one of the more than four hundred species of oak. *Quercus* is Latin for "oak," while *pedunculata* means that the acorns are attached to the branch by stems.

Angelo notes in a whisper that the varietal virus hasn't made any headway as far as cask wood is concerned. It is discussed in geographical rather than botanical terms.

The professor calls the class to order.

"Which one is the lightest?" he asks.

The class hesitates this time, but finally chooses one of two very similar ones.

"Right again!" The professor applauds. "That's Tronçais, a *grain fin.*"

Tronçais is fine-grained. It grows slowly in poor soil and is mainly *Quercus sessilis,* another European species. Its acorns are attached directly to the branch.

"You were hesitant because that other stave is from St. Palais, the forest just over there."

The index finger passes from the vertical to the horizontal in order to point the way.

"It's a *grain fin,* too, and very similar to Tronçais."

Both have a pinkish tinge and are much lighter in color than the Limousin. The other two staves are *mi-fin,* semifine.

Gauthier's accent betrays a more southerly origin. His father was the head cooper at a large Cognac firm, so he grew up near the Limousin forests.

"To get *grain fin,* you need really tall trees so the trunks will be thick enough—at least twenty inches in diameter. Trees from St. Palais have to be at least one hundred fifty years old for *merrain.* A lot of the trees that are being cut there now were planted in the first

[213]

quarter of the nineteenth century! Limousin grows so much faster it can be cut when it's eighty."

The students are swept along by the professor's escalating enthusiasm.

"Look at these two," he says. "The Tronçais grain is so fine you can hardly make out the annual growth rings. With the Limousin, there's no problem."

Gauthier lifts his finger slightly higher.

"Now," he exhorts the class, "look really closely at the Tronçais! The annual rings are finer near the pith because when the tree was young it was shaded by other trees. But then the rings get ever so slightly broader. That's because surrounding trees were gradually cut down and the tree received more sunlight."

The professor observes the class with a severe but paternal look.

"You do know that in a serious forest only the fittest survive, don't you?" he inquires.

He pauses to catch his breath before the final didactic sprint.

"When the tree grows slower, it produces more spring wood and less summer wood. That means more phenol compounds to extract. And the growth varies from year to year, just like grapes and all other plants."

His tone becomes dramatic.

"The history of the climate is written into the wood! And not only in its appearance, but also in its scent. Notice how the wood near the sapwood is much less scented than the wood near the pith."

Gauthier is about to rush on, but he suddenly catches himself. Even though there are no women or children in sight, one never knows! He lowers his voice.

"When a trunk is sawed, they sometimes saw the whole thing straight across and then you get staves made solely of the wood right next to the sapwood."

The professor pauses. Gamba acknowledges his observation with an appropriately scandalized expression.

"That's *dosse*," Gauthier says, uttering the word as a dealer in diamonds might mention costume jewelry from the five-and-dime.

The class is speechless and openmouthed with awe.

"Ah, oak!" exclaims the professor abruptly as he walks into his workshop. "There's no end to learning about it. You can have two trees growing side by side and the quality will be quite different."

He nods toward a bearded young man seated at a desk in the office.

"Ask that gentleman," he says. "He knows all about it."

The gentleman is from a research institute in Burgundy and is studying the effect on wine of such variables as the height on the tree at which wood grows and the direction it faces.

"See those staves over there?" he asks, pointing to a number of small stacks that have been tied and coded on tags. "I've followed every phase from the felling of the trees on. Now I'm going to take them back with me, have them made into casks, and then age the same wine in them. We'll taste periodically and note the differences. It's a twenty-year project."

The researcher gives the class a little tutoring to finish off after the lecture.

"Over sixty substances have been identified that are released into wine by wood," he says. "Now it's even possible to distinguish a stave's geographical origin by chemical analysis. Take eugenol, for example, an aromatic substance found in unheated wood. There's a lot more of it in Allier than in Limousin."

With its rapid-fire information, the tutorial dizzies almost as much as the lecture did. Even the geography is hard to follow.

"The wood from around here and from the Allier is very rich in another aromatic compound, an ester called lactone. That's why it's so spicy."

"Limousin?" asks a student.

"Almost no lactones, but a lot of tannin, which is extracted by the wine in a relatively short time."

"Vosges?" The Vosges is a mountainous region in eastern France.

"Very fine grain. Less aromatic than Allier."

"Burgundy?"

"Kind of intermediate between Allier and Limousin. Neither very aromatic nor very tannic."

[215]

Heads are already spinning, but Gauthier sticks *his* head in the office before anyone has actually fainted. He's ready to show Angelo around.

They go over to the hydraulic axe that Gauthier uses to do the splitting.

"The effect is exactly the same as when its done by hand," he says. "The machine just provides the brawn. And it's precise. I get a cubic meter of staves from five of *grume.*"

Outside his tone becomes more confidential.

"There were some Australians here yesterday looking for staves," he says gravely.

A couple of weeks earlier, an American—a wine producer from California—had stopped by.

"And you know what he wanted?"

Gauthier stops. Incredulity creeps over his face.

"*Grume!*" he exclaims. Logs. Those Americans not only want to make their own casks, but want to split the wood themselves!

Gauthier recovers in time to give his final demonstration, pointing out the features of a stack of staves in the yard. There are alternate layers of three and five of them, with the heart toward the center. Airing is vital. The positions are changed periodically so the seasoning will take place evenly.

"You have to *élever* wood," he says, "just as you have to *élever* wine."

The ground around the stack is black.

"That's all the impurities that have come out of the wood," he cackles. "Better here on the ground than in the wine!"

"When do you cut down the trees?" asks a student.

"Between October and February."

"Do you own the trees, or do you buy them?"

"They're sold by the O.N.F., the National Forest Bureau, at auctions they hold every year in the various departments. The one for the Cher will be held this year in Bourges, on October 12."

THE EVENING before the auction, there's excitement in the air at Gauthier's home, just across the road from his workshop.

Gamba asks him what time the auction begins.

[216]

"At five o'clock."

"In the morning?" Gamba is astounded.

"Yes, sir!" Gauthier replies, deadpan. "Here in France, you know, we work!"

He winks.

"But since they heard that an Italian is going to be there tomorrow, they've decided to start at nine."

Gauthier confesses that he'll have butterflies in his stomach. The auctions determine his supply of wood for the year.

No one but the director knows what the starting prices will be, but Gauthier estimates on the basis of auctions already held in other *départements* that they may be up by as much as twenty percent. He attended the one for the Indre last week at Châteauroux.

"There were about four hundred people there," he says. "Lots of wood. Some pretty good stuff."

Next week, the Allier auction will be held at Cérilly.

"But there's very little Tronçais," he emphasizes. "Very little."

On the coffee table is a booklet put out by the National Forest Bureau describing the lots that will be auctioned in Bourges. It's covered with what look like hieroglyphics.

"We've worked hard on this," Gauthier says.

He and his wife have been going around for weeks, sizing up quality and quantity. They take measurements and even bore holes to get a look at the color.

He picks up the booklet and leafs through it.

"That's not bad," he comments. "That's not bad either, but this lot isn't worth much at all." All of a sudden his face radiates satisfaction. "Ah!" he sighs. "Now, *that's* some really nice wood!"

Gamba is restless. He's anxious to talk about the truckload of staves that Gauthier has promised him.

"I can't get enough wood of the quality I want," Gamba complains.

Madame Gauthier comes in from the kitchen with glasses of sparkling wine on a tray. A quick and forthright woman, she tells him that the French do not like to sell *merrain* to Italians.

"Casks," she says, "sure, that's okay. But not staves."

Gauthier explains that it's not just a question of nationalism.

"It's only natural that we're reluctant to give our best stuff to

[217]

anyone but French coopers. Longstanding friendships and business relationships are often involved."

Gamba raises his glass.

"Here's to good luck at the auction!"

He takes a sip.

"Not bad at all," he says with a grin.

Gauthier is silent, but his twinkling eyes speak for him.

"Of course!" they say. "It's French!"

GAMBA IS OFF TO BOURGES in the early-morning chill. Signs are barely legible through the fog. Picked-over and blackened sunflowers in fields along the highway stand row after row like a spectral army, weary and defeated.

Gauthier is already at the modern Agri-Cher building on the outskirts of Bourges and has managed to get a seat at the front of the hall, which by now is almost full. He keeps looking around nervously to see who's there. Gamba takes a seat farther back, on the opposite side.

On the platform are fourteen officials, half of whom are in uniform. Each of them has a look that seems to appropriate the famous words pronounced by Louis XIV in the seventeenth century: *"L'état, c'est moi!"* *"I* am the state!" They lean over to whisper to one another now and then, but the atmosphere is solemn: the pomp and provincial circumstance that only the French can produce.

The auction starts at nine o'clock sharp. One official announces the lots; another auctions them. The auctioneer starts at a given price, handed to him on a slip of paper by the director, then keeps lowering it until someone yells, *"Prends!"* "I'll take it!" There is no time to hesitate; he moves from one figure to another in less than a second.

Some bidders squeak their *"Prends!"* while others roar. A man sitting in front of Gamba says *"Prends!"* every other lot a split-second too late. Someone protests that he shouted before the person who got the lot. The officials confer rapidly. "Objection overruled," announces the auctioneer, smiling politely. There are wisecracks and snickers after a bidder screeches a piercing

"Prends!" only to realize that he was bidding for the wrong lot. Giggles and gasps erupt when another lot goes immediately for the opening price of over a million francs.

"That's Chaussière again," whispers a man to the woman sitting next to him.

"Who else?" she replies.

Gamba cranes his neck to get a glimpse of Gauthier. He's beginning to wonder when he's going to make his move.

The thirty-eighth lot starts at 410,000 francs. Just as the auctioneer says the "three" of 360,000 francs, Gauthier leaps to his feet. *"Prends!"* he shouts, red in the face.

At forty minutes past ten the auctioneer announces, "Ladies and gentlemen, the sale is over."

Gauthier has bought three lots in all.

"It could have gone worse," he says, patting his face with a handkerchief. "I lost out on a couple of things, but I got some good stuff at a good price. One of the lots is a real beauty."

"Who's that Chaussière?" Gamba asks.

"Ah, Chaussière!" Gauthier grits his teeth and rolls his eyeballs. "He's a big furniture manufacturer from St. Armand. He got all the best wood. Nobody can compete with him."

"Does he sell *merrain?*" Gamba ventures hopefully.

"Are you kidding? He's got customers in Switzerland, a warehouse in Paris, and lots of . . ." Gauthier rubs his thumb and forefinger together: "money."

How could anyone like that be bothered with mere *merrain?*

"I was hoping my brother would grab one of those St. Palais lots," says Gauthier, "but he was waiting for them to give it away." He snickers. "They don't give away anything here."

Madame Gauthier comes over to greet Gamba.

"It was really calm here today," she says. "Sometimes people get all worked up and things get pretty hot."

"That's because the treasury officials were on strike," says Gauthier. "The substitutes aren't so experienced, so they decided to take it easy. Usually it's really rapid-fire."

Leaving the hall, Gamba runs into a small splitter from the Allier who is dejection itself.

"Everything was so expensive," he says with a sigh. "I only

bought one lot. There's less and less wood for staves. The furniture guys just grab it all up."

"You'll do better at Cérilly next week," Gamba says, trying to cheer him up.

FRENCH OAK gets all the headlines in the wine press. Many producers wouldn't be caught with any other kind in their cellar, but that was not always the case, not even in France itself.

"The taste of cask spoils wine," a French publication for the cooperage trade opined in 1875. "Oak from Canada, the United States, and northern Europe releases the fewest foreign elements into wine. This is the kind most suitable for making casks destined to contain fine and delicate wines. Staves made of native oak are suitable only for common wines."

Oak from northern Europe had long been used in Bordeaux. By the early seventeenth century, Hamburg had become Bordeaux's largest market there, and the ships that transported wine to the city returned with staves from forests in east Prussia, Poland, and Pomerania.

Baltic oak is fine-grained and probably gave a less obvious flavor to wine than oak from the forests of Limousin, the closest to Bordeaux. It continued to be used to age the wines of Bordeaux until the First World War.

The American oak that the publication mentioned is *Quercus alba*—white oak. It is less rich in phenolic compounds—tannin and coloring matter—than European oak, but contains more vanillin and related aromatic compounds. Even though it is cheaper than French oak, many producers shy away from it because of the pronounced scent and flavor it imparts to the wine. But perhaps the fact that names like Arkansas, Illinois, and Missouri sound somewhat less glamorous than Allier and other French names also has something to do with that shyness!

"The oak of Croatia and Slovenia has excellent potential," says Gamba, "but the quality has declined sharply in the last ten or fifteen years. They don't exploit their forests rationally. They don't regenerate them systematically, so now the trees are too young and too small. I've had a lot of staves with knots in them that have cracked when we tried to bend them. And, of course, they don't split wood at all. Sawn is all you get."

Though its forests were decimated long ago, Italy itself was still producing a small amount of stave wood until fairly recently. Ottavi, for example, mentions the forest of the Montello plateau, just twenty-five miles north of Venice, as producing oak "comparable to the finest from Slovenia." And there is oral testimony in the Langhe to the world of wood that was. Luciano Sandrone, one of the leading producers of Barolo, remembers older growers telling him about a local wood, *galera,* from which barrels used to be made. *Galera* turns out to be a regional term for *Quercus pedunculata.*

And what of the *barrique*-type cask? Was there ever a tradition of it in Italy before the Tradition of the *botte?* The evidence is scanty, but intriguing.

An example of what might happen if one were to investigate the matter seriously is provided by Giovanni Capelli of the Montagliari estate in Chianti. A few years ago he discovered some family papers dating from the late eighteenth century and learned of a wine his family had made from 1790 until 1917, when phylloxera destroyed their vineyard and they had to replant it. Unlike present day Chianti, which, even after a recent revision of the regulations, still has to be a mixture of grapes in order to be officially approved, it was made of pure Sangiovese and was aged in 200-liter casks called *caratelli.* A true believer in Tradition until his discovery, Capelli quickly converted and is now a staunch defender of the faith of his forebears.

But perhaps even more intriguing is the old saying that "a small cask makes good wine." It must be based on widespread practical experience. The peasants of the past may have been hidebound and tied to Tradition, but theory was not their thing!

Valerio Grasso stands by a *baric,* adjusting the SO_2 dispenser.
Sorì San Lorenzo '89 is being racked.
The SO_2 is needed to protect the wine from excessive oxygen. Guido has checked the level of free SO_2—the fraction that has not

already combined with other elements—and decided the amount to add accordingly. He surveys the scene to make sure everything is proceeding properly.

"Racking doesn't seem like much," he says, "but it's essential. The airing dispels any off-odors the wine might pick up from its sediment. It also disperses carbon dioxide, which would accentuate the perception of tannin and acidity if it remained in the wine. And finally, if racking is done very gently, the oxidation of the tannin is also beneficial. It helps along the process of polymerization. Overreductive wine making—keeping the wine from any contact with oxygen—produces harsh and stinky wines."

As always, the kind of oxidation is crucial. If it's violent, it can be the wine's downfall.

"Especially Nebbiolo's," says Guido. "Because of those unstable anthocyanins, racking is actually detrimental to its color. You can rack Cabernet, for instance, more often."

The wine flows from the *baric* into a big vat, which is a little lower than the level of the floor. A young worker is holding the hose just above the level of the wine already in the vat and keeps raising it gradually as the level rises.

"The vat is lower than the floor so the pump doesn't have to work too much and splash the wine around," says Guido. "It's almost the same as doing it by gravity."

Violence is always lurking somewhere in the cellar, ready to strike. A pump can pummel wine. Kid gloves are needed—not those of a bruising boxer.

"And the worker keeps the hose just above the level of the wine in the vat so the wine coming out of the hose has only a gentle and brief encounter with oxygen."

Angelo has come down to confer with Guido and observes the operation.

"That's right," he says. "The main thing is to avoid the splashing. I remember how, when the wine used to be racked, it splashed around twice. It fell a long way from the barrel into the container where the hose was, and then a long way again once it got to the barrel into which it was being racked."

He has a mischievous smile on his lips.

"Some clients used to complain that, after I had taken over, the

[222]

cellar no longer smelled the same. Sure, my father's cellar smelled wonderful because of all that splashing, but the bouquet vanished into the air."

Angelo makes a "gone with the wind" gesture.

"It was the cellar workers who enjoyed the bouquet, not whoever bought the bottle!"

Grasso is now busy at work filling clean casks with nitrogen. As the wine flows back into them, the nitrogen will be forced out after having served its purpose of protecting it from oxygen.

Fiftyish and with graying hair, Grasso has worked in wineries for twenty-five years and has been here for eight.

"This job takes patience," he says. "Small casks are a lot of work. You need about a minute and a half to empty each *baric* when you rack. Then you have to clean them, dry them, and line them up. And we always disinfect after we remove a row."

He chuckles.

"The place where I worked before was totally different. It was a real processing plant. We handled seven or eight truckloads of wine a day, and it got sloshed around all over the place."

"It takes ten years to train someone really well here in the cellar," Guido says. "We need a man or two down here just to take care of these casks. It takes someone with the mentality of an artisan, not an industrial worker."

WHAT COULD GUIDO be up to now? Standing in a stream of black water with knee-length boots on, he's dousing the stacks of staves with a hose. Yet there's no smoke in sight; there's no fire to fight! Why is a wine maker watering wood?

"This is the third dry winter in a row," he says. "The wood won't season properly if we don't wet it."

He looks down at the murky flow.

"If water has that effect in such a short time, just think what the extractive power of the alcohol in wine would do over a period of months."

Angelo's conviction that seasoning is the most important factor in the quality of a stave is making more and more sense all the time. Of course, the spectacle on the ground is due mainly to the most

[223]

recent loads. The oldest staves have been here for more than three years now, and will be ready to use for this year's vintage. Sorì San Lorenzo '91 will make its appearance in society clothed in custom-tailored oak.

"But the clothes will be discreet," Guido assures.

He's excited about experimenting with his home-seasoned wood.

"Before we use the casks," he says, "we'll treat them in four different ways, including doing nothing at all. Steaming removes some components that we think are negative, but it also undoubtedly removes something positive, too."

There are other plans as well.

"We'll experiment with the malolactic fermentation in *baric*. Now that we have wood we know is properly seasoned, we won't be so worried about it inhibiting the bacteria."

Guido goes inside the cellar. He gets a glass and fills it from a cask.

"Taste this," he says.

The deep-colored wine is spicy and full. It's almost velvety in a youthful way. You could practically drink it now.

He pours out the rest of the wine and fills the glass from another *baric*. This wine is very different. There's more fruit on the nose, but it lacks the richness of the first one. It's angular and rough.

The straight face that Guido has kept until now melts into amusement.

"They're both San Lorenzo '89," he says. "But the first glass was drawn from a new cask, and the second from one that's a year old."

One recalls his words on the evening before the grapes of this wine—or these wines—were harvested.

"Take the same wine," he said, "put it in two different containers, and—presto!—you have two different wines." Little did one know!

"The wine that's been in new wood," Guido explains, "is softer because there's been more exchange between it and oxygen. As the cask is used, the pores get clogged and there's less exchange. It has more body because there are more substances called polysaccharides to be extracted from the cellulose of new wood. They contribute to what we call the 'fat' of the wine."

He pauses as he thinks of what to taste next.

"Ah!" he says, as if suddenly struck by an idea.

He walks over to a cask on the other side of the cellar and draws off some wine into the glass.

"Well?" he asks.

The wine is much denser than the others, but coarse and very astringent. It leaves your mouth coated and puckering.

Guido grins at the grimace.

"You're tasting some of the stuff we *didn't* extract during the fermentation. That's the press wine."

Now you really understand why the red alarm goes on in the fall when grapes for making Barbaresco approach the winery. You don't want that stuff to bomb your wine! In some wine-producing areas—even the most prestigious ones—some press wine is often added to the wine to give it body. Guido never uses any of the press wine, but he has kept a cask just to see how it evolves.

"A wine like San Lorenzo, or even the regular Barbaresco, would only lose some of its finesse without gaining anything from it," he says.

Aging is a phase of wine making in which there is still a lot to be learned.

"It's mostly trial and error," Guido says. "There's a great mass of data, but going from there to actual practice is problematic, to say the least. You just have to taste and taste again as the wine develops, comparing and drawing conclusions as best you can about the variables. And a few things seem clear, at least about the wood. The fine-grain seems best because it releases its components more slowly and makes for wine with more finesse."

So Allier *is* better than Limousin.

"From what I've seen so far, that would seem to be the case—at least for our wines," he says. "But you can't compare a great château like Mouton-Rothschild to a wine from a minor village like Santenay and think you're comparing Bordeaux and Burgundy. Limousin from a certain spot, growing in very favorable conditions, might resemble Allier from a less favorable plot of land. Limousin seasoned for three years would undoubtedly be superior to Allier seasoned only six months."

[225]

Where staves are concerned, it seems, you're never quite out of the woods.

"And at least from a practical point of view, a lot of the talk about differences among particular forests should be taken with a grain of salt," he says. "What guarantee do I have that the wood actually comes from a given spot?"

Guido chuckles.

"To be absolutely sure of what I'm getting, I'd have to cut down the tree and bring it back to Barbaresco myself!"

February 23, 1991

S ORÌ SAN LORENZO '89 bids the *baric* farewell and moves into a *botte* with a capacity of 6,800 liters.

"Just imagine," Guido says, "what this barrel was like when it was new, over twenty years ago. The staves certainly hadn't been seasoned long enough—that would have taken at least seven years!—so there were a lot of coarse tannins and bitter components in the wood. They were bent with steam, which did not provide enough heat to cause the chemical reactions brought about by fire."

One wonders why the wine was not put first into the *botte* and then into the *baric*.

"The newer wood and the greater surface-to-wine ratio mean that the *baric* has a much more aggressive effect on the wine. The density of young wine, with all the fine particles that are still in it, constitutes a kind of buffer that reduces the effect. In fact, when we ferment in a *baric,* as we do with some of the white wine, we don't even treat it with steam. The yeast cells and other dregs buffer the effect of the *baric* even more."

The last of the casks containing Sorì San Lorenzo '89 is being readied for racking.

"The *baric* shakes the wine down first, and then the *botte* smooths off the rough edges," Guido says. "The slow oxidation in the *baric* gets the wine used to oxygen. If wine is always kept in impermeable containers, any contact with oxygen is such a great shock that it gets violently oxidized when it's racked or bottled. But it also has to get used to the reductive state—to the absence of oxygen—that it will find once it's bottled."

May 4, 1992

Guido and I always sit down and taste together before bottling," Angelo says. "We bottle San Lorenzo in the spring of the third year after the harvest, around this time. It'll rest in the cellar until the middle of September, when we'll start shipping it."

Angelo is sitting in the new tasting room on the ground floor of the renovated building that houses the winery office.

Sorì San Lorenzo 1989 is sitting on the table in a bottle filled by hand from the barrel. Guido comes in and pours.

After looking at the color, they sniff, sip, and slosh the wine around in their mouths. Angelo's face does a series of dissolves as expressions fade out and others fade in. Guido closes his eyes. Could he be praying? In moments of despair he has been heard to murmur, "And deliver us from tannin." At a time like this, tannin can even seem evil. The seconds of silence seem endless.

Angelo glances at Guido and receives the same wordless message that he's just sent. He spits out the wine.

"This is going to be something special," he says, "but it would be a shame to bottle it now. The wine isn't ready."

Guido nods in agreement. As they discuss the wine, Angelo

proves to be quite a poet in his own right: a taster-poet, of course, not a poetaster!

He shifts back and forth between metaphor and simile. The wine now *is* and then *is like:*

"A boulder barely sculpted. We're just beginning to get a glimpse of its shape."

"One of those figures of Michelangelo: a slave of stone struggling to get free."

"A spirited steed: magnificent, but bridled and reined in tight."

When a wine is drunk too young—before it has had time to reach its maturity and develop its potential—there is frequently talk of infanticide.

"Infanticide?" gibes Angelo. "That's a pretty hefty infant!"

Sorì San Lorenzo '89 is certainly no Beaujolais nouveau. It has an impressive amount of polyphenols: 2.95 grams per liter. With its 13.69 degrees of alcohol, it is right in line with the wines produced at the beginning of the century by Domizio Cavazza at the cooperative winery. In 1903, 1904, and 1905, for example, the alcoholic content of Cavazza's wine was 13.59, 13.89, and 13.60 degrees, respectively. What is striking in the comparison, however, is the total acidity. Expressed in tartaric acid, the figures for those same three wines are intimidating indeed, at least for a contemporary winelover: 9.07, 7.50, and 8.40 grams per liter, respectively! The much lower acidity of Sorì San Lorenzo '89—5.80 grams per liter—will allow the tannin to be experienced by the palate as savory and velvety rather than harsh.

The year 1989 was hot and dry in Barbaresco. The same year in Bordeaux, which has already acquired quite a reputation for itself, was a bit hotter, and less dry. On paper, Sorì San Lorenzo promises very well indeed.

Angelo is a great promoter of his wines, but he knows that there are no certainties as far as the evolution of a given wine is concerned.

"You can't drink promises!" he exclaims. "Wine is always full of surprises."

"A few more months in *baric* might have done it good," says Guido.

"True," Angelo replies. "But we still need to know more about all that. It's hard to tell when to bottle, too. A wine might be ready with respect to one component, but not another."

When will Sorì San Lorenzo actually be bottled?

Angelo and Guido hardly exchange looks at all. By now they've read each other's mind.

"We'll have to see how it evolves over the summer," says Angelo. "If we're lucky, it could be early September, before the harvest begins. If not, it'll have to be next spring."

They always bottle when it's warm because wine absorbs less oxygen then.

"I hope our clients will understand," Angelo says with a sigh. "Some of them bought it en primeur and paid in advance, and it won't be available for Christmas. It may be over a year before we ship, even if we bottle it in September."

Angelo sniffs and takes another sip. There's nothing he wouldn't give to be able to say with a good conscience, "okay! Let's bottle it!" But he's a hard-nosed sniffer and a tough-minded taster.

"This wine is willful and headstrong," he says. "You can't force it into the bottle if it doesn't want to go."

He looks at his glass.

"It'll tell us when it's ready."

With the bottle as well as the baric, you have to ask the wine.

August 20, 1992

J-E-L-L-O?"

The incredulity makes Guido laugh with glee. He nods and repeats the question as he points to the *botte*.

"What does San Lorenzo '89 have in common with Jell-O right now?"

Could another comeuppance be coming up? In any case, it's quite a letdown. With all the talk about esoteric matters like the malolactic mysteries and those of polymers, the novice has been feeling pretty sophisticated. Jell-O takes him back to the exoteric jabber in the junior-high lunchroom. What on earth could a wine with expectations of greatness have in common with a product like that?

"Gelatin!" Guido exclaims, clarifying the enigma while gelatin clarifies the wine.

The day of decision has come and gone. The wine will be bottled at the beginning of September, and Guido has cut even shorter his already short vacation to guide it from barrel to bottle.

"Most people think it's all over but the shouting now," he says, "but that's what *they* think!"

Many of the wine's fans would already be heading for the exits after having cheered it on from pruning in the vineyard through aging in the cellar.

"This wine's a winner," they would say. "All it has to do now is cross the finish line of bottling: a mere formality."

Little do they suspect that the homestretch is strewn with hurdles.

New red wine is always cloudy because of the particles suspended in it: tiny fragments of the grapes themselves, yeasts, bacteria, coloring matter, fine crystals. Some of them fall to the bottom of the container and remain there when the wine is racked. This spontaneous clarification can be helped along by the wine maker in numerous ways—like exposing it to cold and storing it in small casks, as Guido does. He can also intervene more directly to ensure greater and more stable clarity.

"A cloudy wine is visually unappealing," says Guido. "And the particles diminish your pleasure when you drink it."

Fining is a traditional method of clarifying wine and is carried out with substances that contain protein. Positively charged in the wine, the protein reacts with the negatively charged tannins and other particles, attracting them and forming heavier aggregates called floccules that slowly sink to the bottom of the container.

"Clarification can be deceptive," says Guido. "That's why what the wine does spontaneously isn't enough. The wine seems clear, but particles precipitate in the bottle—when the temperature changes, for example—and it becomes cloudy. Fining ensures that clarity is stable."

Traditional fining agents include ox blood, casein (from milk), isinglass (from fish bladders), and, of course, egg whites.

Guido makes a face and holds his nose.

"I know egg whites are traditional in prestigious places like Bordeaux," he says. "I've tried them, but don't use them. The barrels are hard to clean afterward: you should smell the stench! I find gelatin just as effective, and a lot easier to use."

Guido takes a beaker of unfined Barbaresco from another barrel and pours in the gelatin that he has dissolved in a little warm water. The wine clouds up right away and a mesh forms, which then sinks to the bottom.

"When I did a trial like this with the San Lorenzo here," he says, "it went down so nicely that I'll be able to do without filtration."

Though there's nothing dramatic about Guido's tone, you half expect to hear the opening notes of Beethoven's Fifth Symphony resound throughout the cellar. Filtration is one of the weightiest words in the world of wine. Some people regard it as a heinous crime—a euphemism for enocide. For them, the word "unfiltered" on a wine label is a badge of shining vinous virtue.

"Those people aren't entirely wrong," Guido says. "They're just a bit simple-minded about a complex question."

You sometimes read in wine books and periodicals about wines that tasted wonderful from the cask but were disappointing once they were bottled. A young wine can be alive one day and dead practically the next. Reports of death by bottling seem to regard Burgundy more than any other famous wine.

One explanation is that some grape varieties can take bottling in general, and filtration in particular, better than others. Tannic ones like Cabernet Sauvignon and Nebbiolo seem to suffer less than fragile ones like Burgundy's Pinot Noir.

"Of course," says Guido, "it also depends on how the bottling is actually done. It can be the greatest trauma a wine undergoes. If you don't have the equipment and knowledge to protect it properly, the wine can be overwhelmed by oxygen and brutally oxidized."

A few distinctions are in order.

"When you talk about filtration, you shouldn't lump widely different practices together under a catchall term. Filtration can sterilize wine by removing any yeast and bacteria that may still be in it. That's microfiltration, and for that you need pores as small as 0.40 micron if you want to catch that last bacterium."

Guido uses 150-micron filters. He doesn't want to sterilize the wine, but only make sure there are no traces left in it of the gelatin used to fine it.

"Gelatin is organic stuff," he says. "If there's even a bit left, it could cause a stench."

An onlooker ventures the observation that tight filtration strips the wine of important components.

"You can say that again!" he exclaims. "Like the colloidal matter which confers suppleness. The phenolic compounds are

[234]

smoother when they are bound to those minuscule particles rather than combining with the mucoproteins on your tongue."

But it's not enough to have a certain kind of filter. You also have to know how to use it.

"A lot of wines filtered with cellulose pads taste of cardboard," he says. "But that's not the filter's fault; it's the wine maker's. You have to purge the pad first. It's a bit like staves: they have to lose some of their components before they can be used in a cask. You should always throw away the first few liters that come through a filter pad."

There are other details of great consequence.

"For instance, it's important to have the wine already quite clear beforehand. The clearer it is, the less pressure is necessary to get it through the filter. If some wines are dead after filtration, it's probably because the pump had to work too hard rather than the effect of the filter itself. You can sometimes get the whole job done with fining. It's slower, but actually superior in terms of the future clarity of the wine."

As Guido walks away, he makes his final point about filtration.

"If you've taken proper care of the wine," he says, "you can do without it—if you're willing to take a slight risk."

The gelatin is doing its job. Each floccule that reaches the bottom of the barrel further reduces the danger of off-odors and cloudiness. Soon the wine will be racked off its sediment and then bottled.

All it's waiting for now is the all clear from Guido.

September 3–8, 1992

L IKE STIFF SOLDIERS on parade, the bottles move forward. Flowing down by gravity to the floor below the fermentation room, Sorì San Lorenzo '89 fills each one in turn. Nitrogen has ensured a safer environment for it by expelling most of the oxygen from the bottle just before the wine flows in. Another familiar security guard, SO_2, was already on the job when the wine left the barrel.

"Just a touch," says Guido, "to compensate for the oxygen that inevitably crashes the bottling party. When you bottle young wines, which are still protected by a certain amount of CO_2, you can even do without it. It's sort of like younger and older people: the latter are more vulnerable and need more protection."

The modern wine bottle was one of the necessary conditions for the development of fine wine. Because of their fragility and irregular shape, earlier bottles had been vessels for serving wine rather than transporting and storing it. The new cylindrical bottle made of strong glass not only kept the wine from turning to vinegar. It proved to be a positive factor in its evolution.

[236]

When Angelo started working at the winery, most of the wine was sold in demijohns.

"One day around Christmas in the late fifties," his father recalls, "my mother told me that we had sold almost five thousand bottles that year. That was an unheard-of figure. Christmas was the only time we sold any bottles to speak of."

The decision to bottle was not based on tasting and evaluation of the wine's evolution. It was a purely practical one: the wine was bottled in small lots as orders came. And, of course, lots bottled many months, and even years, apart were quite different from one another. As Angelo says with reference to their 1961 Barbaresco, "Which '61?"

Yet even before the Second World War, a local researcher like Garino-Canina was already pointing out that a bottle is not just another container for the transportation of wine. The reductive environment it provides is essential for the development of characteristics such as bouquet.

With the spread of estate bottling, the bottle was to also become a reasonable guarantee that a wine actually came from the place stated on the label. But this role as a guarantee of authenticity is a relatively recent one. Fantini pointed out that consumers in his day didn't trust bottled wine.

"Who sells in bottles?" he asks rhetorically. "Big companies that buy grapes and wine right and left. Thus there is always a bit of suspicion regarding the origin and authenticity of the wine."

Over many years, beginning around the middle of the seventeenth century, the bottle evolved into the basic shape that we know today. But each major wine-producing region played a variation on that shape and eventually became identified with a standard bottle.

"WE WERE THE FIRST to sell bottles as if they were ties or watches," says Franco Marchini. "Personalized instead of standardized."

Silver-haired and sixtyish, Marchini is the head of Nordvetri, a glassworks located near Trento, in northeastern Italy. In the ultramodern factory, incandescent newborn bottles streak down from above, one after the other, like falling stars.

On his desk is a photo taken in 1939 that shows his father standing next to a machine in Asti, Marchini's hometown.

"It made at most three bottles a minute," he says. "Now we make sixty—one a second."

For a long time after the creation of the modern wine bottle, the container was much more expensive than its contents. Improved methods of production changed that, but progress has not been only quantitative.

Only a hundred years ago, Ottavi emphasized that many bottles were poorly made and corrodible. "Used bottles are much sought after," he wrote, "because they are more reliable."

"Nowadays bottles are filled by machine," says Marchini. "They have to be stronger and perfectly straight. Extra-thick ones like Angelo uses for Sorì San Lorenzo protect the wine from fluctuations in temperature. And we've developed a glass that offers one hundred percent protection against ultraviolet light in the brown version like Angelo's and ninety percent in the champagne-green one. Ultraviolet rays can cause oxidation, you know."

Angelo is here to see about a bottle for his Barolo. Nordvetri developed the unusual bottle that he uses for Darmagi.

"It was unusual at first," Marchini says. "But soon producers were phoning in droves and asking for 'the same bottle as Gaja.' "

Angelo isn't looking for anything like that now.

"A special bottle used to be a way of distinguishing a special wine," he says. "Now it would be closer to the mark to say that the opposite is true."

On a table in the office is a bottle with a strange-looking neck.

"That's right," Marchini says. "It's narrower than standard ones. We made it to order for a producer in Tuscany. He wants it because Antonio Pes, from the cork research institute at Tempio Pausania, in Sardinia, told him that the less cork he puts in his bottle, the less risk there is of having a corked wine. But making this bottle was nothing in comparison with the problems we've had with those of a certain producer of Barbaresco."

Marchini puts on a stern expression and wags his finger at Angelo.

"You really drove us crazy with that cork of yours!" he exclaims.

As EACH FILLED BOTTLE files past, it is sealed with a cork.

The only noninert materials that are allowed to come into contact with fine wine—cork and wood—both come from oak trees. Corks are made from the bark of *Quercus suber*. (*Suber* is Latin for "cork," but the English word derives from *Quercus*.)

For bottle aging and "vintage" wine to be possible, the modern wine bottle was a necessary, but not sufficient, condition. A satisfactory way of sealing the bottle so that the wine could develop for many years was needed. Cork filled the bill. It had been known to the ancient Romans, but it seems that it was then forgotten for over a thousand years. When it was rediscovered in the seventeenth century, the marriage between bottle and cork was celebrated; the history of modern wine could begin.

The selling points of cork as a stopper are impressive: compressibility, resilience, impermeability, lightness, and a high coefficient of friction. Most bark is fibrous, but cork is composed of cells filled with air that measure about one-thousandth of an inch in diameter. One cubic inch of it contains about 2 million cells. More than half the volume of cork is air, which explains not only its lightness, but also the compressibility that allows it to spring back almost immediately to nearly full volume. Under the tremendous force of expansion in the neck, the cells, which are sliced through when the cork is cut out of the bark, act like microscopic suction cups against the glass.

Probably the first person to understand the nature of cork was the English physicist and inventor, Robert Hooke. While looking at cork through a microscope he was led to introduce the term "cell" itself, which first appears in his work *Micrographia*, published in 1665. The book also contains the first representation of cork based on microscopic investigation. Hooke compared the "little boxes" that he saw to a honeycomb and noted that his discovery of the cells "hinted to me the true and intelligible reason of all the Phaenomena of Cork."

Cork, it would seem, is the perfect stopper for wine.

[239]

"CORK!" Guido sighs.

He frequently sighs when he talks about cork, but it's never from relief.

"Cork is not only the last link in the chain," he says. "It's also the weakest. All that work, in the vineyard and in the cellar, can be ruined by one little stopper. It's like losing a big game in the last few seconds because of sheer bad luck."

Guido doesn't willingly let his charges go out into the world with such a fragile barrier between them and all the dangers that are lurking out there.

"What do you mean, 'out there'?" he says indignantly. "The dangers lie in the cork itself. What's needed is a barrier between the wine and the *cork!*"

If you've ever tasted a "corked" wine, you know what Guido means, even though "corked" can mean a number of different things.

A corked wine can be due to alterations of the cork when it is attacked by various molds, either on the tree or after it has been stripped.

Guido is convinced that one of the main culprits is *Armillaria mellea,* a fungus that attacks trees growing in soil with poor drainage because, as with molds in general, humidity is its element.

"The fungus only grows to a height of about a foot on the tree," Guido says. "That part of the bark is okay for other uses, but it should be discarded as far as corks are concerned. Yet the piece-workers who strip the cork even go so far as to cut the trunk underground in order to get more bark. They're like growers who don't know what it means to be selective when they harvest grapes."

Off-odors can be picked up during processing from products, such as chlorine used to sterilize corks; 2,4,6-trichloroanisole is the most infamous example. And since the surface of cork consists of an enormous number of microscopic cells that have been cut, surface contact with the environment is much greater than that of a perfectly smooth surface. Each cell is a microcontainer, and cork easily takes on odors from the environment.

Studies estimating the percentage of wines that are corked have proposed figures varying from as low as 2 percent to as high as 10 percent; 5 percent is the most common one.

"But the problem with cork isn't just corked wines," says Guido. "The problem is cork. Period."

As LONG AGO as 1973, readers of France's leading wine periodical, *Revue des Vins de France,* were no doubt surprised when they came across a half-page advertisement featuring the photos of four men and proclaiming dramatically that "the passion of four generations hangs on the quality of a. . . ." They must have thought that was a pretty heavy burden for a lightweight like cork.

The four men in the photos were thirty-three-year-old Angelo and his father, grandfather, and great-grandfather. The voice of the ad is first-person. Angelo explains that he's looking for "a really exceptional cork." Price is no problem.

Readers must also have wondered who that Gah-zhah was. It's easy to fantasize. The Angelo of the photo looks rather like an Italian version of James Dean. Was he a movie star as well as a *producteur de vin?* And there is also, in the middle of the ad, a photo of a cork on which you can read the letters L-O-R-E-N. Who knows how many Frenchmen thought of Sophia instead of the saint of a certain *sorì!*

"Angelo changed everything," Luigi Cavallo recalls, "even the corks!"

Cavallo's weary eyes come alive with childlike wonder.

"I remember once someone mentioning that in a shipment of a number of cases, two bottles had turned out to be corked. At that time people thought, 'What are two bottles out of so many?' But Angelo got to work on it right way. He went to Sardinia. Things improved."

"GENUINE SARDINIAN CORK can be infinitely better than a lot of the stuff that's sold as Sardinian," says Angelo.

He's on his way to visit producers on the largest island in the Mediterranean after Sicily. The plane will soon be landing in Olbia, the nearest point to the mainland.

Sardinia has special historical ties with Piedmont. A former Spanish province, the island was assigned by the Treaty of London in 1720 to Vittorio Amedeo II of the House of Savoy, who assumed the title of King of Sardinia. Thus the island gave its name to the kingdom that eventually was to unite Italy.

"Many producers process cork they import, sight unseen, from North Africa," Angelo says. "They don't make any kind of selection and often don't even know exactly where it comes from." All cork from the French island of Corsica, about seven miles to the north, is processed in Sardinia, too.

The cork actually grown in Sardinia itself is a tiny fraction of the world production, which comes entirely from the western Mediterranean and Portugal. Attempts to establish forests of *Quercus suber* outside that area have been unsuccessful. With one-third of the cork oak forests and just over half of the cork production, Portugal is far and away the world's leading producer, followed at a distance by Spain and Algeria.

Angelo will be calling on a number of producers in Calangianus, a town in Gallura, the northernmost region of the island.

"I can't get enough corks of the quality I want from one producer," he says.

The ad that Angelo put in the French magazine led to trials with a couple of producers, but he still wasn't satisfied. A few years later he finally convinced a small Sardinian producer, Sotgia, to make him corks that were sixty-three millimeters long—almost two and a half inches—with which he bottled Sorì San Lorenzo '79 and the other two single-vineyard Barbarescos of that vintage.

"Sotgia was stupefied when I first talked to him about those corks," Angelo says. "At that time, the longest ones were those used by a few top Bordeaux estates. And they were eight millimeters shorter."

Once he had the cork, though, he couldn't get it into the bottle.

"At that time there weren't any machines capable of inserting such long corks. I had to have a prototype made according to our specifications."

There were other problems, and other solutions.

"Waiters had trouble pulling them out, so I started importing better corkscrews, like the Screw-Pull from Texas. I was afraid that restaurant owners would find the corks too much bother. But they turned out to be enthusiastic. Even customers who hadn't ordered our wine noticed the cork when it was pulled and asked about it. A lot of owners took pride in explaining that it came out of a bottle of Italian wine."

Angelo was teased about the new corks by his friend and fellow producer, Giacomo Bologna. He chuckles.

" 'Trying to save wine by taking up space with those long corks, eh?' Bologna would say."

The "Fasten seatbelt" sign goes on. The plane is about to land.

"Such long corks don't necessarily give the wine better protection," Angelo says. "But because they are exceptional, they do force cork producers to select their best raw material. Since we started using them, there have been fewer defective ones. But the problem hasn't been entirely eliminated."

ANGELO IS HAVING DINNER at the hotel not far from Olbia where he's spending the night. He tells the owner that he has heard that some Nebbiolo is grown in the area, in a place called Luras.

"Luras!" the owner exclaims, turning up his nose. "That's peasant and cooperative stuff. Really primitive. It wouldn't interest you."

Angelo insists. He wants to know more, but the owner seems anxious to avoid the subject, as if he didn't want to lower the tone of his upscale establishment by talking about such plebeian matters. Reluctantly, he says that Luras is near Calangianus and explains how to get there.

After the owner has moved on to another table, Angelo makes a quick calculation. If he leaves by six o'clock in the morning, he'll have time to look at those vines before his round of appointments begins.

THE ROAD WINDS ITS LEISURELY WAY across the hilly, austere countryside of Gallura. Cork oaks begin to appear here and there. Dumpy and gnarled in comparison, they are hardly recognizable as relatives of their more aristocratic cousins from central France.

[243]

With their reddish-brown trunks exposed, those that have been recently stripped look as though they've been caught with their pants down.

After a wrong turn and several miles on a dirt road, Angelo finally arrives in the village of Luras. He parks the car and goes over to a group of men sitting in what appears to be the village square.

Yes, there are still a few Nebbiolo vines in Luras.

"They were brought over in the nineteenth century by some people from Piedmont," an old man says.

Angelo chats for a few minutes, gets directions, and heads back to the car.

"I just can't imagine Nebbiolo vines out here," he says.

The bumpy dirt road is by now little more than a path leading down a hillside, but there they are. The vineyard is scrubby. The vines have undoubtedly mutated after so many years in such a different climate and soil.

Angelo gets out of the car and stands there gazing at them.

In his *Memoirs of a Tourist,* Stendhal writes about a well-known military figure of his time, General Bisson, who, as a colonel during the French Revolution, ordered his men to halt and present arms as they passed by the Clos de Vougeot. But the regiment's salute could hardly have been such a moving tribute as Angelo's solitary, silent one to these Nebbiolo vines languishing far from the Langhe—exiled aristocrats who have fallen on hard times.

"No other plant gives so much while demanding so little."

The voices of the Ganau brothers seem to blend into one, like their glossy pates in the blinding sun. They are among the top cork manufacturers in Sardinia, and Angelo has arrived in their town. Calangianus: 5,000 inhabitants, 250 cork producers, 90 percent of Italy's production.

Quercus suber is unique in that the phloem—the tissue that transports the sap—is located underneath the regenerative layer known as the cambium, rather than between the cambium and the bark. Thus the bark itself is only a protective covering against hot winds and can be removed without injury to the tree. A new layer grows back every year and the outermost ones cease being part of the living plant.

"The trees are stripped only in the summer, when vegetative growth is at its height, so that the cambium will regrow rapidly," they say. "Otherwise, the phloem might be damaged and the tree would die."

The official season is May 1 to August 31.

"But this year, it started around May 15 because it was so cool that the sap wasn't circulating earlier. And it's over everywhere in Sardinia by the end of July because the sap stops flowing for the opposite reason—it gets too hot."

The single-voiced brothers tell you everything you always wanted to know about the cork tree.

"The tree is first stripped when the trunk reaches a diameter of sixty-five centimeters. It's usually between thirty and forty years old, but that depends on the climate and the soil."

"The first stripping gives you 'male cork,' which is never used for wine corks," they say. "After that you get 'female cork,' but only with the third stripping is it compact and really first-rate."

The minimum period between strippings used to be nine years by law, but it was recently increased to ten.

"Since then," they say, "the quality has improved greatly. In the last few years the cork puts on weight. But if you leave it *too* long on the tree, it gets woody and is no good anymore."

For a while, the brothers alternate.

"But exactly when the cork is at its best depends on where it comes from," says one.

"The best comes from trees that grow in poor soil, because the growth is slow. The annual rings are small and tightly knit. Perhaps mountain cork is best," says the other.

The story sounds familiar. Like *merrain*—and grapes—cork varies greatly from place to place.

"In warm places," continues one of them, "cork takes nine years to mature after the previous stripping. Here in Gallura, where it's cooler, it takes at least eleven. And in a spot like Ala de' Sardi, twelve, and sometimes thirteen or even fourteen years have to go by."

Earnestess fills the air as they pause.

"But when you really know your cork," they say in seeming unison, "you even recognize differences among particular forests."

What could be the Tronçais of cork, the St. Palais of stoppers?

They look at each other. Are they hesitating to reveal a secret? Finally their faces light up.

"Baldu!" they exclaim. "Near Tempio."

BLACK-BEARDED PEPPINO MOLINAS, one of several brothers who own the largest cork factory in Sardinia, is standing in the courtyard of his establishment. He explains how corks are made. As with *merrain,* the first step is seasoning.

"Once the cork is stripped," Molinas says, "it stays outside for at least six months."

Corks are even more confusing than staves. In 1983, a committee composed of scientists, cork manufacturers, enologists, and sommeliers recommended standards for Sardinian cork production. Among their recommendations was that seasoning should last at least one year. According to the Ganau brothers, fourteen months is the minimum. The strips of bark vary in thickness from two to six centimeters. If staves should season at least one year for every centimeter, what is a novice to make of cork seasoning?

The scene in the factory courtyard is not promising. The cork is piled up pell-mell. Boards are touching the ground; the circulation of air is poor. The professor of oak would surely flunk these cork producers!

The cork boards also go through their first classification here. A worker is busy distributing them into different piles with movements so rapid his hands must be doing the thinking.

"About a third of them are discarded," Molinas says. "They'll be ground up and used for insulation."

He leads the way into the factory, where you'd never know you're in sleepy Calangianus. It's high-tech all the way, except perhaps for the tank where the boards are "boiled." According to the norms committee, the water should be at least 140 degrees Fahrenheit even between batches and the concentration of tannin in the water no higher than 6 percent. If the concentration is higher, the cork will absorb tannin. The purpose of "boiling" is to sterilize the boards and render them more flexible.

"The boards are boiled for an hour and a quarter," says Molinas, as Angelo stares at the murky water. "The tanks are cleaned every three days."

After "boiling," the boards are flattened and stacked. But some of those in storage are covered by mold.

"Ah," says Molinas with a shrug. "The white mold is okay. It's the green one you have to watch out for. The cork shouldn't wait more than fifteen days after boiling before being processed, though."

According to the Ganau brothers, two days are the maximum! What is one to believe?

The next step is to cut the boards into strips as wide as the finished corks will be long. They are then punched out widthwise from the boards by machine. As they come down a slide, they are classified.

There are currently three systems of classification.

The traditional, or subjective, one is based on human judgment. It takes into account only the number and diameter of the minute fissures called lenticels. There are five classes, I to V, and discards. Tests have shown that evaluations vary considerably even among experts. One classifier was given the same one hundred corks twice. The first time he put twenty-seven of them into class I and the second time thirty-nine. Six classifiers were given another lot of one hundred corks. The most severe expert put only twenty-seven into class I, while the least severe put sixty-six; the average was thirty-nine.

At the Molinas plant, after each cork has been punched out it is classified automatically by electronic sensors according to the volume of lenticels. This system does not take into account the lenticels on the ends of the cork, nor does it consider such negative features as the red powder or woody streaks frequently found in cork. Thus the automatic system always requires the presence of an expert like the one who, with movements so rapid they are almost blurred, is sorting the electronically classified corks into the appropriate containers. Sometimes electronic evaluations are quite similar to human ones, but at other times the two differ greatly. The advantage of electronic classification is that it always gives the same result in test after test.

The third method of classification, devised by Antonio Pes, is by weight.

"Quality based on the number and diameter of lenticels," Pes has written, "is only of aesthetic value." According to him, the permeability of cork is not due to its greater or lesser porosity, but to the quantity of suberin it contains, a waxlike substance found in the cells. Two corks may have the same dimensions, but different weights, and therefore perform differently in the bottle.

At the Molinas plant, the device that is supposed to weigh the corks isn't even turned on. Angelo's glance is eloquent.

Once the corks have been punched and classified, they are washed, polished, and branded according to the producer's instructions.

"This is how most corks are made today," says Molinas, "but Angelo's and those of a few other producers are made in the traditional way."

A short drive to the other end of town and you enter the world of the *quadrettista*—literally, the "maker of little cubes."

The workroom is straight out of the engraving illustrating the article on cork in Diderot's eighteenth-century *Encyclopedia*. Four men are seated at work benches, cutting parallelepipeds out of boards of cork by hand. They will later be rounded off into their final shape by machine. Working with movements not much slower than those of the classifiers, a good *quadrettista* can make 2,500 *quadretti* a day.

"You get a better cork this way," Molinas says. "The punching machine makes a standard hole on the side opposite the crust and only gets a few of the annual rings. The *quadrettista* eliminates the crust and gets more rings, producing corks of different diameters. He also eliminates defects such as woody streaks."

Molinas grins.

"Of course," he says, "these corks are much more expensive than standard ones."

[248]

ON THE WAY BACK to the airport, Angelo stops off near Arzachena to see two young brothers, Fabrizio and Mario Ragnedda, who make wine with the local Vermentino grape. Most Vermentino is a simple beverage drunk to wash down local seafood and is produced in two versions: yellow and oxidized in the traditional manner, nearly colorless and insipid in the newer technological style. The brothers visited Angelo in Barbaresco some time ago and he promised to drop in on them the next time he came to Sardinia.

Their story is one he knows well: the story of every grower determined to get off the cheap-wine treadmill. The sacrifices. The low yields. The harvesting before dawn to prevent oxidation of the fragile grapes. The incredulousness of restaurant owners when they first hear the price. And, in this case, a happy ending: the breakthrough and the plans for the future.

Angelo is attentive and responsive as they bombard him with questions. The subject of cork comes up. Fabrizio tells about his father-in-law, who strips the bark from the trees.

"He says that everyone always cuts right from the ground. They don't select at all."

What to do? Fabrizio has an idea.

"We ought to choose our own cork on the tree, have it stripped the way we want, and then season it ourselves."

Angelo lifts his eyebrows. An enigmatic smile creeps slowly across his face.

DINNER ON THE TERRACE of the restaurant in Treiso, just a couple of miles from Barbaresco, has been enlivened by the banter orchestrated by Count Riccardo Riccardi. Riccardi works in public relations for a famous producer of vermouth and sparkling wines, but his real vocation is playfully promoting Piedmont. His wife is Tuscan, but even Tuscany is too far south for him.

"Those barbarians!" he exclaims.

With the summer twilight casting its spell over the vine-clad hills, spirits at the table are high.

"Taste this," says Guido all of a sudden, pouring everyone a glass of Gaja Barbaresco 1987 from the second bottle of the evening. It's different from the first one. Both wines are perfectly sound, but the first one had more body. It was fuller and richer in your mouth.

Everyone is amazed. What could it be?

Guido points to the two corks on the table.

"Those!" he exclaims. "And just think, the two bottles are separated by only nine numbers. That means a few seconds apart on the bottling line. The wines came from the same barrel."

But, like Sorì San Lorenzo '89 from two different casks, they are two different wines.

"Many people think cork is a problem only when it causes the odor and taste of what we call a corked wine," says Guido. "But what about differences among perfectly sound wines that are due to cork? Like these two!"

"Bottled wine is in contact with cork," says Riccardi. "It must extract something."

"You bet it does!" Guido exclaims. "And not only is there nothing noble to be extracted from cork in the first place, it's not seasoned nearly long enough, either. If the wine doesn't seep up into the neck of the bottle that's lying on its side, only the base of the cork touches the wine, and the contact is minimum. But if it does seep into the neck, the ratio of cork surface to wine can be greater than that of wood in a *baric*."

Guido pulls out a pocket calculator and starts to calculate. The length and circumference of a cork. The length and circumference of a *baric*. A bottle and a *baric* respectively hold so much wine. Guido is feverish. The crimes of cork exasperate him, and seepage is one of the worst.

"You see!" he exclaims triumphantly. "The ratio can be more than double!"

He's a tough trial lawyer, pleading for a conviction. He pauses so his words will have a greater effect on the jury.

"And that's not all," he says. "A fine red wine might stay in the *baric* for a year or two at most. But it could be in contact with the cork for many years!"

Is cork then guilty? Antonio Pes complains that too often the cork is considered in isolation.

"The bottle is the great absentee in discussions of cork," he writes. "It should be adapted to the characteristics of cork. The neck should not be considered in purely aesthetic terms. Its conicity and diameter are important."

Take two corks, he argues, with the same dimensions and weight and insert them in two different bottles: one with a perfectly cylindrical neck and the other with a conical one. In the first bottle the concentration of suberin and the fatty acids it contains will be the same throughout the cork, but in the other it will be higher near the mouth than near the wine.

"By and large," Angelo says, "producers do a pretty good job of actually making the corks, but it's like with grapes. You can't make a silk purse out of a sow's ear. You can't compensate in the factory for poor-quality cork."

"Yes," says Guido. "They use everything nowadays—cork from areas where it grows faster and is more porous. Twenty years ago most cork was used for purposes other than making wine stoppers. Now the figures are probably reversed, and quality has suffered."

Cork was one of the four major factors that led to the creation of modern wine. While the bottle has gone from strength to strength, and while other countries have joined France as producers of fine wine and England as consumers, cork does not seem to have improved. The story of the marriage of bottle and cork usually implies that they lived happily ever after. But there's no doubt that, like many others, the union long ago settled into a routine and was simply taken for granted, discontents and all.

"We need another kind of stopper," Guido says. "It wouldn't necessarily have to be a crown cap; perhaps some kind of synthetic material. It would take a courageous leader, with the prestige of a Mondavi or Château Margaux. Everyone would follow right away."

Angelo is reflective.

"Bottled wine is a relatively new phenomenon in Italy," he says. "Perhaps earlier we were less sensitive to the phenomenon. Most wine producers still don't have a quality mentality. For very expensive wines, you should be willing to pay even ten times what the most expensive corks cost now if that would give you a serious guarantee of quality. But the whole question is delicate. The idea of opening a bottle of Château Margaux with anything but a cork in it is hard to swallow."

"But there's no getting around the fact that cork isn't inert," Guido insists. "We compare the same wine aged in different kinds of oak or in casks of different ages. Why not do the same thing for corks and other kinds of stoppers, like that friend of Aldo's does?"

A PEASANT WINE GROWER at the Martini and Rossi plant in Pessione, near Turin, would probably feel that he had wandered into the Fiat automobile factory by mistake. The bottles of vermouth—the Martini of your martini—come off the bottling line at intervals that seem to approach those of machine-gun fire.

The closets of Alberto Orrico's laboratory are undoubtedly larger than Guido's lab. Cordial, enthusiastic, and clad, of course, in a white lab coat, Orrico is a friend of Aldo Vacca's from their Turin U. days. He checks the quality of everything bottled at the plant; in addition to millions of bottles of various kinds of vermouth, there are sparkling wines, too, and he has been paying special attention to cork.

"I run two kinds of tests," he says. "First I slice up randomly chosen corks into disks and put them into different containers with the same white wine."

He smiles wryly.

"If you think cork is a neutral material," he says, "I recommend you taste those infusions." He pauses to let the idea sink in. "Then I take a lot of bottles of wine off the bottling line one after the other and close them with a great variety of different stoppers—crown caps, screw caps, corks made out of silicon, natural corks from different lots. A month later we bring in just about everybody who works here to taste them blind."

Orrico wrinkles his brow. He tries to measure his words.

"The one thing everyone always agrees on is that the wines sealed with the real cork are the least appealing. The best results are usually obtained by crown caps and a synthetic cork made with polyethylene. All the wines differ from one another, sometimes greatly. Even people who aren't professional tasters note the differences."

He throws up his hands.

"One of our executives got excited about the synthetic cork, which is made to look like a natural one and is attractive. He tried to convince the association of Asti spumante producers to adopt it, but it was eventually rejected because they were afraid that the image of the wine would suffer."

Similar experiments have been carried out elsewhere: at the prestigious research institute at Wädenswil, Switzerland, for instance. Different closures have been tested for as long as eight years. The crown cap beat all the competition there, followed closely by the screw cap. But unlike Orrico's experiments, the ones at Wädenswil placed imitation cork last. Cork itself finished in the middle of the pack. Many bottles closed with cork were judged just as good as those with metal caps, but others smelled "corked" and had seepage problems.

The jury, it seems, is still out, but conviction may be near.

"Until then," says Orrico, "it's a real lottery."

BOTTLING IS OVER. Within its new glass and cork confines, Sorì San Lorenzo 1989 begins its slow recovery from the shock. In silence and darkness, in the depths of the cellar, it prepares for its debut.

September 10, 1992

ANGELO SLAMS ON THE BRAKES as he spots a highway patrol car lying in wait farther up the road.

"Italian style," he says sheepishly as the speedometer plunges back into the reality of a humdrum highway from its fantasy of Formula One.

Turin has receded into the distance. Angelo is on his way back home yet another time. Thirty years have passed since he set forth in the world of wine, but he's still in a hurry and often on the run. That's the price he's always paid for being a forerunner of the new age of Italian wine.

Arnaud de Pontac, the precursor of them all, also set out to improve and promote his product in the sixties. But those were the sixties of the seventeenth century; the French got a three-hundred-year head start. Perhaps Angelo is trying to make up for all that lost time.

Life has its different tempos. If the road is clear and the visibility is good—Angelo is no daredevil—you can zip along in your car. But you can't rush things in the vineyard or the cellar.

"Sure," he says, "it would have made things easier for us if San

Lorenzo '89 had been ready to bottle in May, but the wine is taking its time. *Pazienza.*" You have to be patient.

Angelo's tense is still the future. Speed makes the future happen faster! Perhaps it also helps to understand that things are always changing. You don't get lulled into the illusion that the view at any one moment is permanent.

"Look at what's been happening in Barbaresco," Angelo says. "Out of one hundred fifty families, forty have set up small wineries and can now take pride in seeing their name on their own label. The emancipation of the small grower from the big companies that used to buy his grapes for a song started even earlier there than it did in the Barolo district. From a social point of view, that's a remarkable collective achievement. Barbaresco is now a solid name to build on."

Other changes are more problematic. Vineyard work attracts fewer and fewer young people and the older generation of workers will soon no longer be around. Federico is worried about the future. How will the job get done?

"You have to think in broader terms than local ones," says Angelo. "The world is changing fast. Look at what's been happening in Eastern Europe. We can't just stand on the sidelines and watch."

Recent visitors to the Gaja winery have sometimes heard a strange language being spoken in the courtyard. They don't understand a word, but they can tell it's not Piedmontese. Italians used to be immigrants themselves; now others are knocking at Italy's door. Barbaresco integrated Giuseppe Botto from Dogliani and Angelo Lembo from Sicily. Why shouldn't it be able to do the same for Selman Mendalliu and Vicktor Lala from Albania? Their hands are now among those that tend the vines of San Lorenzo. Soon, no doubt, their tongues will be speaking to them—in Piedmontese, of course!

"There are some real clouds on the horizon, though," Angelo admits.

The market for fine wine has been hurt by the long recession, and he's worried by the resurgence of the Prohibitionist mood in the United States.

"Producers aren't doing nearly enough to encourage moderation and to emphasize the difference between wine and hard liquor. Wine isn't just another alcoholic beverage. Its place is on the dining table, with food. That's important."

Low speed limits aren't the only aspect of American life that puzzles Angelo. The country of neo-Prohibitionism also supports *The Wine Spectator,* which has the largest circulation of any wine periodical in the world. And the country of Robert Parker, probably the world's most influential wine writer and certainly the one who tastes and writes about the most wines every year, subjects wine to the control of the Bureau of Alcohol, Tobacco, and Firearms.

"What does a wine like Sorì San Lorenzo have to do with the likes of bullets and booze?" He shrugs his shoulders. "We Italians have enough paradoxes of our own," he says, "without worrying about those of other countries."

But Angelo is an assiduous seeker of silver linings, and new markets are opening up.

"Look at the Far East!" he exclaims. "Two billion palates just waiting to discover wine!"

Ten years ago in Japan, consumption was only half a bottle a year per capita. Now that's more than doubled.

"It's still only a drop, but it's going up and up. The Italian restaurants there—the ones run by the *Japanese,* who send their cooks to Italy to work with top chefs—are among the best in the world. And, as everywhere, they're Trojan horses for Italian wine."

Last year at this time Angelo was getting ready for his performance at the tenth anniversary of the New York Wine Experience at the Marriott Marquis on Broadway.

As de Pontac already understood so well back in the seventeenth century, wine needs a stage. Wine needs to make itself known, and what better way than Broadway? This angel will back a show if it promises to be a hit. But it's not easy to make it on Broadway. Backstage in Barbaresco, they've been working hard. There's always room for improvement.

"For instance," says Angelo, "I'd like to be able to experiment with irrigation."

Irrigation is not allowed by the regulations because it is not a traditional practice.

"You bet it wasn't traditional around here!" Angelo retorts. "How could they have irrigated in the past without running water?"

He realizes that a lot of people will be scandalized by his suggestion. Irrigation is often associated with high yields and diluted wines.

"There's a psychological barrier. Irrigation is a word that frightens people. It evokes images of Niagara Falls, of Noah and the Flood! It doesn't have to mean inundating the vineyard and diminishing the quality of the grapes. I'd just like to sprinkle slightly when drought is prolonged."

There are some exciting developments already taking place.

"I'm anxious to see what difference aging in our home-seasoned wood will make," he says.

Their first Barolo since the 1961 vintage will be released next year.

And then there's Guido's new lab.

"Now that it's ready, think of all the things we'll be able to do."

Guido already has an assistant who comes in to do the routine analyses. He himself will have more time to do some of the research he's been thinking about for years.

Yet Guido will never be all chemist; there's the alchemist in him, too. The word "chemistry" itself derives from the Greek for "transmutation," and the transmutation of them all occurs when the base metal of mere must becomes the gold of wine. Guido will always keep you guessing, with all those guises of his.

Enology is to wine as neurology is to mind. It can explain many of the parts, but it can't explain the whole. We can view wine with dual vision, just as we do the sun when it's setting into the sea. We don't have to believe the earth is flat in order to delight in the scene.

Angelo smiles. He's happy.

An angel is a messenger, and Angelo's message is mostly for the market. Yet he's also a true evangelist, spreading the word about wine.

[257]

Wine is the ultimate message in a bottle. It's the most site-specific product of the soil, but its infinite variety of accents only enriches what, like music, is a universal language.

The novelist Sybille Bedford writes about getting the message when barely in her teens. She loved all the things associated with wine—the bottles, the names, the labels, "the link with rivers and hillsides and climates and hot years, and the range of learning and experiment afforded by wine's infinite variety; but what she loved more than these was the taste—of peach and earth and honeysuckle and raspberries and spice and cedarwood and pebbles and truffles and tobacco leaf; and the happiness, the quiet ecstasy that spreads through heart and limbs and mind."

The car is approaching the town of Montà, in the northeastern corner of the province of Cuneo.

"Even though we're still in 'Piedmont'," Angelo says with a grin, "this is where I start to feel I'm home."

The plain of Turin has given way to the dumpy Roero hills. There's Nebbiolo here, too, but the wine is not like Barbaresco. It slips down easily and doesn't live very long. Sandy soil. The importance of site.

Beyond the Tanaro lie the Langhe and very different hills.

"Ah, those hills!" Angelo exclaims. "With all those drought years in a row we've had, the vine would have died almost anywhere else."

The origin of the hills goes back to the Miocene, the fourth epoch of the Tertiary period, perhaps as long ago as twenty million years. The Alps, the Himalayas, and the Andes were all raised then along with the Langhe.

One of the main tasks of the near future will be the replanting of Sorì San Lorenzo. The ungrafted vines of pre-phylloxera days lived a century or more, but now thirty to forty years is a normal vineyard stay for vines that have to earn their keep.

The ripping-up of old vines is a mighty *memento mori*.

"When the time comes to replant again," says Angelo, "I'll probably no longer be around."

After the present vines have been pulled up, the *sorì* will lie fallow for three years. Federico will sow plants like mustard greens to enable the soil to regain its balance after all the years of monoculture. Then he and his crew will replant the vineyard.

Both the uprooting and the replanting will be done in three stages.

"It's risky to do it all at once," Angelo explains. "If you get a bad spell of drought, the young vines could all die because their roots are not long enough to reach the moisture in the subsoil. There's also the commercial side of things. It'll be a number of years before the vines are old enough to produce the kind of grapes we want, and it's important to always have at least a few bottles of San Lorenzo to sell."

Angelo's expression turns intense.

"I want to increase the wine's complexity," he says.

Federico is already hard at work on that. He's been selecting the best Nebbiolo vines from Angelo's holdings in both Barbaresco and Serralunga and planting cuttings from them in a special section of the Pajoré vineyard. There are now one hundred eighty vines there, each with a little white identification tag. When the time comes, he'll take cuttings from them and plant them in rows straight up and down the slope—*rittochino*—in Sorì San Lorenzo.

"We want a varied mix in order to get more nuances. About 40 percent of the new vines could be from San Lorenzo itself; say, 25 percent from other vineyards in Barbaresco, such as Sorì Tildin; 25 percent from Serralunga; and even 10 percent or so from the University of Turin's colonal selections."

He pauses.

"I know our own vines aren't virus-free, and that could cause problems. But it's a risk we have to take."

Angelo looks determined. He's not going to sell out his *sorì* to a selected clone or two. Variety is not only the spice of life, but also the spice of wine.

"I thought one of the reasons for the historical greatness of a region like Burgundy was the great variety of low-yielding clones that had developed over the centuries. They made some big mistakes when all that replanting took place in the sixties."

The car begins its descent toward the valley of the Tanaro. Soon this son of the Langhe will be on native soil.

[259]

In the distance, perched on its hilltop, Barbaresco already beckons. Gone are the construction cranes at the winery that briefly shared the skyline with its ancient tower. Like the church of Combray in Marcel Proust's great novel, *Remembrance of Things Past,* the lofty lookout is all you see from afar. Barbaresco is once again what it always was: a tower "epitomizing the town, representing it, speaking of it and from it to the horizon."

Up there, just down via Torino from the tower and off to the right, this generation of the vines of San Lorenzo is awaiting one of its last harvests. With a saint and an angel watching over them— not to speak of a poet and a wizard—the new vines should have nothing to fear.

But there are important decisions still to be made. About rootstocks, for instance. The considerations are many. Resistance to phylloxera, of course. (The ravage being wrought by the new biotype in California is a warning not to take this matter lightly.) And to drought. Vigor. Will they perform well in Sorì San Lorenzo's calcareous soil? Will they have rooting problems?

Angelo's mind is racing faster than his car. Those vines will be there for thirty years or more, entrusted with "the savor of the earth," with "the secrets of the soil." And in the end, that's where it all begins: with the best grapes in the world.